"*The Rest of Your Life* captures practical Christianity in simple, clear concepts. More importantly, it helps you think through key issues for yourself. Pat writes where we really live and about the things that really matter."

JERRY E. WHITE
President, The Navigators

"One of the biggest burdens in my ministry is how to challenge people who have committed their lives to Christ but do not have the handles on everyday Christian living. Pat Morley has successfully attached handles to 'shoe leather Christianity.' I cannot wait to introduce it to everyone in my church."

H. CHARLES GREEN, JR.
Orangewood Presbyterian Church

"*The Rest of Your Life* hammers home the reality that Jesus Christ can and does change an individual's life. Patrick Morley does a great job of spurring us on to love and good deeds."

DENNIS RAINEY
Director, Family Ministry

"Pat Morley is showing us how to reclaim our culture for Jesus Christ. The key is *leadership*. We each need an objective assessment. We need to think biblically. Leadership starts in the mind. We need accountability and we need to encourage one another. Pat hits on all the bases. This book will be a tremendous help to thousands of people."

CHRIS WHITE
President, Leadership Ministries, Inc.

"Warning: If you read this book alone, you will miss the opportunity to be a 'Great Commission Christian.' If every pastor could pair up his or her congregation to read this book and then challenge each other with the Discussion Questions, reaching the world for Christ would be much more of a reality! We need word-maps like this to leap into action."

BOB FENN
Executive Director, Lay Renewal Ministries

THE REST
OF YOUR LIFE

Other Books by Pat Morley

The Man in the Mirror

I Surrender: Submitting to Christ in the Details of Life

THE REST
OF YOUR LIFE

Patrick M. Morley

Thomas Nelson, Publishers, Inc.
Nashville, Tennessee

Published in Nashville, Tennessee, by Thomas Nelson, Inc., and distributed in Canada by Lawson Falle, Ltd., Cambridge, Ontario.

Scripture quotations are from The Holy Bible: NEW INTERNATIONAL VERSION. Copyright © 1978 by the New York International Bible Society. Used by permission of Zondervan Bible Publishers.

Library of Congress Cataloging-in-Publication Data

Morley, Patrick M.
  The rest of your life / Patrick M. Morley.
    p. cm.
  ISBN 0-8407-6754-4 (hard)
    1. Christian life—1960–   I. Title.
BV4501.2.M58547   1992
248.4—dc20   92-515
                                                   CIP

1 2 3 4 5 6 7 8 9 10 11 12 13 14 15 16 17 18 19 20 — 98 97 96 95 94 93 92

To my parents, Bob and Alleen Morley:

We were four scrawny little tykes,
we four boys.
You not only gave us the gift of life,
you taught us right from wrong,
you gave us enduring values,
you showed us joy, and
you are still always there
when we need you.

I love you very much, Mom and Dad.

I must admit that this book turned out to be a more ambitious undertaking than I first envisioned. The encouragement of a few special people kept me from getting bogged down along the way. Thank you, Patsy, my dear wife, for the thousand times you dropped everything to listen to new ideas, most of which were overstated and hare-brained. Thank you, Mike Hyatt, for your faith in the material. Thank you, Robert Wolgemuth, for your faith in me. Thank you, Chuck Mitchell, for taking care of business. Thank you, Betty Feiler, for keeping the office going. Thank you, Chuck Green, for your helpful comments on the first manuscript. Thank you, R.C. Sproul, for graciously looking over the final manuscript.

AN AUTHENTIC CHRISTIAN LIFE

Whennando de Soto landed his expedition on the shores of Florida, he sent a small party back to the ships to set them ablaze. His confused men watched from the water's edge in horrified disbelief as puffs of billowing smoke swirled into the air. De Soto wanted no man to think there was any turning back. When the sea finally swallowed the last smoldering plank, de Soto turned to his men and said, "Gentlemen, you are home."

Have you burned your boats yet? Or have you kept open the option of turning back? I am at a point in my own spiritual pilgrimage where I want to burn the boats. I never want to turn back. I am tired, fed up with, and, frankly, bored by Christianity that hasn't burned its boats.

Are you anything like me? I'm ready for my life to be radically different. I want people to say of me, "Ah yes, that must be what it means to be a *real* Christian." I want an authentic Christianity that is life changing. I want a genuine faith that will put passion into the years I have left. I want to do something that will count, that will make a difference. I want to live a distinctly Christian life. I'm ready to do something irrevocable—I'm ready to burn my boats.

I could be mistaken, but I think I see a movement of unrest among Christians who are finding their faith has not made much of a difference—men and women who have stopped growing and sharing their faith. I am meeting Christians filled with an in-

1

articulate, ambiguous kind of *angst* that they are somehow missing the mark. I think I see this unrest crystallizing into a widespread movement to find—or recover—an authentic, passionate, life-changing faith. If I am wrong about this, if there is no such movement afoot to recover an authentic, biblical Christianity, then weep for us.

Are you ready to do something extreme, something irrevocable? If you have a desire to break out of the mold of the world, to burn your boats, to get into a radical, life-changing, difference-making, genuine, passionate, authentic, biblical, distinctly Christian way of thinking, believing, and living then welcome to *The Rest of My Life*.

THE PROBLEM

A man said to me, "I'm saved. I don't need to worry about all of that other stuff." Too often people are encouraged to simply "pray a prayer," then told that everything will turn out all right. Well, everything isn't turning out all right. Their lives, rather than changing, have become impotent.

We live in a country saturated with the words of the gospel message. As though it were a weekly allergy shot, our exposure to the gospel often merely desensitizes us to the true message. The meanings of the words "Christian" and "Jesus" and "born again" become hollowed out and gutted of their true, historic meaning.

On Sunday morning one hundred million people will be in church. Sixty million people—one of every three adults—indicate they are "born again." Like me, you may be asking, "Who are all these people? Where are they?" and, "Why hasn't their faith turned the world upside down?" The answer, sadly, is that many of us have so adroitly melded Christianity into our culture that we are completely camouflaged; no one can tell we are there. A landmark Gallup survey indicates that less than 10 percent of Americans are deeply committed Christians.[1]

Thankfully, this percentage translates into many millions of Christians who live deeply committed lives of surrender to the God who is. Yet I believe there are also tens of millions of people out there—cultural Christians—caught in a quagmire of compromise who long to discover an authentic Christian faith. Perhaps they received Christ as a youth many years ago at a summer camp, maybe through their church youth group, or possibly at a Christian campus club meeting. But for ten, fifteen, twenty-five years or more they have been living by their own ideas, and they are tired. Worn out, actually.

Millions of Christians who have lived for years by their own ideas are realizing they are now at a point of crisis: They must decide how they will live the rest of their earthly lives. Will they live it for their own agenda? Or will they live for God?

The choices we make brand us; we are the sum of our decisions. Some of us need to reevaluate the impact those choices have made on our lives. Some of us, I'm afraid, need to take a long look in the mirror and admit that Christianity is not making the difference in our lives that we expected. Instead of becoming discouraged, however, we need to find a faith that will make a life-changing difference.

Everyone's life makes a statement about what is important to him. And for many tired, worn-out, weary Christians the statement is this: "My Christianity doesn't work." What is the statement your life makes?

WHAT THIS BOOK IS ABOUT

Many people these days hunger for a personal, spiritual revival in their own lives and in their families. Many long to recover a passion for the things of God. Many yearn for the sparks of spiritual revolution to ignite in their soul. This, then, is our business together.

To presume that one would be adequate to write a book entitled *The Rest of Your Life* borders on madness. Indeed, the project did overwhelm me at times. However, I now find myself thoroughly excited about the potential of this final work to be genuinely helpful.

We have four missions in these pages, so the book is organized into four parts. The thrust of Part 1, entitled *Making Mid-Course Corrections*, is to draw a picture of the age in which we live and show how deeply it affects our Christian thinking.

Part 2, *Charting a New Course*, challenges each of us to think through where we are on our own spiritual pilgrimage. Then seven "big picture" ideas are offered to focus on while finishing this book, and later when you move on to other things.

Part 3, *Deciding What to Believe*, underscores the importance of building a right foundation of Christian doctrine. A passionate, authentic life is first based upon sound biblical beliefs. Many, if not most, of the problems I have personally encountered among anguished Christians result simply from not having settled beliefs and doctrine.

Part 4, *Cultivating an Authentic Christian Lifestyle*, tries to identify the blueprint for Christian practice and living which we should build on the foundation of our beliefs. What should we be doing if we are going to live a life that makes any difference for ourselves, our families, and in the world?

PURPOSES

I have several dreams for this book. First, I pray that God will use it in a very personal way to help men and women reevaluate and make any needed mid-course corrections.

Second, I hope that by equipping and challenging believers to think and live more biblically this volume will add to the movement already afoot to reclaim culture and lead our nation back to God.

Third, I anxiously pray that Bible study groups, accountability groups, and Sunday school classes will use *The Rest of My Life* for discussion classes. I have learned how delicate an art communication is. The greatest impact and change I have seen in lives has come through group discussion when people have "air time" to flesh out concepts. The best way to "own" an idea is to wrestle and argue with it among some friends.

Finally, most of all I hope this book will be abundantly encouraging. Life can be brutal, and we all need to be encouraged. "An anxious heart weighs a man down, but a kind word cheers him up" (Proverbs 12:25). Encouragement is the food of the heart. In today's rapid-fire culture many of us have hungry hearts.

Yes, we need more insights and wisdom about some things. But, more than anything, most of us simply need to be reminded about the ideas that have slipped our minds. We then need to be encouraged to step back into the mainstream of an authentic Christian life—with passion.

MAKING
MID-COURSE
CORRECTIONS

PART ONE

NEVER MAILED TO ANN LANDERS

CHAPTER 1

D*ear Ann,*

As I glanced at the clock/radio it read 2:00 A.M. I rolled over for the umpteenth time, but I knew it wouldn't make any difference. I knew this night would never end. So I groped through the dark and found my way to the kitchen table to write you this note.

I can't begin to tell you the number of times I have longed to change my life. I've never really been satisfied with the way I've managed the years.

There was the time little Tony wanted me to help him glue a wing on his model airplane that wouldn't fit quite right (you know, Ann, they don't make them like they used to). I told him I'd be right there. I just wanted to finish the paper, but somehow I just forgot. He figured it out fine on his own, but he never asked me to help again.

He's thirteen now. He's grown straight as an arrow. His character is strong, though I'm afraid it's not from me. In spite of my neglect, he has somehow reached down deep inside himself and tapped reserves I didn't know were there. God, how I love that boy. I yearn to hold him in my arms even as I write, but it is, after all, 2:00 A.M.

When Cindy stopped being daddy's little girl and started liking boys, I didn't feel comfortable hugging her like I once did. She is a jewel, and I'm so proud of her. About a year ago I read somewhere that 70 percent of teen-aged girls say they are no longer virgins, and over one million of them become

7

pregnant each year. Those seemed like exaggerated numbers to me, until Cindy's best friend had an abortion. Now I wonder if Cindy is part of the 70 percent.

For twenty years now, Ann, I've slaved away at my career. I'm a strong work-ethic kind of guy. I remember how hard my dad worked for his family, even though we barely got by. I've certainly done better than he did, but I can't help but wonder why his family seemed so much happier than mine. Our home seems to be turning into a house. What is missing here?

Anyway, the reason I'm writing, Ann, and the reason I can't sleep tonight is that I'm afraid. She won't actually come out and say it, but Sue—that's my wife—has lost the flame she once had for me. Oh, I don't mean she has shut me out of her life. It's still the same old Sue that meets me at the door when I get home.

No, actually, I think it's me that has shut her out of my life. I've slowly crushed the enthusiasm she once had for what was happening with us. I haven't really cared that much about what was going on in her life; I have been so busy with my own. I couldn't even tell you who her best friend is or, for that matter, if she even has one. I've been so selfish with my time, Ann. Everything I've done I've done for myself—for my own pleasure.

I know she isn't seeing anyone else—that's not Sue—but what really breaks my heart, Ann, is that I don't think her self-esteem is that good anymore. Over the years I have berated her for her housework, I have criticized how she dresses, and I have blamed her for the faults I see in the children. But worse, Ann, I never say anything nice to her. It's been so long since I looked into her eyes and said, "I love you." The idea even seems awkward now. Truth be known, I love and respect Sue more than anyone I know, but I never tell her that. All I do is criticize.

So, anyway, this afternoon my company dumped me. Cutbacks. It doesn't bother me nearly as much as I thought it would. I haven't told Sue yet.

Now what am I going to do? My company dumped me and I dumped my family years ago. It just seems that the dull, constant pain of regret has trespassed upon my soul—not like a pain from an accident, but more like an unnoticed tumor that slowly, over the years, has spread its malignancy throughout my whole body and soul.

I'm not a bad guy, Ann—really. It's just that after all these years I suddenly realize that I never really knew what I was after, and my life has missed the target. It's as though I pursued the god I wanted, but never knew the God who is. I'm really struggling, Ann.

I have been no stranger to the ways of the world. I bought into this rat race lock, stock, and barrel, and I'm worn out, actually. Oh, I've been part of a local church, even active from time to time. But I think it's all been a game for me. I consider myself a Christian, but my life betrays that I've really been doing my own thing. I've been slow, very slow, to make any changes in my life.

What do I do now with the rest of my career? Do I pull right back into the fast lane, or is there some way for me to reevaluate? I've saved a little money; does that all disappear now?

Ann, I'm talking about the rest of my life here. Can a guy like me have a second chance? How can I find out who I really am, and why I exist? Is it possible to turn my family relationships around? Or is it just too late for me?

This fear that grips me, Ann, well, it's hard to describe. It's like a dull ache in the marrow of my bones; it's like a giant claw that has a stranglehold on my emotions. I wanted my life to count, to make a difference, to be significant. Now I am tormented with the thought that I may just become another statistic.

It's not mid-life crisis, Ann; it's more than that. I'm afraid I've lost my soul. I didn't sell it, Ann. I simply gave it away.

> *Sincerely yours,*
>
> *Robert*

THE NEXT SEVERAL WEEKS . . .

Inexplicably, over the next several weeks Robert kept bumping into men attending a Friday morning Bible study for businessmen. Finally, since he did sense a growing desire to examine his own beliefs and convictions, he let one of his friends drag him through the keyhole to the Bible study one Friday morning.

"Good morning. I'm Jack. Welcome to TGIF Men's Bible Study. It's good to have you with us this morning." The genuineness of this pre-dawn greeting took Robert by surprise. He wondered what possible motive this Jack could have for being so friendly so early in the day. *He must be in the insurance business*, he thought.

"Good morning. I'm Robert," he responded. "What kind of work do you do?"

"I own a small wholesale distribution company. How about you?"

Well, that must not be it. "Oh, I'm between things right now. I've mostly been in management with mid-sized electronics manufacturers," Robert answered, wondering what reaction this would get.

Jack smiled and motioned to a table against the wall. "Why don't you fill in one of these visitor's name tags, Robert, and then we'll get you a cup of coffee," he said.

Robert, though a bit nervous, actually enjoyed the hour-long look into the Bible. When he was warmly invited to come back next week, he somehow believed the offer was genuine. He made up his mind right then and there that he would be back next Friday. Besides, it couldn't hurt to expand his network to help find a new job.

THE NEXT SEVERAL MONTHS . . .

A whole new world began to open up before Robert's eyes. He had never seen men actually caring about each other without ulterior motives before.

Meanwhile, on the inside new thoughts and feelings began to simmer, then boil, but always just beyond the grasp of his awareness. He knew something was changing, but he couldn't put his finger on exactly what. Occasionally a sliver of insight glimmered in the window of his conscious thoughts, but then just as quickly as it appeared it would slip back into obscurity.

Robert noticed some of the men who sat at his same discussion table at the Bible study really seemed to have broken the code. They had a peace which he enviously longed to know. Some of them were struggling, too, but they seemed to know where to look for the answers.

I can't find the answers because I don't even know what the questions are, Robert realized.

When Robert first started attending the Friday morning Bible study, he made it quite clear that he already attended church and didn't want anyone trying to cram religion down his throat. Bill, the discussion leader at his table, honored Robert's wish, but as a result he often felt

---

"After all these years, I suddenly realize that I never really knew what I was after, and my life has missed the target."

---

handcuffed when speaking to Robert. It was as though 98 percent of the helpful information he could share was off-limits. They were living in two distinctly different spheres. He often wondered why Robert bothered to come, but he kept praying for him. "If you ever want to talk personally about things, let me know," Bill told him.

At home the lack of a job led to financial pressures, which led to family pressures. Things were definitely getting worse, not better. The internal pressure on Robert kept building. Robert's eventual phone call came as no surprise to Bill. He was pleased for the opportunity to meet with Robert over lunch and discuss his spiritual condition. After the sandwiches disappeared Robert haltingly labored to express his half-formed thoughts, which seemed to be just centimeters beyond the reach of expression. Bill's heart grew burdened for him. He listened intently as Robert poured out a messy goo of fragmented feelings. Finally, Bill could restrain himself no longer.

"Robert, I have honored your request to not try to 'cram religion' down your throat, but I feel I must express myself to you today," he said honestly. "First, though, let me say that I really see and feel your pain, your frustration, your sense of aimless drifting, and I want to help you.

"It's like this. In my mind's eye I see you in a small, dark room, say ten feet by ten feet. I'm in the very next room, but my room is big, very big, say one hundred feet by one hundred feet and brightly lit. And there are lots of other people—happy people—in my room. Sure, some have problems but all the happy people are helping the others to get through their difficult times.

"You, on the other hand, are all alone, sitting in dark gloom. A door connects your room to mine. I desperately want to invite you into the room where I am, but you have asked me not to. But today I just want you to know that I think you would like it in my room very much. Jesus Christ is the door. He will help you get out of the dark room if you will let Him, if you will turn to Him."

At that moment tears softly formed in the corners of Robert's reddening eyes. After clearing the lump in his throat he responded, "Well, I must say from the way you described my room that you have read my circumstances very well. And from what I've seen of your room, I must admit it looks just as you explained.

"As you say, you have not tried to cram religion down my throat, not even once. In fact, by being able to observe all of you in a non-threatening environment for the past several months I have found myself drawn closer and closer. It's as though I am hooked on a line and some Power is reeling me in," Robert admitted. After taking a deep breath, he was ready. "Would you tell me more about how I can have this personal relationship with Jesus I've heard you talk about?"

THE NEXT SEVERAL YEARS . . .

The Friday morning Bible study helped Robert take a considered look into areas of his life that he had never really examined before in the fast-paced world in which he had moved. He felt deeply touched by the Spirit of God. The impulse to change his ways and live a life pleasing to God escalated within him.

Robert began to think about making a clean break with the past. In his mind he thought through the terms of a fuller, more complete, total surrender of his life to Christ. It seemed to be the next logical step to satisfy his yearning to understand the issues of his inner world. He began to sense what it meant to submit to Christ in the daily details. He felt his heart becoming softer, more tender, more open to living a life of obedience to the God who is, not out of obligation but from a deep sense of gratitude.

"In the hidden place of my heart where no man has ever been, in the secret place where only God has been, there I yearn to really be a man after God's own heart."

One morning, as he pondered the way he had tried to have his cake and eat it, too, spiritually speaking, these words flowed out through the tip of his pen onto a fresh page of the private journal he had started keeping:

Dear Journal,

I find that you have become one of my best friends. I can tell you secrets that I can tell no one else—no one.

I have become very soft and pliable toward the Lord as I have reevaluated my life. Not only have I explored my outward lifestyle, but I have journeyed inward and am beginning to understand who I really am in Christ.

I have always lived by my own best thinking—my own ideas. Now I realize that while I can choose my own way, I cannot choose the results. My decisions have consequences.

Many of my rough edges have been knocked away. I feel more humility, contrition, and tenderness. I am filled up with a repentance I have never known before. I can see so clearly that I don't have all the answers after all—so clearly that it's embarrassing. I've always had an answer for everything. Now I have more questions than answers. It is a radical change.

This newfound humility—well, I really like it. This is the right perspective from which to ponder life. I want to get it right. I don't want the trite, packaged answer. I can no longer brook the clever slogans and sacred shibboleths. I want real meat, real substance.

I tremble at the thought of getting off track again. I am afraid I will again try to grab the reins from God, that I will once again end up taking control of my life. I sincerely want to be a man whose heart is fully committed to God. It is the deepest vein of desire in my soul. In the hidden place of my heart where no man has ever been, in the secret place where only God has been, there I yearn to really be a man after God's own heart.

I want to be a biblical Christian. No fluff. No drivel. No canned answers. No self-centered ambitions. No impure thoughts. No wrong motives. I want to slay the flesh. I long to live by the power of the Holy Spirit. This time I want to make it stick; I want to live the rest of my earthly life for God.

I sense I am on the verge of a breakthrough. I sense God is not finished with me yet, that God has more for me. Now I long to know what it is. I am probing, poking, penetrating, striving to find God's plan for the rest of my life. I think I am going to make it after all.

Robert

ﻬ   ﻬ   ﻬ

DISCUSSION QUESTIONS

1. What part of the letter, "Never Mailed to Ann Landers," do you most identify with personally? Can you explain why?

2. In what ways do you think men and women need to rethink the condition of their spiritual lives? What can be done to help them?

3. "I always lived by my own best thinking—my own ideas. Now I realize that while I can choose my own way, I cannot choose the results. My decisions have consequences." Does this ring true?

   ☐ Agree   ☐ Disagree

   If you agree, give an example of how this principle has affected you.

4. Which room are you now in—the small dark room or the large well-lit room? How is it going in there? (Note: If you are in the small room, this book will gently yet clearly help you walk through the door. If you are in the large room but hurting, these pages will help you diagnose why and offer ideas to become well again. If you are in the large room and happy, this book will help you focus on how to organize the rest of your life in a way that pleases God and serves Him while giving you a satisfying life.)

5. What is an area of your life about which you are deeply troubled? What have you been doing to resolve it?

THE TWO SPIRITS
OF OUR AGE

CHAPTER 2

D*ear Journal,*

What is happening to the world? Everywhere I look I see people in despair, people doing absurd things, materialistic people, and virtual abandonment of moral standards. The world used to be a pretty safe place. What went wrong? What happened to us? I am so confused and frustrated that sometimes I feel like screaming, but there is no one to hear. Can anyone give me some simple categories to explain what's happening to the world?

I am often puzzled about what my role in the world should be. What kind of attitude should I have, and what kind of approach should I use?

Robert

A NUMBER OF YEARS LATER . . .

Many years had raced—no, slipped by—since Robert first placed his faith in Christ. One day his early morning journal entry continued to reverberate through his mind as he drove to work. Midway through the morning he closed his office door, returned to his chair, and sat pensively at his desk.

A reflective, philosophic mood took control of his conscious thoughts—something that didn't happen very often. As he surveyed the balance sheet of his life, he

17

felt his assets and liabilities had come together by almost random, colliding forces.

He felt buffeted on every side by the heartless decisions of overly ambitious people who barely knew his name—decisions that sometimes radically altered the course of his life. No one seemed to know about, or care, that he had a married-but-already-divorced daughter with a small son living in his home. His son was doing well, for which he was thankful. Constantly on his mind was his demure, kind wife who would never make it in the hard-ball, work-a-day world. He never wanted her to have to work when he died; it was a responsibility that gnawed on him, and it was a driving force behind his hard-hitting, time-cramped schedule.

As he pondered his life, his thoughts lengthened and widened to the bigger picture. His mind's eye gazed toward the world silhouetted against the horizon of his thoughts. When he surveyed that world a dark, chilly surge of sadness swept across the landscape of his thoughts like a damp, biting wind. It was a world that seemed out of control, about to explode. So many different worlds.

It isn't all bad, he reassured himself. *Look at the joy you've experienced since becoming a Christian. Look at how you've changed. Yea, look. . . . Haven't been many changes lately, have there, Robert?* He recalled how excited he used to be about his faith. Now he couldn't remember the last time he spoke with anyone about Christ.

The roaring fire of his faith had burned down to a few warm embers, still there, but not the blaze of passion as when he first believed. Robert knew that he had stopped growing spiritually long ago. He had completely separated his faith from his work and social life. All in all, Christianity was still privately engaging to him but an irrelevant factor in his day-to-day world. All this flowed from a single thought many years before: *I'm saved. I don't need to worry about all of that other stuff.*

He couldn't erase the image etched on his mind of a world that drove people to despair. A self-indulgent world of opulence that ignored the have-nots. A dying world of disease that apparently seized its victims at random. A sex-saturated society that sucked out the moral verve from the church. A broken, hurting world in desperate need of God's message of love and forgiveness. A world coming apart at the seams. *There are not many happy campers out there. How did we get to be like this? What does it all mean? What role does God play in things? Isn't He supposed to be in control? And where have I been, anyway?*

THE CENTRAL QUESTION OF LIFE

The history of human thought has focused around one great question: What is the meaning of things, and the purpose of life?

Every young student longs to make sense of his universe, often naively thinking he or she is the first one to ever ponder the subject. I remember being that way, don't you?

At my high school we scrupulously studied the diversity of the world. In history class we looked at the world historically. In English class we explored the world of literature. In algebra class we studied the world mathematically. In chemistry class we examined the elements chart to learn the stuff the world is made of. In geography class we learned how the earth was formed.

Yet no one ever pulled all these particulars into any sort of unified explanation: "What is the unifying idea behind all the diversity in life? What is the meaning of things, the purpose of it all?" As one of those naive young people interested in making sense of things, this drove me to a premature mid-life crisis, and I quit high school in the middle of my senior year. Yes, the search for the meaning and purpose of life can be all-consuming. Whether consciously or not, the search for the meaning and purpose of life is the chief quest of every thinking person's life.

If I promise to keep it *very* short, may I take us through a brief history lesson? Down through the ages man has continually tried to draw a circle big enough to explain the meaning and purpose of life. When a thinker was gripped by a theory of life he would construct a circle to describe it. Then the next fellow would come along and show how that circle wouldn't work after all, but he would, of course, provide the new, correct circle. But then someone else would say, "That is not it either, but here, I have it," and so on.[1] These thinkers were all looking for that one unified stream of thought called "truth," or "reality," that would explain life.

In the sixteenth century the flow of human thought broke into two distinct streams. The Renaissance, which exalted man, became the stream of humanism. The Reformation, which exalted Christ, became the stream of evangelical Christianity. From then till now humanists have attempted to use their *unaided human reason* to draw their circle, while Christians appeal to the *divine revelation of the Scriptures* for theirs.

By the late eighteenth century, due mostly to the period called the Enlightenment, the main artery of humanism burst into scores of little capillary streams of thought. *Humanism* became *humanisms*, like many little echoes. The world had caught a bad case of the "-isms."

The more time that passed, the further these "humanisms" spun away from the truth of God. Finally, from the nineteenth century forward many of the men who shaped the world's ideas found the need for God obsolete. Names that dotted the landscape of that era include Rousseau, Nietzsche, Darwin, Marx, Freud, and Hegel. Then, with no place for God in their equations, these opinion makers despaired of ever finding ultimate truth. In our day, humanism has altogether abandoned its metaphysics, its rationalism, and even the fixed truths of naturalistic science.[2]

These two cleavages in the sixteenth and nineteenth centuries have brought the world to its skeptical knees. Sixteenth-century *Humanism* separated *man from God*; Nineteenth-century *humanisms* separated *man from truth*. Here is the pivotal question for us today: Without God or truth where can one turn to find the meaning and purpose of things?

Except for schizophrenics, utopians, and Christians, the only place for modern man to turn is skepticism, cynicism, and despair. Which is exactly how our non-Christian neighbors feel about things, if we are speaking with them on this level—the level of ultimate reality, meaning, and purpose. Enough, now, of the history lesson. How does all this translate into everyday life today?

Recently fifty men attended a men's retreat in the Ocala National Forest here in Florida. Called the Wounded Warrior Weekend, these men dressed up like Indians, beat on tom-toms, talked to trees, and cried out in existential pain. But what problem does this really solve? This may bring a moment's relief, but what do these anguished men do on Wednesday afternoon when the *angst* returns?

Oh, how I ache for these men. The goal of popular psychology seems to be limited to figuring out who is responsible for your problems. In that way you will know who to blame for the way you are. Figuring out who is responsible for your problems may give you someone to blame, but it will not help you find meaning and purpose for your life.

Today's humanist has abandoned all hope of ever developing a unity to explain life. He microscopically examines only the little questions—questions for which most of us don't need answers. He has despaired of, and thus avoids, life's big questions. And why not? If you don't recognize the need for spirituality, rational thinking, or fixed truth, how can you answer a big question?

"The goal of popular psychology seems to be limited to figuring out who is responsible for your problems. In that way you will know who to blame for the way you are."

The result? Today people do what seems right in their own eyes. "Men have gone in search of many schemes" (Ecclesiastes 7:29). For all our advancements, society teeters precariously on the edge of the moral abyss.

LIFE ON THE EDGE OF THE ABYSS

Somber-faced men with receding hairlines and pale complexions streamed into the Situation Room in the penthouse suite of the Madison Avenue advertising firm. Their crisply-starched white shirts and regimental ties imitated the most minute details of the dress code initiated by the firm's founder. Though not conspicuous enough to occur as an actual conscious thought, these uniforms reminded one of military battle fatigues.

Each man took his seat, and then the field general stalked into the room. The solemn nods of greeting served as the substitute for a salute. The commander stood somberly at the head of the table. A grave, menacing scowl contorted his face, and his grim frown creased a deep vertical furrow in the middle of his forehead.

"Gentlemen," he began. "We lost 2 percent market share in the last ninety days. I'll not hear any excuses for this indescribable setback. It is sufficient for you to know that we are in serious jeopardy of losing this account, which I remind you makes up 17 percent of the agency's annual budget. Beware that if we lose this account, heads will roll. Now let's get to work and devise a scheme to seduce the public back to our client's product. Do I make myself clear? Are there any questions?"

With no questions the chairman rose stiffly then briskly left the room, and pandemonium broke out among the junior executives huddled around the table.

"Good grief," said one. "If we lose this account I'll be sure to go. And we just bought a new house in the Hamptons."

"This is war!" piped an overly eager middle-aged veteran. "We must win the battle for the customer's mind. We must do whatever it takes to sway those people out there back to our client's product."

"Well, let's get down to business then," said another. "I have an idea. What we need to do is portray our product as a panacea that will solve the buyer's hidden needs for acceptance—that his friends will think him wise, attractive, and intelligent only if he buys our product, and a dunce if he buys our competitor's."

"Yea, that sound like a good idea."

The conversation muttered on, the Christians among them capitulated, and the drone of little lies from the merchants of discontent spun into a web of glistening deceit, sure to lure the unsuspecting consumer to flash his plastic card and take one more interest-bearing step toward that elusive commodity: human dignity. These professionals would help the consumer see how intelligent he is to conclude that their product alone will bring him the approval he seeks from his friends, giving him yet another fragile figment of happiness.

THE CHRISTIAN PROBLEM AND OPPORTUNITY

Why is the problem of Humanism a problem for Christians? We must not let ourselves be hoodwinked. We are all deeply influenced by the dominant ideas of our age. Our individual spiritual pilgrimage doesn't take place in a vacuum. As C. S. Lewis noted, we are all much more profoundly affected by the age in which we live than we would care to admit or, for that matter, are even capable of recognizing. Controversies aside, every age agrees upon a great deal more than they disagree about.

The thinkers in any age set the course for culture and society. The thinkers debate the theories, concepts, and ideas which influence a

---

"Our generation lives in an age of profound spiritual crisis. It is an unsettled time."

---

small segment of society: the intellectuals. But then these ideas filter out to the artists, novelists, musicians, dramatists, journalists, and clergy who, in turn, simplify and disburse the ideas to the general public.[3]

Our generation lives in an age of profound spiritual crisis. It is an unsettled time. Like salt water intrusion into a fresh water supply, these capillary streams of thought have, by degrees, trespassed upon the thinking of most Christians.

The system strains and groans like the creaking, rusted hull of an old freighter in a typhoon. Thinking people are terrified over the possibility that she will break up under the fierce, violent pressure of such a vicious storm.

What could the believing world do to again exert a meaningful moral influence on culture and society? It is not enough to say, "I'm saved. I don't need to worry about all of that other stuff." This "other stuff" does matter: It matters in culture and society, it matters to our grandchildren, it matters to God, it matters today, and it matters forever.

Christians are the only group on earth who have a complete circle, or system, of truth—though I'm afraid many don't often know or use it well. We must first understand what's in our circle. It must become as familiar to us as the hammer in the master carpenter's hand. We must penetrate the circle so deeply that we can explain the veracity of what's inside to the most spurious skeptic.

Where do we begin? In the same way a battery must be slowly recharged, so our minds must be carefully, methodically filled with the sound biblical principles of faith and practice. No more "I don't need to worry about all that other stuff." Christians who would live an authentic Christian life must replace secular thinking and categories with a biblical base, model, and paradigm. This game we are playing is for keeps, and the final score gets posted forever.

CHRISTIANITY AND HUMANISM

The spirit of Christianity exalts God, while the spirit of Humanism exalts man. These two spirits, of course, are present in every age in some form. They represent a perpetual tug-of-war between the secularized and the sacred, the humanistic and the holy. Exactly what is Humanism?

Though Humanism is not a monolithic set of beliefs, it is the grandfather of all the other "-isms." Humanism is the main artery which leads to all the capillary "-isms" of our times. Here is a working definition:

> Humanism is the life view that man, who at the level of his basic nature is good, establishes his own moral values apart from the influence of anyone (including God), and he self-determines his destiny; he is the "master of his own fate." Man is responsible only to leave the world a better place. Truth is relative, and whatever goal man chooses to pursue is good.

Christianity and Humanism represent two clear, distinct options for each of us individually and for society as a whole. On one side is Christianity and, on the other, under the umbrella of Humanism, is everything else. We might diagram it like this:

CHRISTIANITY　　　　　　　　**HUMANISM**

The difference between Christianity and Humanism is total and complete. The wall between them symbolizes a complete separation. They are two separate spheres, not merely different points along a continuum. They are radically different and opposite systems of how to approach life, meaning, reality, values, ethics, justice, relationships, eternity, God, and man. As systems, they have no points in common and a wall of ideology separates them.

Certainly some humanists smolder with hostility toward Christians, but so do some Christians toward humanists. By and large most humanists are actually very nice people. Sure, there are exceptions, mostly egoists out for personal gain. Humanists are not invaders from outer space; they are our next door neighbors. They, too, want to leave the world a better place. Frankly, most humanists are not ideologues, but they have merely defaulted into their life view. In other words, they are simply products of their age.

Humanism has plainly grandfathered many ills: abortion, euthanasia, the sexual revolution, and more. And humanists have trashed many aspects of education, science, law, and justice. At another level, though, the world owes a great debt to humanists. They have been stewards of the environment, science, medicine, and government while for a century the Christian world has been in a Rip Van Winkle's snooze. Humanists are not out to destroy the planet, but to save it. They may end up destroying it, but that will not be what they set out to do.

CHRISTIANS AND HUMANS

While it is important—crucial, really—to keep up the wall between Christianity and Humanism, it is equally important to tear down the walls between Christians and humans. The symbol looks like this:

CHRISTIANS ⟶ HUMANS

We tend to get this backwards. We build walls where we should tear them down—in our relationships; and we tear down walls where we should build them up—in our beliefs.

Humanity longs for a Savior. The Barna Research Group reports that 81 percent of born-again Christians say "having a growing relationship with Jesus Christ" is a top priority. But guess what else? Forty-seven percent of *non*-Christians also said "having a growing relationship with Jesus Christ" is a top priority.[4] Wow! That is every other non-Christian! The message? Many people would gladly receive Christ as

Savior if we would simply stop calling them names and love them with the love of God.

One reason we have built walls where we should not, and have not built walls where we should, is that many of us don't fully understand Jesus' teaching in John 17.

Jesus said we are *in* the world but we are not *of* the world—"in but not of." In times past and present, a preoccupation with this concept has handicapped the full intention of Jesus' teaching in John 17, producing a separation of our faith from everyday life.

Our Lord said, "They are still *in* the world. . . . They are not *of* the world. . . . My prayer is *not* that you take them out of the world but that you protect them from the evil one. . . . As you sent me *into* the world, I have sent them *into* the world" (John 17:11, 14–15, 18, italics added).

So not only are we to be *"in* but not *of"* the world, but also *"into* but not *of"* the world. We must fathom the full duty of a true disciple. The full teaching of Jesus is *both* "in but not of" *and* "into but not of." These are two different ideas, not merely the same idea expressed in two different ways. Here is how they look with symbols:

"IN BUT NOT OF"

Christianity   Humanism

"INTO BUT NOT OF"

Christians   ⟶   Humans

"In" But Not Of

"In but not of" is our *relationship* "with" the world. Biblical Christians are to be "in" the world but not "of" the world. It pertains to our *character*—the kind of life we lead. We are aliens and strangers in the land, pilgrims passing through on our way to the Celestial City.

Christians and non-Christians live next door to each other like wheat and tares. We are to live by them without becoming like them. "Let both grow together until the harvest" (Matthew 13:30). Unfortu-

---

"Perhaps it is time for us to rethink how we will spend the rest of our lives."

---

nately, twentieth-century Christians have parked on this idea, adopting the value of "live and let live." And we have largely separated ourselves from not only the non-Christian world, but also from the *undecided* world—those to whom we are to take His light.

"Into" But Not Of

"Into but not of" is our *mission* "to" the world. Biblical Christians are to go "into" the world. "Into but not of" is an active role; it pertains to our *conduct*—the kind of impact we have. We are called to be salt and light to a broken world full of death and decay. The purpose of salt is to preserve. We are to preserve culture by challenging and encouraging the highest possible good. The purpose of light is to drive out darkness. We are to bring God's message of love and forgiveness to a dark, broken world.

In this century we Christians have lost our influence in culture and society. Authentic, biblical Christianity has become a minority report. Can you think of a single arena in which the Christian life-and-world view is affecting culture in any triumphant way?

Consider the worlds of law, medicine, science, education, the arts, the media, politics, sports, entertainment, commerce, and philosophy—even religion. Not one of these arenas operates from a distinctly Christian base. It is, in my view, because we lost sight of John 17:18: "As you sent me into the world, I have sent them into the world." We do not have a sense of being "sent."

Here is the irony: *We are there.* Christians are in each and every important arena of American life, but most are silent.

The root problem is that many Christians in positions to influence culture are what Os Guinness calls *undiscipled disciples*. They know Jesus but little else, and they are spiritually impotent—spiritual pygmies, really. Guinness says, "The problem is not that Christians are not where they should be. The problem is that they are not *what* they should be *right where they are*."[5]

More than anything we need a second Reformation to challenge cultural Christians (our largest denomination) to rethink the beliefs by which they live so they can impact society and culture in a meaningful, biblical way. A spiritual *revival* will put us back in touch with Christ personally, but only a *reformation* of our belief system will give us the competence to bring the life-changing knowledge of God back into our culture and society.

Perhaps it is time for us to rethink how we will spend the rest of our lives. Perhaps it is time for us to speak out as our world dances precariously along the edge of the moral abyss. Will we continue to capitulate, or will someone in those meetings begin to call out as a voice in the wilderness? Are you yet willing to let Christ send you out "into" the front lines of society to speak for Him there?

Thank God for the remnant in each of these arenas making a difference. Thousands of faithful believers in big and small companies, trade and professional associations, business groups, and communities sponsor outreach prayer breakfasts. Countless elected and appointed officials, college professors, lawyers, scientists, teachers, homemakers, and business people attend Bible studies and seek to share the gospel with their peers.

However, these thousands must become tens of thousands. These modern day apostles are today only voices in the wilderness. To bring about a true reformation of society and culture, hundreds of thousands of us must rush to their aid as though a rescue party.

The kingdom of God is not a temporal kingdom. Reformation cannot legislate spiritual fervor and moral good. We are not to forcibly superimpose Christianity upon the culture. Rather, out of a grateful heart filled to the overflow with Christ's love and forgiveness, we are to live with such integrity and perform our work with such excellence that people are compelled to consider our lives.

Only when we have faithfully lived "in" the world, will we be invited to speak. We must accept the invitation, cross the line that separates merely being "in" the world, and go "into" the world and speak bravely. The world will be won to faith in Jesus Christ only in proportion to our faithfulness to be both "in" the world and "into" the world.

The moral order is like a stalled plane plunging toward earth. If only one in ten Christians would go "into" the world—not merely remain "in" the world—and speak boldly for the Christian life view, what would happen? Like the trembling copilot who courageously grabs the vibrating stick, that one Christian would soon reverse the moral, spiritual, and relational plunge of the past century and save us all.

Authentic Christianity penetrates like dye down deep into the fabric of culture and society. It shows a marginal difference exists between our lifestyles and those who make no claim on Christ. Authentic Christianity answers the call of God to be not only "in but not of " the world but also to go "into" the world. If we will only embrace authentic Christianity, the results will electrify the world.

ǝ　ǝ　ǝ

DISCUSSION QUESTIONS

1. Describe your own personal search for the meaning and purpose of life. Has it been an easy or difficult pilgrimage? How do you think God may have led you along this journey?

2. "We are all much more profoundly affected by the age in which we live than we would care to admit or, for that matter, are even capable of recognizing. Controversies aside, every age agrees upon a great deal more than they disagree about." Do you agree or disagree? Explain your answer.

3. Have you ever said or thought in so many words, "I'm saved. I don't need to worry about all of that other stuff." If so, what effect do you think that approach has had on your life? Do you still hold to that idea? Why, or why not?

4. Do you think about life in biblical categories? When problems or decisions come up do you think about them biblically? If not, how could building a biblical base, model, and paradigm affect the rest of your life?

5. "Christianity and Humanism represent two clear, distinct options for each of us individually and for society as a whole. The difference between Christianity and Humanism is total and complete. They are two separate spheres, not merely different points along a continuum. They are radically different and opposite systems of how to approach life, meaning, reality, values, ethics, justice, relationships, eternity, God, and man. They have no points in common and a wall of ideology separates them."

   ☐ Agree   ☐ Disagree

   Comment.

6. "While it is important—crucial, really—to keep up the wall between Christianity and Humanism, it is equally important to tear down the walls between Christians and humans. We tend

to get this backwards. We build walls where we should tear them down—in our relationships; and we tear down walls where we should build them up—in our beliefs."

☐ Agree   ☐ Disagree

Comment.

7. Read John 17:11,14–15,18. What are the two different concepts Jesus is teaching in this passage?

verses 11,14–15: _____ But Not _____

verse 18: _____ But Not _____

Explain the difference. How significant is this difference?

8. In what practical ways can you be more "into" the world?

THREE
DANGEROUS
IDEAS

D*ear Journal,*

I know just enough about the "-isms" to be dangerous. Dangerous because I probably think I know more that I do. Dangerous because I probably underestimate the degree they influence my thinking. Dangerous because of the subtle effect they have on my own Christian beliefs. Dangerous because they pull me into the world. Dangerous because I don't really know enough to talk intelligently with someone who actually knows why they are not a Christian.

Robert

CHAPTER 3

A WORLD UNDER PRESSURE

Robert had the convertible top down as he snaked through rush hour traffic. The car in front of him wanted to make a left-hand turn, but the approaching traffic streamed as far as the eye could see. Robert could easily have pulled into the adjacent lane and gone around this car. Instead, he passively leaned against his horn, never changing the expressionless look on his face.

So much of life seemed pointless to Robert. He often felt depressed; the sorrow, the pain, the anguish troubled him. The seeming lack of fixed truths vexed him. His consuming passion for more and more things puzzled him. Later, a penitent Robert wondered, *Why do I think the way I think and do the things I do? I live on the ragged edge.*

People today are under a great deal of pressure. They are colliding with the future predicted by Alvin Toffler in his book *Future Shock*. We have become *the change society*, absorbing an ever accelerating litany of changes each passing year. And what is the basic problem?

We have created a culture which requires more energy than people have to give. Many people are finding they simply cannot manage the pressures of so many changes so quickly. The real problem, of course, is that it's not just happening to *them*. It's happening to us, too. Let's slow down for a few moments to see why we, too, often suffer the same maladies.

The world runs on ideas. Ideas are the fuel upon which dreams are built and nations shaped, and by which lives are shattered and kingdoms crumble. In the marketplace of ideas, here are three particularly dangerous ones.

THREE STRANDS OF HUMANISM

Although Humanism sums up all the other "-isms," humanists don't all think alike any more than all Christians do. Some qualify as card-carrying fatalists, while others join the human potential movement to create their own destiny. From egoistic to altruistic, atheistic to agnostic, hedonistic to stoic—every humanist carves out his own set of beliefs.

Nevertheless, three pervasive "-isms" in particular deserve further explanation to help us see how subtly they influence our thinking:

CHRISTIANITY 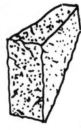 **HUMANISM**

Existentialism
Relativism
Materialism

Existentialism addresses the *meaning* of life; relativism, the *values* of life; and materialism, the *comfort* of life.

"We have created a culture which requires more energy than people have to give."

The condensed explanations that follow are published in the same way someone would produce a medical handbook for the home. They are only meant to help self-diagnose ourselves in the most general sort of way. If you are hurting, though, you may find the pain in your otherwise healthy life comes from one of these vexing viruses, "-isms" as common as the cold. You may want to ask your pastor or Christian bookstore for further reading suggestions.

1. THE EXISTENTIAL WORLD

Do you ever walk out of a theater with that uneasy-but-can't-quite-put-my-finger-on-it feeling? If so, you probably lack the categories to describe the ideas which propelled the plot. People find it immensely satisfying not only to know *what* happens, but *why*.

Existentialism towers as one such idea which has seeped and oozed into almost every crack of culture, particularly visible in art, literature, and entertainment. Christians who attend movies and plays, who read books and listen to opera, who watch television and visit art galleries are bombarded by plots laced with this "-ism." For example, 90 percent of the men in a large Bible study I attend saw *Dances with Wolves*, a decidedly existential script.

The opening scene of *Dances with Wolves*, the 1990 winner of seven Academy awards, including Best Picture, portrays a seriously wounded Union officer who, all alone, must make an important choice: Should he let his wounded foot be amputated or find death at the hands of the Confederate soldiers?

He mounts his horse, shuts his eyes, holds out his arms as though soaring in flight and then, to dramatically scored slow motion, he rides in front of the blazing muskets of the Confederate troops. When they astonishingly fail to kill him (we are all astonished—him, them, us, everyone), he repeats the ruggedly courageous, daring (insane) ride. And once again the Confederate soldiers and the audience are stupefied that they still can't seem to hit their brave target.

Mystically, darkly inspired by this, the Union troops rally, chase off the Confederates, and the lieutenant becomes a hero, all because (as he points out in the voice over) he was impotent to commit suicide. This scene sounds absurd when thought through, but the deceptively romantic lure of cinema makes us see him as somehow heroic and noble at the moment. Later, he bravely rebels against authority (he deserts the Army) and finds his peace by becoming an Indian. It is the making of an existential hero.

Existentialism Explained

The existentialist is a rugged individualist who pulls himself up by his own bootstraps. He believes that a man's destiny lies within himself. As Jean-Paul Sartre observed, the first principle of existentialism is, "Man is nothing else but that which he makes of himself."[1]

The starting point for secular existentialism is the belief that everything is permitted; after all, man is free. His freedom is the foundation of all his values. Though he is free, however, he is left alone in his freedom, responsible for his condition, without excuse. There is no legislator besides himself; in fact, he is abandoned to make his own subjective decisions. He can count on no one but himself and, thus, not only is man free, he is condemned to be free.

Man's freedom places the entire responsibility for his life squarely upon his own shoulders. And not only for himself, he is also responsible for the welfare of all men. Fate forces him to face a hostile world and make his important life decisions with limited knowledge—and that terrifies him because he has no way of knowing whether he is right or wrong.

But since this responsibility is too large—too overwhelming—man is burdened down by anguish and sorrow. It is easy to see why the existentialist despairs of life. It is a cruel fate that men created by God with a longing for meaning and purpose would never find it. Condemned to a hall of doors, man finds that each succeeding door to meaning slams shut just as he arrives, keeping meaning always elusive and just beyond his grasp. He stands alone, so all he can do is try to be brave. Sartre vividly summarizes: "In life, a man commits himself, draws his own portrait and there is nothing but that portrait."[2]

Walter Kaufmann concludes existentialism is not a philosophy, as such, reducible to one set of tenets, but a label for several widely different revolts against tradition. The existentialist abhors neat, compact schemes placed over his individuality. Does this sound hauntingly, personally familiar? Portions of existentialism strike raw, sore nerves in every human being. Because existentialism so succinctly frames the problem of modern man apart from God, it has wedged itself into the framework of our most basic beliefs. Though no longer an organized movement, this "-ism" deftly gives shape and form to the wounds man feels, helping him to express the bitter disappointment of his soul.

Do you see how, indeed, we are all more profoundly affected by our age than we would care to admit or even be capable of recognizing? Many of us were existentialists before we believed in Christ, and maybe we didn't know it. Some of us probably still are.

The Existentialist and God

It is not that the existentialist doesn't believe in the existence of God; he probably does. Most humanists at least accept some form of deity, although an agnostically distorted idea of God. He likely thinks all roads lead to heaven and labors to be as good as he can. This, too, leads to sorrow because, he wonders (without expecting an answer), "How can anyone ever know for sure?"

The secular existentialist rebels openly against the God who is, thus he has no fixed reference point or moral guide. Thinking himself alone, his situation is at once both tragic ("Is this all there is?") and absurd ("I am responsible for something that doesn't matter anyway").

Existentialism and Despair

What is the appeal of existentialism? Why is it so common? The broad, popular appeal of this "-ism," *even when not known and practiced by name,* springs from the "we're in it together" factor. "It's us common folk against the system." Existentialism addresses the problem of pain: "Life is hard, and then you die."

Life does often lead to sorrow, pain, and grief. Should we be surprised that a step-by-step guide on how to commit suicide, *Final Exit*, turned into a national best selling book? What then do men do with their despair? After all, life is part suffering; it does have anguish. Jesus Himself said, "In this world you will have trouble" (John 16:33), and "Each day has enough trouble of its own" (Matthew 6:34). Existentialism seeks to provide an answer to the problem of pain, although usually apart from God and almost never Christianly. It declares that life is meaningless. Sartre's famous line expresses the resulting grief: "Life is a useless passion."

For those without Christian hope, the notion that we must be brave and leave the world a better place appeals to our universal inner urge for dignity. Every now and then someone heroically ascends from the futile ranks for a brief moment and articulates that frustration which so often defies expression.

In the 1976 movie *Network*, Howard Beall, network news anchor, becomes one such hero by helping people articulate their rage. After falling on hard times, Beall was fired. In despair he announced that since his show was the only thing he had going for him, he would blow his brains out on national television. The next day he admitted his announcement was an act of sheer madness, then he goes on to decry the pointless pain, the humiliation and decay, the futile frustration of life, and the lack of human dignity. "Things have got to change," he points out passionately.

Then, after taking a deep breath as though to gain strength, he rails, "All I know is that first you've got to get mad. You've got to say, 'I'm a human being, my life has value!' So I want you to get up now. I want you to get up right now out of your chairs. I want you to get up right now and go to your window, open it, and stick out your head, and yell, 'I'm mad as h _ _ _, and I'm not going to take this anymore!'"

The film dissolves to street scenes across America. Young couples, old couples, people everywhere raising their windows, sticking their heads out, and yelling, "I'm mad as h _ _ _, and I'm not going to take this anymore!" One young husband and father beats on his charcoal grill as he vents his rage. One can't help but identify—even feel better, if we're honest. This succinctly summarizes the existential motif. But here's the problem: What do you do tomorrow . . . when the pain returns?

At least existentialism is honest; it deals with the sorrow of life head on. Perhaps that's why it is so appealing to the common man. It doesn't pretend that sorrow and pain are not there, like many positive thinking programs and escapist religions.

"For those without Christian hope, the notion that we must be brave and leave the world a better place appeals to our universal inner urge for dignity."

Existentialism, though, is merely a futile accommodation to the despair produced by a fruitless search for the meaning and the purpose of life.

Christianity and Despair

Although coming to radically different conclusions, existentialism and Christianity alone among the "-isms" and religions of the world face sorrow head on.

Christianity squarely addresses the sorrow of life and provides an answer that resolves the issue. Despair is, in fact, a recurring theme in life, but Christian despair differs from existential despair in two ways. First, Christian despair cries out to God, not to the empty silence of agnostic air. Second, Christian despair eventually yields to hope. It is not consigned to a life sentence of meaninglessness:

> We also rejoice in our sufferings, because we know that suffering produces perseverance; perseverance, character; and character, hope. And hope does not disappoint us, because God has poured out his love into our hearts by the Holy Spirit, whom he has given us. (Romans 5:3–5)

Christian despair doesn't last; it is temporary. In humble faith the agonizing Christian fully expects a reply from the God who is. Consider these men of the Bible who despaired even of life itself, though God revived them:

Moses: "I cannot carry all these people by myself; the burden is too heavy for me. If this is how you are going to treat me, put me to death right now." (Numbers 11:14–15)

Samson: With such nagging [Delilah] prodded him day after day until he was tired to death. (Judges 16:16)

Elijah: "I have had enough, LORD," he said. "Take my life." (1 Kings 19:4)

Job: "I despise my life. . . . Let me alone; my days have no meaning." (Job 7:16)

Jeremiah: "Cursed be the day I was born! . . . Why did I ever come out of the womb to see trouble and sorrow and to end my days in shame?" (Jeremiah 20:14, 18)

Jonah: "Now, O LORD, take away my life, for it is better for me to die than to live." (Jonah 4:3)

Paul: "We were under great pressure, far beyond our ability to endure, so that we despaired even of life." (2 Corinthians 1:8)

Jesus: "My soul is overwhelmed with sorrow to the point of death." (Matthew 26:38)

Despair, loneliness, anguish, and sorrow are not exclusive existential themes; they are *life* themes. Existentialism so closely identifies with these themes, however, because it so directly addresses them. Christianity and existentialism are the two thought systems that provide an answer to despair.

Christianity joyfully declares there is hope: "Praise be to the God and Father of our Lord Jesus Christ, the Father of compassion and the God of all comfort, *who comforts us in all our troubles*" (2 Corinthians 1:3–4, italics added). Conversely, existentialism sadly whimpers that there is only more despair, so try to be brave.

One last thought. Some of us, if we are candid, will probably find at least a little of this thinking in our own life view, too. To be the genuine Christian article we need to whittle down to genuine Christian beliefs. To do less could be dangerous.

2. THE RELATIVE WORLD

Perhaps no bromide has more dominated this century than the notion: "Everything is relative." In the first sentence of his ground-breaking work, *The Closing of the American Mind*, Allan Bloom captures the mood of the age:

> There is one thing a professor can be absolutely certain of: almost every student entering the university believes, or says he believes, that truth is relative.[3]

The doctrine of relativism postulates that there is no absolute truth—what Francis Schaeffer called "true truth." Let's begin by admitting it; things do at first seem that way. In our advanced scientific world old paradigms fall like dominoes; new discoveries catapult us forward.

For example, in the 1840s Vienna housed a famous medical center. But on the maternity ward one of every six women died. When young Dr. Semmelweis ordered that physicians and students begin washing their hands after performing autopsies on the dead women and before making pelvic examinations on the living women, the mortality rate plunged to one in eighty-four. Later, when eleven of twelve women examined on the maternity ward died, the doctor instructed everyone to wash his hands between each examination of well patients, also, and mortality dropped even more.[4]

Here's the point: Semmelweis didn't *invent* truth; he *discovered* the truth. In fact, God had already told Moses the safest way was to cleanse hands after handling the dead or infected. Semmelweis's methods, for which his peers severely ridiculed him (he even lost his job), advanced medical science toward the truth and away from error. It was truth discovered, not truth overturned.

Science is in complete harmony with Christianity. Science never leads us away from truth but toward truth. Nothing science discovers is new truth. Scientific accomplishment moves toward truth; it does not *create* truth. The old theories fall on their own weight for the very reason that they are found out to be *untrue*. People, however, without thinking deeply, may begin to think truth is relative.

Standards and Authority

With roots leading back to Hegel and seemingly ratified by constant change, this is an age when most people doubt that truth is fixed. Whatever works for you is "fine." Whatever works for me is "fine." Such relativistic thinking has caused a crisis of standards and moral authority. What, or who, defines right and wrong? Without an independent standard, each man is free to set his own rules.

Relativism is the standard of no standards. It is feeling driven, wispy, and completely adjustable depending upon the whim of the moment. Relativism is a synonym for ambiguity. Relativists have a spongy foundation. The personal identity crisis so many sense, mostly non-Christians but Christians too, traces back to an unsettled notion about the fixed nature of truth.

The Authority of Christianity

Two foundational questions sincere truth seekers must ask are these: "By what *standard* do I evaluate my life?" and its corollary, "To whom or what *authority* do I submit my life, my plans, my dreams?" Relativism answers these questions by simply saying *you* set your own standard and *you* are the final authority for your own life and actions.

We must proportion our lives to the perspectives, principles, and priorities of Scripture. The Bible governs as the final authority in the life of a biblical Christian for faith and practice, for doctrine and life, for belief and behavior. Martin Luther was willing to be marked a heretic over the matter. He said at the Diet of Worms:

> Unless I am convinced by the testimony of the Scriptures . . . I am bound by the Scriptures I have quoted and my conscience is captive to the word of God. I cannot and I will not retract anything. . . . Here I stand, I cannot do otherwise.[5]

Relativism has certainly diffused into the Christian world. From the nineteenth century until now, liberal theologians (relativists in the church) continually challenge the authority of the Scriptures as the inerrant, infallible Word of God. This deep, still accelerating debate has left the church in division. When the church (especially the pulpit) abandons the Bible as its moral authority, from where will society find clear moral direction?

The humanistic world cannot be expected to accept the Bible as its final rule of authority. The Christian world can. When Christians depart from the authority of Scriptures the resulting fractures and fissures eventually lead to a collapse of moral authority. We seem perilously

---

"Everyone must choose to be a relativistic man pleaser or an absolute God pleaser. And the wrong choice will be dangerous."

---

close, often setting policy based on cultural expectations and norms rather than biblical precepts. Take, for example, the denominational debates over human sexuality and abortion.

Without the guidance and restraint of Scripture, we will not naturally gravitate to the highest possible good but, like water, we will find the path of least resistance. Everyone must choose to be a relativistic man pleaser or an absolute God pleaser. And the wrong choice will be dangerous.

3. THE MATERIALISTIC WORLD

What do the automobile, the airplane, the telephone, the radio, the television, the stereo, the condo, and the computer have in common? None of them existed one hundred years ago. Pause and imagine, if it is possible, not having a phone, a car, or a T.V.

We live in a wonderful world of progress. The dark side of this progress, however, baits people into the idolatry of putting money and things before God. An unbridled desire by some of us for ever-increasing material prosperity creates an addiction to *a lifestyle of thorns*: "What was sown among the thorns is the man who hears the word, but the worries of this life and the deceitfulness of wealth choke it, making it unfruitful" (Matthew 13:22). As one tired man with dark rings under his eyes said, "My problem is that I want it all."

Society, culture, and even government send us signals that tell us to live for the moment, that time is running out. For example, consider the use of debt. Government tacitly approves the acceptability of using debt (a mortgage on future income) to finance our current lifestyles. They have unleashed the trend-setting example that debt is okay. How? By balancing their budget by running the federal charge cards up to (and over) the maximum limit. Think it over. To what extent do you view debt as a *necessary* component of a happy life?

The Lure of Affluence

When carefully examined, the basic proposition of materialism is exposed as the exact opposite of the basic proposition of Christianity. "You can't serve both God and money." Closely consider this Webster's Dictionary definition of materialism: "The theory that *physical well-being* and *worldly possessions* constitute the *highest value* and the *greatest good* in life" (italics added).

Is that true? Do physical well-being and worldly possessions constitute the "highest value" and the "greatest good" in life? Obviously, no thinking Christian should agree with this idea. Yet, upon reflection, we must acknowledge that our lifestyles often reveal that we have woven in a fat thread of materialism. Continual stress and worry over our circumstances betrays an undue attachment to the things we have, or wish we had.

Christians have a deep bias toward materialism because it is a foundational philosophy of all the world. Whether capitalist, communist, or poor, most people presume they can be happy if only they can achieve what Dr. Francis A. Schaeffer referred to as *personal peace* (read "physical well-being") and *affluence* (read "worldly possessions"). Calling these the two impoverished values of the age, Dr. Schaeffer diagnosed a textbook case of materialism.

Is more really better? In *City of God*, St. Augustine cleverly contrasted the pursuit of riches with a more modest approach:

> Let us imagine two individuals. Of these two men, let us suppose that one is poor, or better, in moderate circumstances; the other, extremely wealthy. But, our wealthy man is haunted by fear, heavy with cares, feverish with greed, never secure, always restless, breathless from end-

less quarrels with his enemies. By these miseries, he adds to his possessions beyond measure, but he also piles up for himself a mountain of distressing worries. The man of modest means is content with a small and compact patrimony. He is loved by his own, enjoys the sweetness of peace in his relations with kindred, neighbors, and friends, is religious and pious, of kindly disposition, healthy in body, self-restrained, chaste in morals, and at peace with his conscience.

I wonder if there is anyone so senseless as to hesitate over which of the two to prefer. What is true of these two individuals is likewise true of two families, two nations, two kingdoms; the analogy holds in both cases.[6]

Can there be any doubt that our great nation is on the first path and not the second? Think it over. Which path are you on? your family? your country?

"Continual stress and worry over our circumstances betrays an undue attachment to the things we have, or wish we had."

Hopefully, ours will be the age when man finally realizes that a better machine does not necessarily mean a better life. The satisfaction of the soul comes spiritually, not by things.

What Jesus Says

Though our age lures us away from Christ and toward mammon, life is complicated by the plain fact that we do need *things* to exist. About "things" Jesus said, "Your heavenly Father knows that you need them. But seek first his kingdom and his righteousness, and all these *things* will be given to you as well" (Matthew 6:32–33, italics added).

Notice that Jesus doesn't say "seek *only* his kingdom," but "seek *first* his kingdom." Jesus sets out an order to follow, a way of thinking, a path of priority. Jesus is not opposed to possessions. He wore a robe worth casting lots over, and He was buried in a rich man's tomb. It is not the *possession* of things that is sin, but an *obsession* with things.

We would be hard pressed to have no material thoughts, but we must guard against unthinkingly branding our lifestyle with the "-ism" suffix. There is a huge difference between needing material things and subscribing to the philosophy of materialism. To need material things is to be human, but to subscribe to materialism is to consciously believe things are "the highest value and the greatest good in life," an indefensible position for a true Christian.

A pleasant trend is that some people are feeling the prick of this thorn and deciding to quit the materialistic rat race. In her book *Downshifting*, Amy Saltzman points out an increasing trend to ease back on working hard for success in life by taking lower pressure work, which she differentiates from dropping out. She calls this concept, quite cleverly I think, "downshifting." Does downshifting to a less demanding lifestyle make sense to you?

It would well serve the kingdom of God if all Christians reevaluated their material desires and decided to narrow their interests. Divided interests lead to a divided heart. When we narrow our focus and simplify our lifestyle, our Father will give us concentrated spiritual energy to advance the kingdom of God in our own hearts, in our families, and in the broken, hurting world.

God makes some men wealthy, and this should be a blessing to them and us. Wealth received as a gift from God and managed as a steward will accelerate the fulfillment of the Great Commission. The tempting tendency toward materialism, though, must be vigilantly guarded against. "Though your riches increase, do not set your heart on them" (Psalm 62:10). It is a thorny, dangerous idea.

Existentialism, relativism, materialism—America has a bad case of the "-isms." Ideas are not dead things buried under the sediment of time, but living things, squiggly things, dangerous things, often contagious things. Many sincere Christians have been infected by these three dangerous ideas—ideas as common as the cold. Have you caught a case of the "-isms?"

ᶻ☙   ᶻ☙   ᶻ☙

DISCUSSION QUESTIONS

1. Give a working definition for each of the following:

   - humanism
   - existentialism
   - relativism
   - materialism

2. Describe one way each of these ideas has influenced your daily life.

3. Which "-ism" has *most* influenced your life, and how? Is it one discussed or some other one?

4. "We have created a culture which requires more energy than people have to give."

   ☐ Agree   ☐ Disagree

   Explain your answer.

THE FIFTH GOSPEL

D*ear Journal,*

I can see that I have not lived by a distinctly Christian life view. Instead, I have blended my new Christian views with my old humanistic views. To be honest, I'm not quite sure what view I'm following. Frankly, I have been so caught up in the way I wanted my life to turn out that I have "twisted" many things to fit into my plans. What a fool I've been. I wish I had never heard of the human potential movement. I think I have lost my objectivity. If a guy isn't careful it could ruin his life.

Robert

CREATING A FIFTH GOSPEL

When I received Christ I had big plans for my life. Regrettably, I must confess that in many ways I sort of *added* Christ to my life as another interest in an already busy and otherwise overcrowded schedule. Since I knew where I was headed, I would make my plan, then pray for God to grant it. The formula was this: *Plan, then pray.*

Because I had already made up my mind about what I wanted, I would read the Bible and scrupulously scour those crinkly pages looking for proof texts. Many of us live that way: We decide what we want, then go look for evidence to support the decision we have already made. It doesn't sound very objective when we see it in black and white, does it?

When I would see a verse that ratified my plans I would underline and often memorize it. But when I saw a verse that veered off in a direction I didn't want to go, I would figuratively pull out a large mental eraser and smudge that pesky verse right off the page.

I began to follow the God I was underlining in my Bible. Frankly, I never intended to edit the Bible into my own version. Nevertheless, over the first ten years of my spiritual pilgrimage I created a fifth gospel: Matthew, Mark, Luke, John, and Patrick. My thinking was not based upon the objective authority of God's Word. Instead, that insidious invader named self-deceit had wormed his way into the mainstream of my mind.

This produced a terrible result. I built an empire on the shifting sands of borrowed money. I was having my cake and eating it, too. When I finally came to my senses our faithful Lord forgave me, but then proceeded to crush the business with trustworthy, caring blows. All in all, it was very humbling. Richard Armour wrote a little poem that summarizes my experience with money. He said:

> That money talks, I'll not deny.
> I heard it once; it said good-bye.

We are the sum of our choices, and our choices have consequences. Fortunately, the blood of Christ will cover over any sin if we only ask. Still, though completely forgiven, we must often bear long-lasting consequences for our poor choices. We can choose our way but not the result. My new formula is this: *Pray, then plan.*

Here's the problem with making a fifth gospel: It will inevitably lead to a spiritual crisis. Our subjective self-deceit may be deliberate, it may be naive, or it may be from sloth; but the result remains the same.

I think if we are honest with ourselves, many of us will see that we have created a fifth gospel (or maybe we have four and a half). The age in which we live is a virtual incubator for creating a fifth gospel. It is a "me, now, fast" world. How do we create this fifth gospel?

SYNCRETISM

If I were limited to one, overarching observation that captures the mood of our Christian culture today, I would say it is *syncretism*.

Syncretism is not an everyday word for Christians. It should be, and I hope you will help make it so. Syncretism simply means trying to merge two or more life views into one. Webster's Dictionary defines it

---

"Syncretism . . . is cultural Christianity, and throughout biblical history it made God very angry."

---

this way: "The attempt or tendency to combine or reconcile differing philosophical or religious beliefs." The Greek root word literally means "union, or to unite." Syncretism is trying to blend together or "unite" different belief systems, to layer beliefs on top of one another.

Said simply: Syncretism is making a fifth gospel. It is trying to have our cake and eat it, too. It is trying to have the best of the Christian life view and the best of a humanistic life view at the same time. It is to worship Christ, but not give up our idol. It is cultural Christianity, and throughout biblical history it made God very angry. This diagram captures the problem of syncretism:

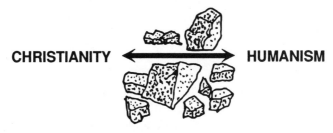

CHRISTIANITY ⟷ **HUMANISM**

The single greatest problem in Christendom in our time is that Christians are willing to tear down the wall of belief that separates Christians from humanists like a sort of Berlin Wall, wrongly thinking that harmonizing Humanism and Christianity will somehow win humanists to Christ. That isn't any way to win souls. Instead we become syncretized into humanistic Christians—or Christian humanists.

The layering of differing beliefs in syncretism is a problem more prone to appear in an eclectic, diverse, heterogeneous culture like ours than in a regimented, homogeneous one.

Syncretism is the black hole of Christianity. Many Christians flirt with syncretism by dancing capriciously along its brittle rim. But if you slip and fall over the edge, you can disappear.

A CASE STUDY IN SYNCRETISM

His wealth garnered him the number one spot on the Forbes 400 list by an unmatchable margin. His countrymen chose him to be their President. The leaders of the world came to seek his counsel. His military prowess earned him the position of chairman of the Joint Chiefs of Staff.

Through his commercial genius he ascended to become the chief executive officer of the largest corporation. Through his uncanny trading skill he became the world's foremost merchant. His formidable fleet of trading ships sailed throughout the world making him the leading shipping magnate.

His religious devotion marked him as a spiritual giant among his peers. Through his towering intellect he became the most profound teacher in his land. Because of his trained ear he was recognized as the most accomplished songwriter in his homeland. So keen were his insights that he became the most prolific classical writer of his era. He reigned as the poet laureate of the land. He was the leading patron of the arts.

His relentless quest to classify nature marked him as the greatest scientist of his time. Through his mammoth construction projects he was revered as a master builder. His architectural interpretations became the world's most important buildings.

Trying to comprehend this man's wisdom, wealth, and accomplishments would be like trying to visualize an amalgamation of Andrew Carnegie, Abraham Lincoln, General Douglas MacArthur, Bernard Baruch, J. Paul Getty, J. C. Penney, Aristotle Onassis, Dwight L. Moody, John Harvard, Leonard Bernstein, Charles Dickens, Robert

Frost, Louis Agassiz, Albert Einstein, and Trammel Crow. He was the prototype Renaissance man.

Word of his wisdom and accomplishments spread throughout the world. Who is this man? The correct answer is, of course, Solomon. The wisest, wealthiest, most honored man to ever live was Solomon. "There will never have been anyone like you, nor will there ever be" (except Jesus, 1 Kings 3:12).

When an aging King David neared the end of his reign he issued this charge to his son:

> "My son Solomon, acknowledge the God of your father, and serve him with wholehearted devotion and with a willing mind, for the LORD searches every heart and understands every motive behind the thoughts. If you seek him, he will be found by you; but if you forsake him, he will reject you forever." (1 Chronicles 28:9)

SOLOMON'S MISSION AND METHOD

Solomon was the first philosopher, preceding Plato and Aristotle by six hundred years. For his life's mission he chose "to search out and set in order the scheme of things" (see Ecclesiastes 7:25; Ecclesiastes 12:9–10), the business of every philosopher. Solomon set out to draw the circle which would be big enough to explain the meaning of things, and the purpose of life.

His method was to search out every earthly avenue to find the orderly scheme of things that would bring the particulars of life into some organized whole, or system. This is no different than what every philosopher through the ages has attempted (except for our current skeptical age), but with two notable differences.

First, Solomon was the wisest man who ever lived, so he brought to his quest the greatest skills of any thinker who has ever thought. He had the advantage of resources, power, and wisdom like no other man before or since. Solomon had the money, brains, and ability to extend the reach of his inquiry into every corner of the cosmos.

Second, Solomon painted with a broad brush. While others may attempt to master a single specialty (or two), Solomon left no earthly avenue unexplored, no worldly way unexamined. While today's secular thinkers, by and large, have given up hope of understanding the big picture, Solomon expected to discover a circle big enough to explain everything. While today's wise men myopically dissect trivial issues, Solomon was searching for the big ideas.

Solomon had it made: power, prestige, fame, and fortune—a running start. Yet a sense of meaning eluded him. In Ecclesiastes 1:12–2:10 Solomon labors the extremes to which he went to find the meaning of life. He tried to find it by devoting himself to *study* (education) and *exploration of the world* (science)—but found no meaning. He entertained *worldly wisdom*—and found no meaning. He tried to find it in *the bottle*—again, no meaning. He tried to find it through *accomplishments* by building houses, vineyards, gardens, parks, and reservoirs—still, no meaning.

He tried to find it through accumulating *wealth*, acquiring herds and flocks, silver and gold, slaves and singers—no meaning. He tried to find it in *carnal pleasure* and became a playboy—no meaning. He entertained *madness and folly*—no meaning. He developed *a great reputation*—no meaning. He threw himself into his *work*—no meaning. Solomon applied himself wholeheartedly to find meaning in ten worldly ways:

- Study (Education)
- Exploration the World (Science)
- Worldly Wisdom
- Alcohol
- Achievement
- Wealth
- Sex
- Madness and Folly
- A Great Reputation
- Work

Can you think of any other worldly way men and women pursue the meaning of things, and the purpose of life?

After experimenting with every earthly option to find meaning and happiness, Solomon recorded his findings in an orderly manner in the book of Ecclesiastes. And what did he conclude from his nefarious exploits?

SOLOMON'S FINDINGS AND CONCLUSIONS

Solomon drew two sets of conclusions. First, he concluded what every secular existentialist has ever concluded: "'Meaningless! Meaningless!' says the Teacher. 'Utterly meaningless! Everything is meaningless'" (Ecclesiastes 1:2).

> ## "The message of Ecclesiastes is simple: Apart from God life has no meaning."

When he surveyed the work of his hands and his achievements Solomon concluded that "everything was meaningless, a chasing after the wind; nothing was gained under the sun" (Ecclesiastes 2:11). In despair he summarized, "So I hated life" (Ecclesiastes 2:17).

The message of Ecclesiastes is simple: *Apart from God life has no meaning.* Solomon said, "No one can comprehend what goes on under the sun. Despite all his efforts to search it out, man cannot discover its meaning" (Ecclesiastes 8:17). Apart from God he could not draw the circle that was big enough to give life meaning.

Solomon, acting as a sort of forerunner for us, anticipated the crushing despair that we, too, feel when we cannot find an ordered explanation for life.

The Scriptures foretell the befuddlement that world-wise thinkers will come to. They cannot draw a circle big enough to explain the meaning of life because their circle does not include the God who is. "'I will destroy the wisdom of the wise; the intelligence of the intelligent I will frustrate.' Where is the wise man? Where is the scholar? Where is the philosopher of this age? Has not God made foolish the wisdom of the world?" (1 Corinthians 1:19–20).

Solomon was a spiritual man, but he was a syncretist. His heart was devoted to God, but not "fully" devoted. He tried to find the meaning of life by blending Christianity and Humanism into one circle. Solomon tried to have his cake and eat it, too. He made a fifth gospel. When he saw that apart from God life had no meaning, Solomon still had one more avenue open to him.

Though he found all earthly avenues meaningless, though the wisest man who ever lived could not set in order the scheme of things without God, though he hated his life, Solomon was able to develop a second set of conclusions and recommendations for mankind. When he redrew his circle to include God as God is, the meaning of life came into focus. And what did he say? "Now all has been heard; here is the conclusion of the matter: Fear God and keep his commandments, for this is the whole duty of man" (Ecclesiastes 12:13).

Humanism fails by drawing a circle *without* God, while syncretism fails by drawing a circle around *the God we want* instead of *the God who is*. The Christian circle—which includes the God who is—is the only circle big enough to explain the meaning of things and the purpose of life.

The Scriptures record that in the end Solomon ruined his life. Though Solomon came to the right conclusion, his syncretism ruined his life. His searchings, however, benefit all mankind, because we can choose not to follow in his footsteps. But for Solomon his choices had consequences. He died a disillusioned man.

How did such a grand beginning go down to such a terrible finish? Did it happen overnight? Exactly how did Solomon ruin his life? For that matter, how does anyone ruin their life?

HOW TO RUIN A LIFE

God especially warned the Israelites against intermarriage with the culture. Over and over again God cautioned them, "Don't intermarry with the culture." Why? Because our Father knows that to intermarry with the culture is that devastating, first syncretistic step toward worshiping other gods and idolatry.

Intermarriage with the culture will turn our hearts after other gods. "You must not intermarry with them, because they will surely turn your hearts after their gods" (1 Kings 11:2). To intermarry is syncretism. It is to become a cultural Christian. And it leads to idolatry and the worship of other gods.

Can you recall the first and second of the Ten Commandments? You recalled correctly: "You shall have *no other gods* before me. You shall not make for yourself an *idol* . . . for I, the LORD your God, am a jealous God" (Exodus 20:3–4, italics added). No other gods; no idols.

> ## "The Christian circle—which includes the God who is—is the only circle big enough to explain the meaning of things and the purpose of life."

Solomon didn't ruin his life overnight. Rather, it started with one small, almost imperceptible step over the line God had drawn. And what happened? Absolutely nothing. So in his mind Solomon redrew the line in the new place. Later, he stepped across that new line, too, and again, nothing happened. *Maybe it doesn't matter after all,* he thought. So, slowly, over the years, he began to dance more and more boldly, more and more closely, near the edge of the brittle rim to the black hole of syncretism. He became more and more desensitized to sin.

Not overnight but slowly, down through the years, by compromise and self-deceit, Solomon fully syncretized—intermarried—with the culture. He chose his way, and it produced an inevitable result. The Scriptures record, "As Solomon grew old, his wives turned his heart after other gods, and his heart was not fully devoted to the Lord his God" (1 Kings 11:4). As he grew old, it happened—not overnight.

Solomon underestimated the jealous anger of God. In the end, "The LORD became angry with Solomon because his heart had turned away from the LORD" (1 Kings 11:9). Isn't it ironic: The wisest man to ever live decided not to live a wise life. He lived a life of syncretism, and one day he disappeared.

A LACK OF WISDOM

Syncretism is an open gate which leads to the two things God hates most of all: worshiping false gods and idolatry. The psalmist defines syncretism and its consequences this way: "They mingled with the nations and adopted their customs. They worshiped their idols, which became a snare to them" (Psalm 106:35–36).

Some of us have intermarried with the culture; we have syncretized; we have adopted the wrong customs; we have made a fifth gospel; we have been snared.

The single greatest opportunity for syncretized Christians is to reevaluate and redraw the line in a right place, far away from the brittle edge of syncretism's black hole. As Paul said, "Don't you know that a little yeast works through the whole batch of dough?" (1 Corinthians 5:6).

In the next section, "Charting a New Course," we will explore how we can be sure our lines are drawn in the right place, and how to wisely chart a new direction toward an authentic, passionate, difference-making faith.

ﷺ   ﷺ   ﷺ

DISCUSSION QUESTIONS

1. To what extent would you say you have created a fifth gospel? What effect has it had on what you have believed and the way you have lived?

2. Explain syncretism (review the subheading "Syncretism"). How has syncretism affected your thinking?

3. Read Ecclesiastes 7:25 and 12:9–10. What was the purpose of Solomon's life?

4. Read Ecclesiastes 1:12–2:11. What were ten earthly avenues Solomon explored as he attempted to search out and set in order the meaning of things? Which of these have you tried? What have been your own conclusions?

5. Read Ecclesiastes 1:2; 2:11; and 2:17. What were Solomon's first set of conclusions? What kind of circle did these conclusions represent?

6. Read Ecclesiastes 12:13. What was Solomon's second set of conclusions? Why two sets of conclusions? What is the difference?

7. Read Exodus 20:2–4; 1 Kings 11:2; and Psalm 106:35–36. How do you ruin a life? To what extent have you harmed your life by syncretism?

CHARTING A NEW COURSE

PART TWO

BORN AGAIN "AGAIN"

CHAPTER 5

D*ear Journal,*

My Christian friends all seem to be getting very different results from their faith. Some are growing strong, others appear lukewarm, still others don't see the impact faith should have on how we live. This puzzles me. I'm sure many have syncretized with the culture—I can see that I have. Some obviously only need to keep fine tuning an already vibrant faith, but others of us need to make some major mid-course corrections. I suppose we all need to make a significant reevaluation of our spiritual lives from time to time. One thing I know for sure—I don't want the tepid, lukewarm faith of a cultural Christian. Do I need to be born again "again?"

Robert

CONFUSION IN THE CULTURE

A Gallup survey asked, "Would you say you have made a commitment to Jesus Christ or not?" A remarkable 66 percent of adults over age eighteen indicated, "Yes."[1] How can this be? How could this statistic be true? With the way culture has declined in recent decades we must wonder, "How could two out of every three people I see each day possibly be Christian?"

The pressures of the modern world—the change, the pace, the responsibilities—drive people in a host of directions to search for the secrets of meaning and purpose. They often end up exploring in the spiritual realm, as a *Newsweek* cover story points out. Entitled *And the Children Shall Lead Them, Young Americans Return to God*, the article postulates a religious revival in America. When we grow up, the researchers found, we want to establish values, roots, and traditions for our children—and religion ranks high on the list of how to go about it.

When we compare the state of our culture to the notion of a religious revival, we find a puzzling riddle that drives us to ponder "Revival to what?" To quote *Newsweek*,

> Unlike earlier religious revivals, the aim this time (aside from born-again traditionalists of all faiths) is *support* not *salvation*, *help* rather than *holiness*, a circle of spiritual equals rather than an authoritative church or guide. A group *affirmation of self* is at the top of the agenda, which is why some of the least demanding churches are now in greatest demand. (italics added)[2]

Simply stated, what we are experiencing is not a *spiritual* revival, but a *demographic* revival. The life philosophies people grew up with haven't produced. The circles they drew didn't work. Life has not cooperated. The hollow, vacant philosophies of our age simply have not had the structural integrity to resist the pounding storms of rapid change.

And so people are looking for a new circle to explain the meaning of things and the purpose of life. People want to find a life view that brings sense to the dissonance and diversity that confronts them each day. People are searching for contentment, and many of them are ending up in the church.

THE PEOPLE IN THE PEWS

Obviously, not everyone who professes Christ lives Christianly. The more arresting question is, however, are they Christians at all? Yes or no? Let's examine why different people get different results from the faith they profess and see what it means. Following are some useful "slots" to help us think about our walk with God.

A caution at the beginning is in order. Let's remember that God alone knows whether someone is part of the kingdom or not. "Man looks at the outward appearance, but the LORD looks at the heart" (1 Samuel 16:7). This is not meant to be a grid through which we filter our friends. Instead, this is a tool for self-examination and for understanding the biblical categories in a general way, not in an applied, specific way to those around us.

"People want to find a life view that brings sense to the dissonance and diversity that confronts them each day."

The world has two kinds of people: believers and non-believers. Among those who *profess* to be believers we see three kinds of people: biblical Christians, "defeated" cultural Christians, and "counterfeit" cultural Christians.

Biblical Christians are easy to spot. They seek to love God with all of their heart, soul, and mind. They strive to be imitators of Christ. Sure, they sin. But then they quickly confess and purpose to change. They long to live a life pleasing to God in accordance with His will.

Cultural Christians, on the other hand, vacillate between brilliant periods of profound obedience to Christ and dark days of being choked by life's worries, riches, and pleasures—like Solomon. In this century we have become a nation of *cultural Christians*.

Cultural Christianity means to pursue the God we want instead of the God who is. It is the tendency to be shallow in our understanding of God, wanting Him to be more of a gentle grandfather type who spoils us and let's us have our own way. It is sensing a need for God, but only on our own terms. It is wanting the God we have underlined in our Bibles without wanting the rest of Him, too. It is God relative instead of God absolute.

Here is the pressing question: Are cultural Christians *really* Christians? The correct answer is that some are, and some are not. Some people go through temporary periods when they are *defeated,* but others are *counterfeit.*

My own experience is that many people have "prayed a prayer" but never "found faith." *Prayer* doesn't make us born again; *faith* does. Many others have sincerely received Christ by faith, but they have not become growing disciples of Christ. They have "found faith" but have never been challenged to grow spiritually, and they are deeply disillusioned and discouraged about matters of faith and life.

"Defeated" Cultural Christians

The malady of "defeated" cultural Christians is *backsliding*. They don't produce as much fruit as they should. "He himself will be saved, but only as one escaping through the flames" (1 Corinthians 3:15).

A Christian is either a Christian or not, but he may be a good one or a bad one. He can choose to live, to the best of his ability, a life of obedience and be a biblical Christian. When he backslides into a moment—or lifestyle—of defeat he is still at all times a Christian, but he does not experience the power, peace, and joy of the Holy Spirit in his life.

Note some of the terms frequently used in our culture to describe this group of Christians. They all basically refer to the same thing—a temporary lapse:

- cultural Christian
- carnal Christian
- backslider
- lukewarm Christian
- nominal Christian
- defeated Christian

There may even be temporary periods when they produce no fruit (though this should cause them great concern). Here are six biblical scenarios which describe temporary times when a Christian may not produce fruit at all though still be a believer:

1. The concept of the prodigal son (Luke 15:11–32).

2. The concept of the son who said he wouldn't go to his father's field but later did go (Matthew 21:28–31).

3. The concept of land producing thorns and thistles and in danger of being cut off, but confident of better things for you (Hebrews 6:8–9).

4. The concept of the man who hears the Word but lets life's worries, riches, and pleasures choke it (Luke 8:14).

5. The concept of giving a fig tree not producing fruit one more year to produce (Luke 13:6–8).

6. The concept of becoming a lukewarm Christian by thinking "I have acquired wealth and do not need a thing" (Revelation 3:14–22).

Richard Baxter, the gifted seventeenth-century Puritan writer, noted three types of "defeated" cultural Christians. The first group he called *the young and weak*. Though perhaps in Christ for a long time they have grown little. Then as now, he noted this as the "most common condition of the godly." Because they are slow to learn, they still need milk, not solid food (Hebrews 5:11–14).

The second group are *those who labor under some particular corruption* which makes them trouble to others and a burden to themselves. "Too many such persons," says Baxter. These have addictions to pride, worldliness, sensual desires, or other evil passions (Colossians 3:5–8).

The third group is *declining Christians who have lost their first love*. Whether falling into some scandalous sin or merely abating in zeal and diligence, these backsliders need double doses of the compassion that comforts and the truth that will set them free.[3]

"Counterfeit" Cultural Christians

The affliction of "counterfeit" cultural Christians is *apostasy*. R. C. Sproul succinctly defines apostasy as "a *profession* of faith but without a *possession* of faith." Most non-believers realize their lives have missed the mark. It seems natural, then, that many of these hurting people would seek the benefits of Christ.

When someone who knows their life has missed the mark hears the wonderful news of Jesus they have two choices: They can seek to know

Jesus, or they can seek only the *benefits* Jesus offers. The former seeks the God who is, the latter the God he wants.

The man who wants to enjoy the benefits of Christianity without actually receiving Christ into his life doesn't have genuine faith. He is what we might call a "counterfeit" cultural Christian. He has no root; therefore, he does not have real faith. He *professes* faith but does not *possess* faith. And because he never really believed, when his "faith" (actually, *lack* of faith) is tested, he falls away. He becomes apostate.

Here is the problem: Many who fall away remain in the church. Whether for social or business reasons, they enjoy the wholesome atmosphere of being around Christian folk. They continue to "profess" to be Christian.

Many of these counterfeits are exceptionally decent people. They're downright likable. They may even produce fruit, though it is not the fruit of repentance that flows out of the abundance of a grateful heart.

It's hard to tell a counterfeit from the genuine article. In fact, the *more* counterfeit a thing is the *less* counterfeit it will appear. The counterfeit dollar that safely passes into circulation is the one that looks the most like the real thing. Even non-Christians can spot the conspicuous counterfeit. But to spot the accomplished counterfeit may well be impossible.

Some counterfeits know they don't believe the claims of Jesus to be true. Others have belief, but in a god which is not the God who is. I would venture a guess that many "counterfeit" cultural Christians, relying on a false religion, don't have a clue that they have a counterfeit faith. Others wait desperately for someone to tell them the true gospel. And it's our job to tell them.

Recently a drug manufacturer announced the study results of a new wonder drug for migraine headache sufferers. The research showed that within one hour of taking the drug a whopping 70 percent of the test patients had little or no pain. Remarkably, in the control group that received a placebo, 29 percent of the test patients showed the same improvement.[4]

Scientists testing new drugs always have a control group. Those in the control group take what they think is the real thing, but it is not; it is a placebo, a "sugar" pill. It has no active ingredient; it is not real medicine. The *placebo effect* simply means that a certain percentage of people taking *any* potential cure will show signs of improvement if they think they are taking real medicine.

"The man who wants to enjoy the benefits of Christianity without actually receiving Christ into his life doesn't have genuine faith."

Though the placebo will produce the benefits of the real medicine for a while, sooner or later the effect wears off. They are, after all, not taking the real thing. It won't work forever; it is not a permanent solution.

A certain percentage of people professing faith in Jesus Christ don't take the real medicine—the real cure for what ails them. They don't place their faith in the Savior of the Bible for their salvation. Instead, they place their faith in their good deeds, or some vain imagination of what Jesus must be like. It is a faith that has no active ingredient. It is a placebo.

"Counterfeit" cultural Christians often show temporary improvement. "Those on the rock are the ones who receive the word with joy when they hear it, but they have *no root* [it was a placebo]. They believe *for a while*, but in the time of testing *they fall away* [the effect wears off]" (Luke 8:13, italics and parenthetic remarks added). Unfortunately, they have not truly received Jesus. Their interest was not in Jesus the Savior, but Jesus the Benefactor. They took a placebo. And like any placebo, sooner or later the effect wears off—even the placebo effect of the gospel.

Non-Christians

We must mention one more group in order for our understanding to be complete. There is another group sitting in the pews—the non-Christians. These are people who have never made a profession of faith. They may think they are Christians or they may know they are not. Not only do they not *possess* faith, they have never *professed* faith either.

What is the difference between a non-Christian and a "counterfeit" cultural Christian? The difference is the profession. The "counterfeit" cultural Christian has made a profession of faith, while the non-Christian has not.

Here's the point to remember: The term "counterfeit" cultural Christian is a misnomer. It is a term of convenience. This person is actually not a Christian at all. As to salvation, there is no difference between a non-Christian and a "counterfeit" cultural Christian.

The following outline makes a good synopsis of our discussion:

I. Believers
  A. *Biblical Christians*
  B. *"Defeated" Cultural Christians*
    1. Backsliders
    2. Temporary
    3. Seduced by syncretism
II. Non-Believers
  A. *Non-Christians*
  B. *"Counterfeit" Cultural Christians*
    1. Apostates
    2. Profess Christ, but don't possess Christ
    3. The placebo effect of the gospel

GETTING ON TRACK AGAIN

Some of us, I'm afraid, need to be born again "again." No, I'm not trying to start a new heresy. The plain facts are that someone who has been truly born again is born again forever. No one who makes a true profession of faith need look again on that one-time-for-eternity decision. A genuine "profession" of faith yields an unshakable "possession" of faith.

But I do think some of us need to take a long look in the mirror and admit our syncretism, that we have created a fifth gospel, that we have become like Solomon (at least a little), and recommit our lives to be authentic, biblical Christians in the broken world. We ought to admit (where it's true) that, even though we know Christ, we have been living by our own ideas.

"As to salvation, there is no difference between a non-Christian and a "counterfeit" cultural Christian."

Soren Kierkegaard, the passionate nineteenth-century writer, said that to become a Christian in Christendom we must first disengage from our illusions. The problem is to become a Christian when one is already a Christian of a sort.[5] Is your faith authentic? To what degree have you been a Christian "of a sort?"

Robert Talks to God

Dear Lord, . . .

> *Yes.*

Uhhh, is that really You, Lord?

> *Yes. You did call My name, didn't you?*

Yes . . . I guess I just wasn't *really* expecting an answer.

> *That's a real problem in your generation.*

What's that, Lord?

> *People not expecting an answer.*

Yes, yes, I can see that is true. Lord, I really did have something I wanted to talk over with You.

> *What is it?*

Well, You see, I have been getting back in touch with who I really am lately, and I must confess to You, I don't like what I see very much. I think I am guilty of being more like the world around me than I sense I should be. I don't know the biblical Jesus very well, but more of a contemporary Jesus I have somehow adapted to the times.

That's a good observation. Most people never get as far as you have. What's your next step?

Well, now that I have gone this far, Lord, I want to go all the way. I want You to take the scales off my eyes. Let me see You like I have never seen before!

Are you sure you think you are ready?

Oh, yes, Lord. No question.

Are you 100 percent certain?

Lord, You know that I am.

No reservations, then?

None, Lord. Show me the truth.

All right then. What kind of car do You think I would drive today?

Car? What does that have to do with seeing You more clearly?

If you are going to really know Me, you need to know how I would handle things, where I would go, what I would do, where my priorities would be. Does that make sense?

Why, yes. Yes, I guess it does.

So what kind of car would I drive?

Well, er, I don't think it would be a luxury car, maybe a used something or other. Come to think of it, You are so radical, You may not even own one at all.

That's not far from the truth.

Hmmm. I wonder what neighborhood You would live in. What kind of work would You be involved with. Gee, this is interesting. I never thought about the biblical Jesus in contemporary terms before.

Kind of interesting, isn't it?

Yes, Lord, it is.

Listen carefully. Do you have a pencil handy? Write this down: The biblical Jesus and the contemporary Jesus are the same Jesus.

You mean all those things You said to men back then still apply?

You are not far from the kingdom of heaven.

So then I am supposed to feed the poor, visit sick people, share my possessions, maybe even sell some? Do You have any idea how hard I have worked to get where I am?

And while we're on the subject, what about this loving other people stuff? It's getting just a little crowded down here, You know. I have to send up flares just to get someone to let me cut across to the right-hand lane so I don't miss the turnoff to my house.

And what about this job? They've got me working sixty hours a week. There's no time left over for visiting my wife, much less any sick people. What do You want me to do—get another job?

You bring up some interesting points. What do you make of it all?

I find it hard to believe, frankly. How could Jesus expect me to respond the same way today as people did two thousand years ago? I mean, there are cultural differences. Huge differences.

True, the culture has changed, but don't you remember that "Jesus Christ is the same yesterday and today and forever"?

But they didn't even have cars back then.

A car is a good thing. You live in the suburbs. You need a car. Remember: "Every good and perfect gift is from above, coming down from the Father of the heavenly lights, who does not change like shifting shadows." Cultures change, but I don't change. Do you understand Me?

Sort of. I'm beginning to. Cultures change but You don't. So when I interpret You from the culture instead of the Bible the image I see is more of a God adapted to the times. The image is distorted.

Precisely. Distorted by shifting values and strange teachings. All based on human wisdom, I might add. Most people distort my Word because they let the world inflame all sorts of ambitions and passions within them.

What a mess. My life looks more like a compilation of television ads than a biblical Christian. I'm a carbon copy of my times. I've merged Christ into the culture. I guess You might say I'm a cultural Christian. What do I do now, Lord?

Well, you really only have two options. Are you quite certain you are ready for this?

Yes, of course. I want to know. Why wouldn't I?

Okay, then. Your first option is to stop playing games with Me. It really upsets Me. I'm tired of your saying one thing and doing another. If you want to see Me as I really am, you must become like Me for the benefit of your generation. Love Me. Deny yourself. Take up your cross daily. Serve others. Come after Me, not that new luxury import car you have been eyeing.

You know about that?

Yes, but that's not all I know about. Whether you buy that car is not the point. I blessed you so you can afford everything you have, but that's not the only reason I blessed you. I gave you ability to earn a nice income for the sake of My kingdom. Frankly, I'm concerned about the attitude of your lifestyle.

Those extra funds you have been accumulating were originally intended to feed the poor, equip the saints, and win other broken people into My kingdom. When you don't tithe you are robbing from Me. Since you asked, I want to make this point very clear: You can't have it both ways. I know you need money, but you can only have one master. You must make a choice. You cannot serve both money and Me. I have said this before, you know.

And what's my other option?

If you wish, I will put the scales back over your eyes.

If you have been living the life of a "defeated" cultural Christian—perhaps you have syncretized—and long to get back to the Jesus of the Bible, then let me encourage you to tell Him about it. He loves you. He longs to restore you. "A bruised reed he will not break, and a smoldering wick he will not snuff out" (Isaiah 42:3). Rededicate yourself to Him afresh—become born again "again." Here is one way of expressing your desire:

Lord Jesus, I need You in my life right now more than I ever have. I acknowledge that I have been seeking the God (or gods) I have wanted and not the God who is. I have been a cultural Christian. I long to get back to You, to know and follow Your plan, purpose, and will for my life. I repent and open the door of my life. I ask You to forgive me and again take control of my life and make me into the kind of person You want me to be. Help me by the power of Your Holy Spirit to be a biblical Christian. Amen.

Where do we go from here? How can we continue our deep resolve to walk with God rightly? Here is how: If we come daily to the foot of the Cross, keep short accounts with God, confess our sins regularly, and daily seek to follow Christ in the power of the Holy Spirit and become more like Him, then we will know what it means to be a biblical Christian.

"No one has a perfect walk. But deep inside the soul of the biblical Christian burns a longing to live an authentic life that is pleasing to God."

No one has a perfect walk. But deep inside the soul of the biblical Christian burns a longing to live an authentic life that is pleasing to God. Once we become a biblical Christian, does this mean we are set for the rest of our lives? No, every Christian goes through occasional periods of defeat. Yet, through growing in our knowledge of God and self we can increasingly become imitators of Christ in a genuine demonstration of faith, love, obedience, and service.

If you realize that you have been living the life of a "counterfeit" cultural Christian, or even a non-Christian, and if you sense an inner desire to change, be encouraged. It is the Holy Spirit who gives you the desire to believe. A later chapter describes the content of the gospel and how you can settle the issue of your eternal destiny.

Most troubles people have are not from a lack of knowledge, but from a lack of wisdom. Wisdom marks the boundaries of how to apply the truth and knowledge of God we acquire to the particulars of our daily lives. In the next chapter we will take up the subject of finding wisdom.

🌭   🌭   🌭

DISCUSSION QUESTIONS

1. What is the difference between a cultural Christian with a "defeated" faith and a one with "counterfeit" faith?

2. How does the concept of "the placebo effect of the gospel" strike you? Explain your answer.

3. Which of the following "slots" best describes where you have been on your own spiritual pilgrimage?

    I. Believer

      A. Biblical Christian

      B. "Defeated" cultural Christian

    II. Non-Believer

      A. Non-Christian

      B. "Counterfeit" cultural Christian

4. If you are a Christian, reflect on the following continuum and place an "X" at the spot that best describes where you have been and a "check mark" where you would like to end up in the near future. What steps can you take to get there?

"DEFEATED" CULTURAL CHRISTIAN ├───────────┼───────────┤ **BIBLICAL CHRISTIAN**

SEVEN STEPS
TO A WISE LIFE

Dear Journal,

Can I ever relate to Solomon? I think I have
experimented with every single thing in which he
tried to find meaning. I have not been very wise. But
I'm not stupid, either. I don't want to ruin my life. I
don't want to live a syncretistic life. Where should I
concentrate to develop spiritual wisdom and
maturity? Where can I best invest my time? What
are the key principles to keep my life on track?

Robert

CHAPTER 6

THE TWO PARTS OF WISDOM

John Calvin, who played such a leading role in the de-
velopment of Western thought during the Reformation,
was also described as "a genial man with a talent for
friendship."[1]

He devoted his entire life to trace out and organize
the subjects of the Bible into logical, orderly patterns.
He continually added to his thoughts—so much so that
his final tome, *The Institutes of the Christian Religion*,
contains over fifteen hundred pages. All serious theologians have had to consider Calvin.

The impact of his work on all religion, not to mention the sheer length of it, give the opening words of
Calvin's *Institutes* special, elevated significance. They
are worthy of careful consideration. He wrote, "Nearly

all the wisdom we possess, that is to say, true and sound wisdom, consists of two parts: the knowledge of God and of ourselves."

The knowledge of God and the knowledge of self. With the pursuit of these two great themes we can soar high on light-feathered wings toward the horizon of eternal peace, meaning, and purpose. The secret of spiritual objectivity, growth, and wisdom is to seek the God who is and to carefully examine our own lives.

Finally, we have enough to balance out our earlier diagram and show the important strands by which Christianity towers above Humanism, relegating its pitiful power to dim, dreary shadows:

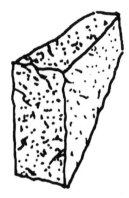

CHRISTIANITY

Knowledge of God
Knowledge of Self
Truth
Salvation
Purpose, Meaning
Wisdom

HUMANISM

Existentialism
Relativism
Materialism

These are the building blocks of a happy, fulfilling life. How do we go about it? What is the end we seek? The highest answer is wisdom. "Wisdom is supreme; therefore get wisdom" (Proverbs 4:7). By this we do not mean a worldly sort of wisdom, but the wisdom of God.

Wisdom—knowing ourselves and the God who is—will connect us to the eternal plans of the One who made us. Let's survey seven major ways Christians can guard against creating a fifth gospel through syncretism. And, of course, these become a suggested list of steps that lead to a wise life.

1. STUDY GOD'S CHARACTER

Over the years I have heard several deeply spiritual people say, in one form or another, "If you really want to have a closer walk with God, the best thing you can do is to study His attributes." I have found this to be true.

When we penetrate the splendors of the character and attributes of God, a whole new rich world of spiritual understanding opens up to us.

We study the attributes of God to discover who He really is. When we don't pursue Him we become mere cultural Christians. Cultural Christians pursue the God they want instead of the God who is. God is not who we first thought Him to be. He is who He is, and unchanging. No task is more noble than to surrender our expectations and presuppositions before the throne of His grace and mercy so that we may *know* Him . . . so that *we* may know Him . . . so that we may know *Him*.

Our initial impressions of God were shaped by our culture: where we were born, who our parents were, the religion we practiced, our natural abilities, our disappointments. The very word "Father" is extremely loaded, the meaning so intertwined with our experiences with human fathers. This means we will spend extra hours undoing concepts from our old circle, as well as filling up our new circle with the correct doctrine of God.

Few people are pursuing a passionate life of devotion and study of God. How many can you think of? Our age is a biblically illiterate age. According to the Barna Research Group, 93 percent of American households have a Bible, while only 12 percent read them every day.[2]

If we have a *syncretized* notion of the God who is, we do not know God, but god. How well can you describe the character and attributes of God?

2. LEAD AN EXAMINED LIFE

A young Christian man about to turn thirty lamented, "I have become a very hard-boiled and cynical person. I'm Jekyll at home, but Hyde at

> *"When we run at the frenzied pace of the rat race we, too, lose our clarity and focus."*

the office. I'm afraid that if I don't make some radical changes now I may never be able to."

For many people what looked like a groove turns out to be a rut. If we burrow along in a rut too long, one day we look up and can't visualize ourselves scaling the walls to freedom. A friend commented, "A rut is simply a grave with both ends knocked out."

I don't know about the circles in which you travel, but everywhere I go these days I find that people are tired. They are not only physically tired, but mentally, emotionally, psychologically, and spiritually tired. Christians have no special inoculation against this. When we run at the frenzied pace of the rat race we, too, lose our clarity and focus. Tired people don't examine their lives—they don't have time to do diagnostics.

The fastest way to a fifth gospel is to be deceived by leading an overly busy, unexamined life. One of the most revealing biblical word studies I've ever done is on the word *deceit* and its sister words. Here are five different deceivers:

1. The *heart* is such a willing party to self-deceit. "The heart is deceitful above all things" (Jeremiah 17:9).

2. The *old man* is a devious deceiver. "Your old self, which is being corrupted by its deceitful desires" (Ephesians 4:22).

3. *People* purposefully manipulate each other. "Wicked deceivers surround me" (Psalm 49:5). "Let no one deceive you with empty words" (Ephesians 5:6).

4. *Satan's minions* muster deceit. "[The beast] deceived the inhabitants of the earth" (Revelation 13:14).

5. And, of course, that snake *Satan* himself is the Master Deceiver. "The serpent deceived me, and I ate" (Genesis 3:13).

What a depressing scenario this would be if God did not offer help to overcome the tentacles of deceit. The antidote is to lead an examined life, regularly reviewing our ways.

As I said in *The Man in the Mirror*, the number one shortcoming of man at the close of the twentieth century (as it has been at the close of every century) is that we lead unexamined lives. An unexamined life is inevitably a *syncretized* life. Would you say you have done a good job in self-examination or not?

To help you think about your life in self examination, I have included a self test entitled "A Self Examination," (see figure 6.1). Why not give this a try? There is no better time than now. Keep it completely confidential—between you and God alone. Be painfully honest in appraising yourself. Then reflect upon your answers as you move through the rest of these pages. Think of practical changes you can make. Make a mental note to look at this self-examination again when you finish the book.

3. MAINTAIN PRIVATE DEVOTIONS

Richard Dobbins, founder of Emerge Ministries, works with pastors who have fallen into sexual sin. He notes a single common denominator among every fallen pastor with whom he has worked. Dobbins, who has counseled hundreds of morally failed pastors, says, "I have never seen one minister guilty of sexual sin who kept a daily personal devotion time."[3] In other words, in the days, weeks, and months leading up to their moral failure their public ministry continued but their private watch before Christ stopped. Dobbins says the difficulties arise when we confuse our *walk with God* and our *work for God*.

If the pastor must be vigilant to keep his private devotional life fresh, how much more vulnerable is the layman who must each day face a hostile world filled with temptation? When we crowd out private, personal moments with our Lord we begin to run on the reserves, and soon the fumes. We do not have the power of the Holy Spirit to live a life worthy of the calling we received unless we are filled to overflowing. When we drink deep the things of God, we will have enough of Christ to refresh ourselves and some left over to share with others, too.

Nowhere does the Bible say we *must* read our Bible every day. However, the Bible does say that the person who *does* meditate on the Word daily "is like a tree planted by streams of water, which yields its fruit in season and whose leaf does not wither. Whatever he does prospers" (Psalm 1:3). And the Bible says, "Pray in the Spirit on all occasions with all kinds of prayers and requests" (Ephesians 6:18).

A Self Examination

Reflect on the following continuums and place an **"X"** where you think you have been and a **"check mark"** where you would like to end up in the near future. Put an **"*"** next to the area needing the most attention.

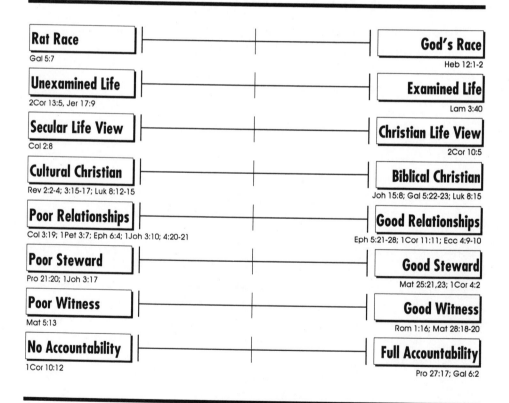

Rat Race		God's Race
Gal 5:7		Heb 12:1-2
Unexamined Life		Examined Life
2Cor 13:5, Jer 17:9		Lam 3:40
Secular Life View		Christian Life View
Col 2:8		2Cor 10:5
Cultural Christian		Biblical Christian
Rev 2:2-4; 3:15-17; Luk 8:12-15		Joh 15:8; Gal 5:22-23; Luk 8:15
Poor Relationships		Good Relationships
Col 3:19; 1Pet 3:7; Eph 6:4; 1Joh 3:10; 4:20-21		Eph 5:21-28; 1Cor 11:11; Ecc 4:9-10
Poor Steward		Good Steward
Pro 21:20; 1Joh 3:17		Mat 25:21,23; 1Cor 4:2
Poor Witness		Good Witness
Mat 5:13		Rom 1:16; Mat 28:18-20
No Accountability		Full Accountability
1Cor 10:12		Pro 27:17; Gal 6:2

Figure 6.1: Self Test

The Scriptures don't say you have to read the Bible and pray daily. Instead, they say we should continually meditate on the Word and pray about everything. The biblical concept is continual devotions. Actually, the concept of a daily quiet time is a cultural accommodation to busy, crowded schedules. Because most of us do have such hectic schedules, the idea of a few minutes devoted exclusively to Bible reading and prayer is valuable. Daily private devotions is not a *requirement*, but it is *wise*. Ask any fallen pastor.

Personally, I have known many people who have had great struggles even though they maintained a close, intimate walk with Jesus. But I have never seen one of these go undelivered in due time. "The man who looks intently into the perfect law that gives freedom, and continues to do this, not forgetting what he has heard, but doing it—he will be blessed in what he does" (James 1:25).

On the other hand, I have known many Christians who suffered deeply simply because they did not pursue the presence of the Lord through regular personal devotions in their hour of adversity. Without regular time with God, the seeds of *syncretism* take root. Do you maintain a traditional time of private devotion? Without being legalistic, what kind of commitment to time alone with God is realistic for you?

Consider establishing a maximum time limit for your devotional life, not a minimum. This will keep down the guilt. If you have never had a quiet time before start with a maximum of five minutes. Only allow yourself to go beyond your maximum if you are on fire for more. Read one chapter of the New Testament and pray a prayer (like the Lord's Prayer). Don't expect to make it every day, but pick a time and place regular enough that you can reasonably make it about five of seven days a week. If you read one chapter of the New Testament five days each week you will complete it in one year (260 chapters). Increase your daily time limit only as you feel you can't keep the lid on it any more, but go slowly. If you will set realistic expectations, then you can design a program doomed to succeed.

4. THINK DIFFERENTLY

Many of us add Jesus to our lives as another interest in an already busy and otherwise overcrowded schedule. Call this the gospel of addition.

The gospel of Jesus Christ is to *add* Him, but also to *subtract* some things—what the Bible calls repentance. Salvation includes *conversion* and *repentance*. Paul said, "I preached that they should repent [subtract sin] and turn to God [convert—add Christ] and prove their repentance by their deeds" (Acts 26:20). The gospel of Jesus Christ comes by faith and repentance.

Repentance literally means "to think differently." God wants us to think differently. To do this we "add" some things to our lives and "subtract" some things. God is working out the details of our character. He wants to work some things "in to" our character and some things "out of" our character. When we add Jesus but don't subtract sin, we are not following God's gospel, but a *syncretistic* fifth gospel.

In what ways have you "thought differently"? Are you as far along as you would like to be? How can you advance further?

5. ACCEPT BIBLICAL AUTHORITY

A Christian woman told me that she was planning to leave her husband and three children to pursue a professional career. Then she asked my advice.

"What do you understand the Bible to say about this?" I asked.

"The Bible says I should not divorce my husband. I know that. That's why I feel so torn. I just feel that this is something I have to do but I have been wavering back and forth for months," she said ominously. "My best friend thinks I'm crazy."

We live in an overstimulated, sensual time. The exaggerated emphasis on "feelings" is the hallmark of relativism. However, the believer cannot trust feelings. Feelings must be brought under the moral authority of the Scriptures. Feelings betray. Feelings lead to *syncretism*.

Any feeling that guides us into a decision that is counter to the Word is born of the flesh and must be checked. The Bible must be viewed as our final authority, not wavering emotions. "For the word of God is living and active. Sharper than any double-edged sword . . . it judges the thoughts and attitudes of the heart" (Hebrews 4:12).

One of the most significant crises in our culture is rebellion against authority. One day recently, while driving to the Little League baseball field, I encountered a group of boys on bicycles. One boy in the group shouted some unheard-by-me snide remark at this "oldster" while the others laughed knowingly. I kept driving, though brooding.

A minute later a boy crossed in front of me at an intersection. The light was green for me, but red for him. When I slammed on the brakes he sneered at me as if I was the dumbest person who had ever walked the face of the planet. Maybe he was right—because I certainly felt stupid. What I wanted to do, of course, was run the little fellow over, but I just knew people wouldn't understand.

The problem is that these cute little urchins grow up. And when they do, they love to resist authority. They bring the same rebellious attitudes to the church and the Word of God. When someone—like the church—does ask them to submit to authority, they simply won't do it.

Is there a little "urchin" inside you? Do you struggle with an authority problem? Why is submitting to the Word as moral authority so important?

6. DISTINGUISH THE BIBLE FROM CULTURAL NORMS

Today girls call boys on the telephone. So what? I think we dreadfully mistake violations of the rules of culture for violations of the Bible. In

> ## "To convert a difference of opinion about cultural norms into a spiritual issue is madness."

our culture most parents grew up in the era when only sleazy girls called boys. Today kids don't feel the same way their parents once did. To convert a difference of opinion about cultural norms into a spiritual issue is madness.

When we become Christians we tend to bring our culture with us. Such has always been the case. In the first century two kinds of people were becoming Christians: Jews and Gentiles, the religious and the non-religious. Both groups tended to bring their cultures with them. They tried to make the gospel into Jesus Christ *plus something*.

Some of the Jews brought the law with them and tried to distort the gospel into Jesus Christ plus law. Today we would call them legalists. Some of the Gentiles brought Greek philosophy with them and tried to make the gospel into Jesus Christ plus good ideas. Today we would call them syncretists.

When we attempt to bring the old order of the world into the new order of the kingdom of God, we distort the way God wants us to live the rest of our lives. The kingdom of God on earth is a whole new order, a whole new way of living. When we blend our new Bible and our old culture together we won't be able to discern what are the distinctly Christian ideas.

Those of us truly committed to Christ can live one of two ways. We can "do our own thing," or we can live for the will of God. Sadly, many people who have received Christ as Lord struggle against Him. They are living by their own ideas. They are Christian in spirit, but secular in practice. They have not sought the will of God with dogged determination. Instead, they have been doing as they pleased, and their lives are not turning out as they had hoped.

One secret of living by a distinctly Christian life view is to not confuse your Bible with your culture. When we are moralizing about someone's behavior (a no-no by itself) ask this telling question of yourself, "Am I bothered because this violates the *Bible* or because it doesn't fit into the expectations of my *cultural norms?*" A briefer version may simply ask, "Where in the Bible does it say you can't do that?"

Someone doesn't have to perform to our standards to live Christianly. Where does it say in the Bible you can't wear long hair? If someone dresses like they still live in the fifties (or sixties), why are they ostracized?

When we try to enforce the current trends of our own culture as the standard for acceptable behavior (whether too strict or too tolerant), we fall into the trap of building on the wrong base. Judging people based upon their culture is a symptom of *syncretism*. Do you base your views of people on the Bible, or do you evaluate people based on the changing norms of culture?

---

7. DEVELOP PERSONAL ACCOUNTABILITY

He fumbled to explain the deep financial morass into which he had gotten himself. The more he spoke the more emotional he became.

Finally, though I did not mean to hurt him in any way, I interrupted and asked, "Do you think you are going to make it?"

At that he fell apart. "I don't know. I just don't know," he moaned.

People succeed or fail four ways: spiritually, morally, financially, and relationally. Do you know anyone who ever set out to fail on purpose? Obviously, no one ruins their life on purpose. Yet people all around us fail regularly. Why?

"Integrity is a one-to-one correlation between my Bible, my beliefs, and my behavior."

When my hometown was small no one escaped notice. The high visibility restrained a lot of sin. Sometime in the past decade, however, the city grew in size and passed a *threshold of anonymity*. Today someone can move about virtually anonymously, escaping scrutiny, at times slipping through the cracks.

In our era almost all Christians lead anonymous spiritual lives. Today's Christians seem to be able to float in and out of the church without having to be accountable for their lives. Without accountability we have no one to whom we must give an answer for our lives. We have not given anyone permission to ask the hard questions. Our lives become shrouded in the ambiguity of trite responses to questions asked by people who might actually care if we would be honest with them.

Modern pressures mean less time to think about our own lives, as well as less time to be interested in the lives of others. With so many problems of our own we often don't have the energy to express interest in how others are *really* doing. So they often fail, and so do we.

The overarching goal of accountability is to help people succeed in life. This only can come to pass by leading a life that pleases God. How do we accomplish such a feat? By living a life of integrity. *Integrity is a one-to-one correlation between my Bible, my beliefs, and my behavior.* Walking transparently before some brothers or sisters creates the highest probability for leading a successful life with integrity. Isolation from the valuable views of maturing Christians contributes to failing in life, not succeeding.

The trend line points toward less accountability, not more. Our generation faces an enormous explosion of possible choices, excruciating time demands, and unparalleled personal stress. At the same time there is a pronounced move toward individualism and anonymity, and away from institutionalized norms. Funny. At the precise time when we need some friends to help us make the right choices, we are culturally moving toward isolation from each other.

We live in a culture which increasingly approves of privacy ("It's nobody's business but my own") and individualism ("Do your own thing"). The growing tendency to make religion a private matter has led to a sort of *compartmentalized Christianity.* People view what they do in religion as one compartment or cell, what they do at home as a different compartment, and what they do at the office as an altogether unrelated matter. They apply different values and standards to different compartments. Often no single thread of continuity ties these compartments together into a whole.

It is a mistake to presume that if someone is private at the office that they have meaningful personal relationships in their homes and neighborhood, or vice versa. Many people operate without any meaningful personal relationships or accountability whatsoever. They have a dull edge. They are not sharpened by accountability's queries. They are not as objective as they ought to be. They are living by a fifth gospel. Is it any wonder they *syncretize* Christianity with Humanism?

Do you have anyone to whom you are accountable? How would the quality of your spiritual pilgrimage profit from an accountable relationship?

⁂   ⁂   ⁂

Many of us could live more wisely. We tend to create a fifth gospel by *syncretizing* our beliefs with ideas from the world. We break the chain of integrity: from Bible to beliefs to behavior. We have explored seven steps to a wise life that can help us maintain a sharp edge to our spiritual objectivity:

1. Study the character of God.

2. Lead an examined life.

3. Maintain daily personal devotions.

4. Think differently.

5. Establish the Bible as your final moral authority.

6. Don't confuse the Bible with cultural norms.

7. Maintain an accountable relationship.

These powerful principles mark the corners of a life filled with wisdom. They point the way to knowing both one's self and the God who is. Where these principles are applied no fifth gospel will be found, but an authentic, life-changing faith.

The next section, "Deciding What to Believe," explores the biblical doctrines that when finally grasped by men and women through the ages have shaken the earth's foundations. The final section, "Cultivating an Authentic Christian Lifestyle," offers helpful suggestions on how to be so radically changed that people feel compelled to say of you, "That must be what it means to be a *real* Christian."

⁂   ⁂   ⁂

DISCUSSION QUESTIONS

1. "Nearly all the wisdom we possess, that is to say, true and sound wisdom, consists of two parts: the knowledge of God and of ourselves."

☐ Agree   ☐ Disagree

Explain your answer.

2. Which of the following principles do you apply on a regular basis? Explain how these have helped you to know yourself and to know God better.

☐ Studying the character of God.

☐ Leading an examined life.

☐ Maintaining daily personal devotions.

☐ Thinking differently (repentance).

☐ Establishing the Bible as my final moral authority.

☐ Not confusing the Bible with cultural norms.

☐ Maintaining an accountable relationship.

3. Which of the seven areas in question 2 do you consider to be weak spots? What changes would you like to make? How important are these principles to the success of the rest of your life?

DECIDING WHAT TO BELIEVE

PART THREE

AN APOLOGY FOR DOCTRINE

D*ear Journal,*

For the life of me I can't understand why, but somehow I never grasped the extent to which my beliefs determine my behavior. Frankly, I've been lazy. I never thought learning doctrine was all that important. Besides, my work keeps me very busy—who has the time? I figured as long as I believed in Jesus, that everything would turn out okay. Well, it hasn't. I have monumental problems, and now I can see how most of them are the direct consequences of choices I've made which were not biblical at all.

Robert

CHAPTER 7

WHAT IS DOCTRINE?

At one level the Bible touches every facet of life and faith. At another level, though, the Bible can be compressed into a few major subjects or themes about which we can form basic positions, or doctrines.

Webster defines a doctrine as "a particular principle, position, or policy taught or advocated." In short, Christian doctrines are the core beliefs of our faith.

Some are afraid of doctrine; they think it will ruin their faith. A woman said, "We used to attend a 'feeling' driven church, but we sensed something was missing. We moved to a Bible-based church and were, frankly, surprised. We gained the rock of Truth, but we were able to keep our feelings, too."

In this section of the book we will delve into that nucleus of doctrines which most deeply impacts the rest of our earthly lives. They address the deep questions about the purpose and meaning of life, questions such as these: Who is God? Is He knowable? How can He be known? Is man by nature basically good or bad? Why is there brokenness and pain? Why do men need to be saved? How can a man be saved—by faith or by works? Or is it some combination of the two?

Obviously our look will be limited. But I hope these short primers will stimulate some new thoughts if you are a seasoned believer or stir up the desire to know more if you are young in your faith.

WHY DO WE NEED DOCTRINE?

Remember how you used to squirm in class when the teacher would ask a question but you didn't have the answer? Remember how you hoped upon hope she wouldn't call on you?

Similarly, have you ever nearly collapsed in a panic attack when someone asked you, "As a Christian, what do you believe, and why do you believe that way?" Many times we have settled on *how to live* (our practices and behavior) but don't have a firm grip on *what we believe and why* (our doctrine and beliefs). Why is it important to know the principles and beliefs behind our behavior?

Chuck Green, my pastor, says, "The Bible is either true or it isn't, and you either believe it or you don't." The main reason we need to know what we believe and why is because *it is true*. Francis Schaeffer often said, "There is only one reason to become a Christian and not two—it is true."

If Christianity *is* true, then we have the answer for a broken, hurting world. Indeed, Christians are the *only* group who have been able to draw a circle large enough to explain the true meaning and purpose of life. To know doctrine, then, is to know the truth about life—about the way life *is*, not the way we wish it might have been.

A second reason we need doctrine is *to lead a balanced life*. To lead a balanced life is to first know what to believe and, then, as a result, how to live. The truth about how to lead a balanced life is found only in the Bible.

Most of us don't have time to deeply penetrate the Bible for insights, so we sit under seasoned Bible teachers. Bible teachers must make choices about what they will teach in order to create the proper balance between "what to believe" and "how to live." They must choose from among four teaching thrusts:

1. Truth: What to believe.

2. Proof: Why to believe it.

3. Application: What to do as a result.

4. Implementation: How to live it out.

Bible teachers who over-emphasize "what to believe" to the exclusion of "how to live" are often thought of as cerebral, dull, and boring. But those who over-emphasize "how to live" leave us wondering, "Why should I do that?" The experienced Bible teacher tries to show us the

---

"What we believe determines our behavior."

---

balance between both. We need both if we want to be a biblical believer. If we leap past the "what to believe and why," then we won't have the base or foundation we need to make adjustments when life zigs instead of zags. We won't be able to think for ourselves.

The purpose of doctrine is not to barricade people inside the truth as though in a prison but, rather, to so clearly mark the boundaries of what is true and what is false that God's people can move about freely. Jesus said it this way: "If you hold to my teaching, you are really my disciples. Then you will know the truth, and the truth will set you free" (John 8:31–32).

The purpose of doctrine is not to bind people up—exactly not that. Rather, the clear purpose of doctrine is to set us free to reach our full potential in Christ. Only when the boundary lines are clearly marked can we move about in freedom and not fear the pitfalls of being outside the truth of God's Word. Doctrine graciously unlooses the strangulating cords of spiritual ignorance and legalism that paralyze people. Doctrine sets us free.

Why do we need to be so particular about the details of what we believe? *What we believe determines our behavior.* As the subtle, underlying motivators of all that we do, our beliefs are of paramount importance. Not of secondary significance—to be relegated to the "if I find time" category—doctrine is the rudder that sets the course of our life. We are responsible for what we believe and the choices that result.

What we believe counts forever. Our role in the eternal destiny of our neighbors depends on what we believe. Are the lost *really* lost? Doesn't God have a plan to save everyone? Are the good deeds of the person who is kind to all, always helps the needy, and leads a (somewhat) moral life sufficient for salvation? Why or why not? How (and whether) we reach out to lost people depends upon how we answer these and similar questions. These are questions of doctrine and belief.

What we believe determines how we minister. Is God sovereign? If He is sovereign, is He good? If He is both sovereign and good, how do we explain the innocent child struck down by a car or painful, debilitating diseases? How could God possibly be both all-powerful and good at the same time? How (and whether) we comfort and encourage people is determined by our answers to these and similar questions. These are the questions of doctrine and belief.

DOCTRINE AND PRACTICE

In giving advice to his young protégé Timothy, Paul exhorted him, "Watch your life and doctrine closely" (1 Timothy 4:16). Paul understood the distinction between "what we believe"—our doctrine, and "how we live"—our practice. They are different, but inextricably connected. What is this distinction, and what is its significance?

In our Christian life we deal with *matters of faith* and *matters of practice*. Faith is what we believe, our doctrine. Practice is the effect of what we believe has on how we behave, and how we live.

The all-important first step in living Christianly is to build a Christian base. By Christian base we mean matters of doctrine, faith, belief, and knowledge of the truth; these subjects form the foundation of our life view. It is what we believe. Unless we build a correct Christian base we will not have the categories to live a correct Christian life.

The base we build determines the life we live. Only a Christian base will produce a Christian life. By Christian life we mean matters of practice, behavior, and life. It is how we live. What we believe necessarily and inevitably determines how we live.

The title of an article in this morning's newspaper (and you can pick any day) focuses on the relationship between belief and behavior. The title and subtitle to the article tell the story: "Teen Sex in an Age of No Rules: With the Influence of TV Shows and Birth Control, 'Going All the Way' Is Now a Natural Part of Dating." If my great, great granddaughter should curiously peruse this book in one hundred years, I wonder what kind of culture she will be growing up in. "Honey, whatever it is like, always remember that what you believe necessarily determines how you live. Give attention to building a distinctly Christian life view. 'Watch your life and doctrine closely.'"

Our faith, beliefs, and doctrines form the grid through which we filter our decisions of practice, behavior, and life. In other words, we practice what we believe and we believe what we practice. Our behavior is a reliable indicator of what we believe.

Let's summarize:

Matters of Doctrine	Matters of Practice
Building a Christian Base	Living a Christian Life
Faith	Life
Belief	Behavior
What We Believe	How We Live

Frankly, I have lost sleep over including this section in the book. I'm afraid as Christians we have no burning passion to settle the issues of what we believe and why. I'm afraid we have put too much faith in our teachers and nibble around the edges of truth instead of cutting into it ourselves. I'm afraid our visits to the gospels are vicarious, not personal.

I'm afraid we are willing to settle into a nominal, tepid, cultural Christianity because we have our life insurance. I'm afraid we will apply rigorous discipline to learn how to earn a living, but not how to live. I'm afraid we think we can be saved, then continue to live as though nothing happened.

I'm afraid that we lose our enthusiasm for the things of God because of the urgencies of everyday life. I'm afraid we think receiving Christ is the end of our spiritual pilgrimage, not the beginning. I'm afraid we think we can pray a prayer and then everything will take care of itself. I'm afraid we expect God to be a gentle grandfather-type always willing to rescue us from our poor choices. I'm afraid we sense no personal responsibility for the gospel. I'm afraid we think someone else will tell the ubiquitous "they" about Jesus.

I'm afraid that we are very busy with our careers and don't have the time to invest. I'm afraid that we think we are too old to grow or have lost the zeal to learn. I'm afraid that we think we are covered by the blood of Christ, so why bother. I'm afraid that we are so new in Christ that we think we will never be able to understand it all anyway. I'm afraid that we don't think God is watching us so why worry. I'm afraid that we have simply become lazy.

Those are my fears but, far and away, my greatest fear is that you will not work through this section. I'm afraid you will think, "I'm saved. I don't need to worry about all of that other stuff." Please don't. We will try to answer the questions, "So what? Why do I need to know this?"—hopefully giving you practical, personal reasons to learn this information. Would I be overstating the case to say that the future of Christian civilization as we have known it depends upon your worrying about this stuff? Time will tell.

THE BENEFITS OF DOCTRINE

Historically, whenever the people of God have been gripped by the earthshaking doctrines of the Bible they have set their worlds ablaze for the kingdom of God. A right knowledge of God will inevitably lift our vision for the rest of our lives to heroic proportions.

To finally understand the problem that Jesus Christ solves is revolutionary. To finally comprehend the intricate relationship between faith and works outfits a person with life-changing power. To finally understand how a person is saved radically alters the way we see other people.

> ### *"Whenever the people of God have been gripped by the earthshaking doctrines of the Bible they have set their worlds ablaze for the kingdom of God."*

To finally know that God is utterly faithful, trustworthy, and sovereign releases the last remnants of doubt and fear. To finally know the unconditional love of God in Christ gives the heart an unshakable assurance of its destiny. To finally see how the deep and radical effects of the Fall hamper mankind frees us from charging God with wrongdoing. To finally penetrate the forgiveness of Jesus enables us to be free—fully and finally—from all moral guilt for the sins that have haunted us.

THE GOAL OF DOCTRINE: AN INDEPENDENT FAITH

Young adolescents blindly accept what their parents tell them as true. One day, though, they become teenagers and realize they must establish their own independent identity apart from Mom and Dad.

The main job of teenagers is to find out who they are—their identity. They must draw for themselves the line that sets the boundaries of their beliefs. To find out precisely where this line should go, teenagers experiment with their behavior, often drawing lines in the wrong places. Said simply, sometimes teenagers find out who they are by finding out who they are not.

Sometimes teenagers choose radical, outrageous behaviors that fall outside the perimeter of who they ought to be. They may come to their senses after the first try, or not until many painful years pass by. Sooner or later, though, they realize that the behavior falls outside the boundaries of their identity, so they abandon it. Other times they are confirmed in a behavior, and so add the underlying, motivating belief to their identity and character.

Over time, through trial and error—make that trial and success—the well-adjusted teenager's identity grows from vague, indistinct feelings of ambiguity to the surefooted, concrete, expressible confidence of knowing who he is, what he believes, and why.

When we first believe in Christ we become what is sometimes referred to as a "baby" Christian. While maybe a silly term to some, it certainly fits. At some point we must grow up and establish an independent faith, not one blindly accepted, but carved out of our own experience and study. We must become spiritual teenagers, seeking to independently draw for ourselves the lines that mark the boundaries of our beliefs.

Sure, we will occasionally draw the line in the wrong place. Like teenagers, *we often find out who we are by finding out who we are not.* It's okay to experiment; that is how we find out who we are in Christ. The question is this: Have you located the cornerposts that mark the perimeter of authentic, genuine Christianity?

NONNEGOTIABLES

Some doctrines, like the sovereignty of God and the deity of Christ, permeate almost every page of Scripture. These basic doctrines form the core of what we might call *nonnegotiables*. Other (often less pervasive) doctrines may also receive "nonnegotiable" status by particular sects, movements, and denominations. If you took a poll, you would quickly learn that people's lists of nonnegotiables vary widely.

We each ought to have a list of nonnegotiables—a primary list and a secondary list. The primary list holds those doctrines from which we can brook no difference (e.g., the character of God or the resurrection of Christ). These are the doctrines for which you are willing to give your life.

A secondary (perhaps longer) list of nonnegotiables, though, should be those doctrines which may be very dear to you personally but, in charity toward your brothers and sisters, you allow for honest differences of opinion (e.g., the ministry of the Holy Spirit, infant vs. adult baptism, free will vs. election). These are nonnegotiable to you personally but, in wisdom, you don't start wars over them. R. C. Sproul aptly calls these "intramural debates."

And then there ought to be a third list: a long list of matters which may be extremely important to you personally but don't mean a hoot if someone else doesn't feel the same way (e.g., differences in worship style or drinking caffeine). Not only would you not die over these, you don't even bring them up in conversation. Quizzically, the most major disputes often take place over the most minor doctrines. Could that be a strategy of the evil one?

Should our list of nonnegotiables be long or short? May I suggest your list be as short as conscience will allow. As one friend has said, "You can have a long list if you want, but you won't have much fellowship."

Jesus did not have a long list.

FOUR RUBRICS OF DOCTRINE

What are the most important doctrines to settle in our minds? Max Anders distills the Bible down to "eight great subjects": The Bible, God, Christ, the Holy Spirit, Angels, Man, Salvation, and Future Things.[1] In the next five chapters we will discuss doctrines about a number of these subjects from the viewpoint of classic, traditional, orthodox, evangelical Christianity. We won't be settling the debates which have for centuries gone unsettled, but neither will we shy away from debates of gravity, like whether men are saved by faith or works. Here are four rubrics for this section of the book:

- *The Doctrine of the Bible:*
  Chapter 8, "Thinking in Biblical Categories"
- *The Doctrine of God:*
  Chapter 9, "The God Who Is"

- *The Doctrine of Man:*
  Chapter 10, "The Radical Effect of the Fall"
- *The Doctrine of Salvation:*
  Chapter 11, "The Content of the Gospel"
  Chapter 12, "The Relationship of Faith and Works"

Can we exhaust everything just tallied? No, of course not. But we can stimulate ourselves to think more deeply about the things of God. Some are already thinking deeply about these subjects and will enjoy seeing one more perspective. At the other extreme are those of us who have never really pushed ourselves to think in biblical categories. We have enjoyed the comfortable orbit, but we hate it, don't we? Let's do it; let's burn our boats.

None of these chapters is meant to be the final word on the doctrine it presents. I have made no attempt to be comprehensive. I have attempted to write in such a way that you will be stimulated to do additional studies. The underlying assumption is that the reader is already an evangelical Christian who accepts the Bible as the authoritative Word of God. If you are not in that category (yet), then you may want to also explore other texts written for inquirers and skeptics.

I hope you will criticize and argue and question and doubt and wrestle with each doctrine. Don't accept anything uncritically. The Apostle Paul said that those who have something to say should speak, "and the others should weigh carefully what is said" (1 Corinthians 14:29). Instead of this being the ending point it should be the beginning, or another stop along the way.

愛 愛 愛

DISCUSSION QUESTIONS

1. What are the beliefs for which you would be willing to die?

2. Assume someone asks you today, "You're a Christian. What do you believe, and why do you believe it?" Would you be prepared to give them an answer? Read 1 Peter 3:15. Why is it important to be able to give an answer?

3. "Most Christians don't have well-developed doctrine."

   ☐ Agree   ☐ Disagree

   Explain your answer.

4. What is doctrine? What is the difference between doctrine and practice?

5. Why is doctrine important? Can you give an illustration of how knowing doctrine has helped you? Can you give an illustration of how not knowing doctrine has harmed you?

6. Have you ever heard this statement (or words to this effect)? "I'm saved. I don't need to worry about all of that other stuff." What does this attitude communicate? How would you modify the statement to reflect a wiser approach? To what degree has it reflected your own thinking?

7. Has doctrine been a topic that has occupied much of your time and energy? Why or why not?

THINKING IN BIBLICAL CATEGORIES

D*ear Journal,*

As I have thought it over, I can see that what I have believed has profoundly influenced how I have lived. Surely there is a direct link between belief and behavior. I sense a desire to clarify what I believe so that I can be building on the right foundation. I can see that for my "life" to be godly my "doctrine" must first be godly.

The problem for me, though, is that I have always found the language of the Bible foreign—beyond the grasp of my everyday vocabulary. I don't understand the biblical categories in which I should think. What are the categories I need to build a Christian base of thinking? What do I need to know to think biblically? And is the Bible really the authoritative Word of God?

Robert

A CHRISTIAN LIFE VIEW

When Robert first became a Christian, virtually every doctrine and concept came as a new idea. He found it difficult to grasp many concepts the first time around, for that matter the first several times around. He felt as though he was enshrouded in a thick, impenetrable fog.

Robert lacked a good foundation of Bible knowledge and vocabulary. Whenever his pastor preached a sermon that burned a hole through some of the fog, the rest of the fog would not hold its place, but within hours would spread over into the cleared out space. *This is surely no thunder and lightning experience*, he thought. His mind kept saying, however, *Be patient, Robert. Be patient.*

Later, as Robert became more familiar with the Bible, the thick fog that had always separated Robert from thinking in distinctly Christian categories began to burn off. The Bible acted as a bright, hot sun that melted the mist away. A quiet excitement for learning more about God through the Bible welled up within him. He had come a long way, though it had taken many years.

Every person operates from a *base*, or *life view*. This base may be Christian, humanistic, or syncretistic. Some carefully chisel out their life view; others merely assume the default values of the cultural majority.

Many Christians do not operate from a distinctly Christian life view. Instead they have built on the shifting sands of shallow thinking; they live by their own ideas. Some Christians, not anchored in the Word, watch in exasperation as the cross currents of trendy thinking guide their most important choices.

Others, new to the faith, must deal with the painful consequences of past errors. Several men at a retreat were standing around at a break, congratulating a very wealthy man for being so rich and so Christian at the same time. He had paid a great price to become so successful, however. "I would give it all up if I could only have a relationship with my son," came his sobering reply.

Our choices have consequences but they often don't show up until we are deeply into a wrong way of thinking and living. It's never too late to change, of course, but the pain can be excruciating. The value of painstakingly developing a biblical way of viewing life cannot be overstated.

How do we find the boundaries of a Christian life view? We do so by letting the Bible carve its indelible mark on our heart, mind, and soul. "The word of God is living and active. Sharper than any double-edged sword, it penetrates even to dividing soul and spirit, joints and marrow; it judges the thoughts and attitudes of the heart" (Hebrews 4:12).

The Bible is Christ's teaching and the sword of the Holy Spirit. The sanctifying saber of God's Word will lop off every syncretistic idea that is not part of a distinctly Christian life view—if we listen. The Bible alone, apart from human additions, marks the perimeters of a Christian life view.

THE AUTHORITY OF THE BIBLE

In a world with limited resources you must pick your issues carefully. You can't fight every battle. The sixteenth-century reformers understood this principle.

"Some of the greatest tragedies have come not by the wicked intentions of evil men, but by the misguided good intentions of otherwise fine men."

The leaders of the sixteenth-century Protestant Reformation narrowed their focus to two central, nonnegotiable issues. The first was *salvation by faith alone*. The second was *the authority of the Scriptures*.

Why was the authority of Scripture so important to them? The problem they saw was not that men *abandoned* the Bible, but that they placed their own authority alongside the Bible as a sort of coequal authority. They saw that since the mind suffers from the effect of the Fall, men make mistakes.

Some of the greatest tragedies have come not by the wicked intentions of evil men, but by the misguided good intentions of otherwise fine men. Think of almost any church split. Invariably, good people come down on both sides of whatever issue. There is one supreme opportunity to override man's propensity to err. The Bible must be the final rule of authority for all matters of faith, doctrine, and life. Why the Bible?

The Bible claims to be the authoritative, infallible Word of God. Consider these ten points:

1. *God is the source of all Scripture.* "All Scripture is God-breathed and is useful for teaching, rebuking, correcting and training in righteousness" (2 Timothy 3:16).

2. *The Word of God is without error.* "Every word of God is flawless; he is a shield to those who take refuge in him. Do not add to his words, or he will rebuke you and prove you a liar" (Proverbs 30:5–6).

3. *The Word of God is infallible.* It is incapable of error. Not only is it *without* error, it *cannot* err. "The law of the LORD is perfect, reviving the soul" (Psalm 19:7).

4. *The Word of God is eternal.* "Heaven and earth will pass away, but my words will never pass away" (Matthew 24:35).

5. *The Word of God is effectual.* It produces the intended result. "My word that goes out from my mouth: It will not return to me empty, but will accomplish what I desire and achieve the purpose for which I sent it" (Isaiah 55:11).

6. *The Word of God is truth.* "Sanctify them by the truth; your word is truth (John 17:17).

7. *The Word of God is trustworthy.* "The statutes of the LORD are trustworthy, making wise the simple" (Psalm 19:7).

8. *The Word of God teaches, encourages, and warns.* "For everything that was written in the past was written to teach us, so that through endurance and the encouragement of the Scriptures we might have hope" (Romans 15:4). "These things happened to them as examples and were written down as warnings for us, on whom the fulfillment of the ages has come" (1 Corinthians 10:11).

9. *The Word of God reveals the way to everlasting life.* "But these are written that you may believe that Jesus is the Christ, the Son of God, and that by believing you may have life in his name" (John 20:31).

10. *The Word of God gives believers assurance of their salvation.* "I write these things to you who believe in the name of the Son of God so that you may know that you have eternal life" (1 John 5:13).

Does the fact that the Bible *claims* to be the authoritative, infallible Word of God prove these claims are true? No, of course not. An *internal* claim can't prove a thing is true. But, it is not insignificant that the Bible does make these claims.

Do you have to believe what the Bible claims about itself to be a true Christian?

THE BILLY GRAHAM STORY

In many of his interviews Billy Graham refers to a time in his life when he struggled about whether he could believe the Bible was the authoritative Word of God. He attended a little conference with some top professors and intellectuals high up on a mountain in California. They told him their doubts and showed him what they called the contradictions in the Bible.

He was young. He had only been out of school for a short while and was having his first experiences in preaching. These men were persuasive, and he began to doubt. Yet he struggled against those doubts. So he went out into the mountains, found a tree stump, and laid his open Bible on it.

"Oh, Lord," he said, "I do not understand everything in that book, but I accept it by faith as Your Word." He has never had a doubt since. Billy Graham believes the Bible is God's authoritative, infallible book. He knows that when he quotes the Scriptures he is quoting the Word of God.

I had the awe-inspiring privilege of visiting the mountain-top memorial that commemorates the life-changing experience of Billy Graham. Here is the text of the plaque:

In Honor of Billy Graham

Who had a life changing encounter with God here at Forest Home when as a young preacher he knelt with a Bible in his hands and promised God he would . . . take the Bible by faith and preach it without reservation.

From that time his preaching was marked by a new and God-given authority. Preaching the Scriptures in the power of the Holy Spirit he has seen multiplied thousands turn to the Lord Jesus Christ in repentance and faith.

Other Opinions

Not everyone, of course, feels the same way as Billy Graham. Robert Ingersoll once said, "In twenty-five years, the Bible will be a forgotten book."[1] He died in 1899. Who was Robert Ingersoll, anyway?

Voltaire said, "Another century and there will not be a Bible on earth."[2] He died in 1778. I wonder if his bones have turned to dust yet?

So do you have to believe the Bible is God's Word to be a Christian? I don't know. You decide. But why take a chance?

The doctrine of the authority and infallibility of the Bible ought to be a nonnegotiable. How else can we reliably hear from God? When we stray from the Bible we miscalculate in one of two directions.

LAW, LIBERTY, AND LICENSE

To not live by biblical principles leads in two life-breaking directions. The path of *antinomianism* (*anti-*, "against" + *nomos*, "law") is the path of *licentious behavior*. It is taking advantage of the grace of God. It says Christ is my Savior, but I am Lord of my own life—"all that other stuff doesn't matter."

Equally devastating is the path of *legalism* which makes rules and regulations where Christ has not. Christians who end up needing counseling usually suffer from too many legalistic rules that stifle the joy of family life. The problem? Too much law, not enough grace.

The perfect path is the *grace* that gives us freedom and liberty two ways: freedom from bondage to sin and freedom to obey Christ in the power of the Holy Spirit. As Paul put it: "You, my brothers, were called to be free. But do not use your freedom to indulge the sinful nature" (Galatians 5:13). The following continuum is an illustration:

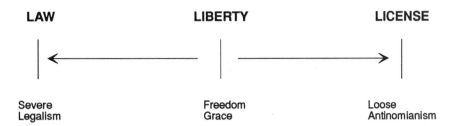

LAW   **LIBERTY**   **LICENSE**

Severe   Freedom   Loose
Legalism   Grace   Antinomianism

Legalism is imposing a law where Christ did not make one, and antinomianism is granting grace where Christ did not intend to. For example, the Bible doesn't speak to the proper length for a high school cheerleader's skirt (yes, my daughter is a cheerleader). When someone sets up an arbitrary rule (e.g., not above the knee) and then calls it *a test of spirituality*, he has become a legalist. On the other hand, someone who ignores the Bible's admonition to be modest may have become an antinomian.

In his book *The Grace Awakening* Chuck Swindoll gives a strong exhortation to not apply a biblical standard where one does not exist. He gives a great list of issues which often become taboos, even though the Bible is silent about them:

- Going to the movies or live theater
- Wearing cosmetics
- Playing cards
- Watching television
- Going to the beach
- Not having a "quiet time" every day
- Going to a restaurant that sells liquor
- Wearing certain clothing
- Driving certain cars
- Wearing certain jewelry
- Listening to certain music
- Dancing . . . square, ballroom, disco—whatever
- Holding a certain job
- Wearing your hair a certain way (assuming you have hair)

- Having lovely and elegant possessions
- Getting a face lift
- Drinking coffee
- Eating certain foods
- Working out in leotards[3]

Never make someone else's cultural preference a test of their commitment to Christ. And never make for yourself a cultural norm out of anything which would not be pleasing to the Lord. The best insurance against wrong living is right doctrine. When our doctrine is wrong our practice will get lost on one of two wrong roads: Legalism Lane or Antinomian Avenue.

BIBLE TERMINOLOGY

The Bible has its own terms to describe what happens when we become Christians and thereafter. Part of building a Christian base includes being able to distinguish among these biblical terms.

Understanding Bible terminology helps build categories or "slots" in our minds which can give us increased confidence about our own spiritual pilgrimage, as well as provide useful tools to help when speaking to others. This brief survey (perhaps the briefest ever given!) should help you to distinguish the different phases of your walk with Christ.

Perhaps the easiest way to do this overview is chronologically. The following figure shows a time line depicting the sequence of salvation for a Christian:

SALVATION

Birth, conversion, and death are the three epochal moments in a Christian life. Sanctification, on the other hand, is a *process* that begins at the *moment* of our conversion and ends at death, which is when our glorification in heaven begins.

Salvation

Salvation is the umbrella term that captures the totality of our turning to God from sin and entering into the kingdom of God.

Salvation is a *current* salvation. The kingdom has come. Once we are saved, we are saved for all eternity. But, in another sense, it is also an *ongoing* salvation marked by obedience: "Therefore, my dear friends, as you have always obeyed . . . continue to work out your salvation with fear and trembling" (Philippians 2:12). It is a secure salvation, but not one to be taken for granted. And in a third sense it is a *future* salvation: "The goal of your faith, the salvation of your souls" (1 Peter 1:9).

Said differently, the kingdom has "already" come in one sense. But in another sense the kingdom has "not yet" come, at least not in the full glory that will accompany Christ's return.

Two other terms represent Bible concepts that are particularly important: conversion and sanctification. They are both God's work given freely by His grace, though we, too, are urged to be diligent in turning from sin and to God. While our conversion comes in the twinkling of an eye, sanctification is the lifelong process of growing conformed to the image of Jesus. Let's briefly look at both.

Conversion

Conversion is a total, radical, final, unconditional break with the past in a once-for-all surrender and turning to God, accompanied by a pledge of total obedience.

Conversion means that we "think differently" about God, turning *from* sin and *to* Christ. It is something we do—it is a human task, but not without the enabling of God's Holy Spirit—it is a gift.

Conversion includes all those terms that often seem to be used interchangeably, but actually express distinctions that are worth noting:

- *Calling*, a divine summons to salvation
- *Regeneration*, a quickening by the Holy Spirit to faith
- *Grace*, the kindness of God by which He gives us faith
- *Faith*, the gift of God by which we trust Christ

- *Repentance*, to think differently leading us to turn from sin
- *Conversion*, radical change turning the heart toward God
- *Forgiveness*, act of God that pardons, removes guilt, and renews
- *Justification*, our declaration of righteousness before God
- *Reconciliation*, peace with God through Christ's work
- *Adoption*, admission by God into the family of faith

Sanctification

Once we become a convert to Christianity, our sanctification begins. Sanctification is the *declaration* and *process* by which God makes us holy.

To be sanctified means "to be set apart." Jesus Christ is perfectly holy, and God "sets us apart" to be conformed into that same holy image of Jesus through sanctification.

When we are converted God *declares* us holy, or sanctified. To be declared sanctified is to be placed within the boundaries of the right-of-way of the road named "Christian." But it is a road yet to be traveled, not the final destination, and so we must go on from there as pilgrims in the world; thus, sanctification is also a *process*.

Once we are positioned on the Christian road we don't always drive in the right lane. Sometimes we sin and find ourselves crossing the center line, even landing in the ditch, but we are still within the right-of-way, and are still at all times a Christian. Here is a central point: When we sin we don't lose our sanctification but, rather, our *fellowship* with God.

Our sanctification is multi-dimensional in that we *are* sanctified, we *are being* sanctified, and we *will finally be* sanctified. Said differently, we are initially sanctified *positionally*, we are continually being sanctified *experientially*, and we will finally be sanctified *ultimately*.

THEOLOGY: A FOUR-SYLLABLE WORD

The word "theology" can be intimidating. Some see it as the exclusive province of bookish intellectuals who roam about the halls of ivory towers. Some think it is a four-letter word. Actually, everyone who looks into the character of God is involved in theology. Theology is simply the study of God. Theologians, then, are people with special training to study God, but anyone who reads a Bible practices theology.

To study God is a noble pursuit, but even among good-hearted men differences still arise. Why do we well-meaning people come to different conclusions about the nature and character of God? Generally

---

"When we sin we don't lose our sanctification but, rather, our fellowship with God."

---

speaking, sincere Christians agree upon far more than they disagree about. Some illustrations may help to lessen your concern over many perceived differences.

Personality Versus Theology

First, picture a quartet of four gifted voices singing *How Great Thou Art*. One is a bass, another an alto, another a soprano, another a tenor. Two are ladies, two are men. They could not be more different, yet there they all are singing the same song, in tune, on key. In fact, the harmony they make together is far more soothing than any one of them alone. And it is beautiful. Although individually they may sound as if they are different, they are not really.

This is one way theology works. Different people articulate their theology according to the distinctives of their own personalities but, if they are true to Scripture, they are all singing the same song. If you listen closely you will hear the harmony. A Bible verse can have one and only one *meaning*, but may have many *applications* (read: voice, pitch, and timbre). There are a thousand sermons in every verse.

Perspective Versus Theology

Joshua, the central character in the book of the same name, tells an inquirer,

> Each person looks at life through a different vision. Three men can look at a tree. One man will see so many board feet of valuable lumber

worth so much money. The second man will see it as so much fire-wood to be burned, to keep his family warm in the winter. The third man will see it as a masterpiece of God's creative art, given to man as an expression of God's love and enduring strength, with a value far beyond its worth in money or firewood. What we live for determines what we see in life and gives clear focus to our inner vision.[4]

Imagine you and three of your friends are sitting at a table. In the center of the table is a ceramic eagle. You ask each person to describe what the eagle looks like. One person gives a perfect description of the eagle's tail feathers. Another notes the majesty of the wing span from the side view. Your third friend describes the fierce, steely eyes visible only from the front view.

This is exactly what the four gospel writers did. They each saw Christ from their own perspective. Not only did they look on Christ from different *physical* angles, but also from different *cultural* perspectives. Matthew was a wealthy Jewish tax collector; Mark was a modest missionary and associate of Peter; Luke the Gentile doctor was an evangelist and close companion of Paul; John the Jewish fisherman was part of Christ's inner circle.

They saw Christ differently. Matthew unfolded the story of Christ the Shepherd King of the Jews. Mark exclaimed the good news about Christ, the Son of God. Luke presented the humanity of the Lord to the Gentiles. John focused upon the deity of Christ. The point is this: These different accounts are not accounts of the differences in *Christ*, but differences in the *writers*. In fact, we need all four of these different partial perspectives to arrive at the one correct overall perspective.

We should take care to see that variety in personality and perspective is not automatically taken to be a difference in theology. Even if there is a difference, unless it is a significant nonnegotiable, the best course is to keep your own counsel. Let people apply the Scriptures to their own life situation under the guidance of the Spirit.

TWO CONTRASTING APPROACHES

At a Bible study I attend, two types of newly converted men join our group. The first is eager to have a ministry, to make applications to everyday life, and to enjoy the fellowship. These men are ready to run with the horses. In all fairness, it's difficult to fault men who have never had to defer gratification for not wanting to hit the ground at a full gallop.

The second type of new convert sees the vision of an abundant life, but also senses the need to walk before they run. They recognize the importance of properly setting the cornerstones before building on the foundation. They have a desire to understand the basic principles and tenets of the Christian faith. They understand that to *serve* the Master they must first *know* the Master.

As noble and attractive as running with the horses may be, the importance of building a Christian base of doctrine, faith, beliefs, principles, and tenets based upon the Bible cannot be overestimated.

ᔥ   ᔥ   ᔥ

DISCUSSION QUESTIONS

1. "Every person operates from a base, or life view. This base may be Christian, humanistic, or syncretistic. Sadly, many Christians do not operate from a distinctly Christian base."

   ☐ Agree   ☐ Disagree

   What are the potential consequences of not living from a distinctly Christian base?

2. Describe a decision you made from a non-Christian base which you now wish you could do over. Were the consequences immediate? Why do you think it often takes so long for the ill effects of our choices to catch up with us?

3. "What we believe necessarily and inevitably determines how we live."

   ☐ Agree   ☐ Disagree

   Explain your answer.

4. Give an example of legalistic behavior from your own experience. Again from your own experience, give an example of licentious behavior. If you did not already have these "categories," how can they help you in the future?

5. Are you still confused by biblical terms? Give a working definition of salvation, conversion, and sanctification. What have you learned about these concepts that is new? How can having mental categories like "conversion" and "sanctification" help you in the future?

6. Can you think of a time when you thought you had theological differences with someone, but they were really only differences of personality or perspective?

THE GOD WHO IS

CHAPTER 9

*D*ear Journal,

It's funny. I know that I used to worship false gods. After all, in the human potential movement we always exalted self, money, success, prestige, and performance above everything else. I admit it. I was out for me, myself, and I. When I became a Christian, I assumed that would pretty much settle the matter. But I sense that I am still not fully in tune with the God of the Bible. Who is He? I mean, who is He really?

Until recently I never thought much about the importance of studying the character and attributes of God. Now I see it is a crucial step in becoming a biblical Christian.

Robert

THE GOD WE WANT

When I became a Christian I knew *who* I wanted God to *be* and *what* I wanted God to *do*. Because my preconceived notions about God were so strong, I conscientiously preserved my distorted view of God. I brought an image of God as I wanted Him to be with me. As I grew in Christ I added some new correct doctrines to my view, but clung to those notions I considered "old favorites."

After walking with Christ for ten years I discovered that I was not carefully and scrupulously following the God of the Bible. By then the tentacles of self-deceit were wrapped tightly around my brain like those overgrown roots that buckle concrete. So advanced was my syncretism and so severe was my addiction to materialism that it took two-and-one-half years of diligent, daily, disciplined study and repentance with many tears to rebuild a distinctly Christian life view.

One day, as I was recovering from my idols, my syncretism, and my fifth gospel this thought occurred to me: *There is a God we want, and there is a God who is—and they are not the same God. The turning point of our lives is when we stop seeking the God we want and start seeking the God who is.* The cultural Christian seeks the God he wants, but the biblical Christian seeks the God who is.

Each of us in our own spiritual pilgrimage must come to terms with the God who is versus the God (or gods) we want. It is easy to unwittingly serve the nameless gods we want. This search for the one, true God is the most valuable undertaking a Christian can make. It is the principal thing.

God is faithful, and He will deliver true believers from self-deceit and restore them. How well I know. At the end of my two-and-one-half-year journey I recommitted my life to Christ in a fresh way. I repented from seeking the God I wanted. That was February, 1986. Then in May, Congress passed the Tax Reform Act of 1986 which significantly altered the way capital formed around real estate (my field). Actually, it didn't "alter" the way capital formed; it "stopped" capital from forming.

Immediately, God began to correct my character. I thought I had signed up for a little remodeling and redecorating—maybe even a new addition. Imagine my surprise when the bulldozers showed up and leveled me all the way to the foundation! I had so syncretized that God had to start over. Thank God I had the right foundation.

Seemingly insurmountable business problems engulfed my life. Many friends, though never actually saying so, seemed to be thinking, "He must be under God's curse!" No, I was under God's blessing. *Before* February, 1986, when God permitted me to be swallowed up by my own ambitions, certainly *then* I was under God's curse. But after giving my life wholly and totally to the pleasure of His will, God's first task was to faithfully remove the cultural Christianity from my life. He had to remove the shakable kingdom I had built so that the unshakable kingdom could shine through. Through faithful, caring blows God proved His love for me by smashing to bits those created things which I had built up as a wall between us.

"The turning point of our lives is when we stop seeking the God we want and start seeking the God who is."

My material assets plummeted, but my spiritual assets climbed, and in some strange way I sensed that my overall personal net worth had soared like an eagle toward the heavens. When the dust settled, the wall had fallen, and I could see God in a way I never dared imagine. He is the God who is.

The removal of a shakable kingdom built with the hay, stubble, and straw of selfish ambitions and vain deceits, far from being a curse, is a blessing. Whatever the price to be rid of our idols, it is worth the investment.

If someone had told me what would happen, I would have said, "I could never go through something like that. The discipline is too severe." Yet, in some inexplicable way, the way back from cultural Christianity, while filled with moments of deep anguish, was pure joy. Not so severe, it was a blessing, not a curse.

Here is a great promise to each of us: *God never over-disciplines.* "He does not treat us as our sins deserve" (Psalms 103:10). He does not repay in kind. His discipline is for our blessing, not cursing. His yoke is easy and His burden light. He rewards each of us when we long for an authentic relationship with Him. Here is an entry from my journal, February, 1991, exactly five years after I surrendered to seek the God who is:

> God never over-disciplines. Hebrews 12:10: "But God disciplines us for our good, that we may share in his holiness." I have the sense that God has finished chastening me for my addiction to materialism, my

syncretism, my desire to serve both God and money, my desire to have the God I wanted, my desire to make plans and have God bless them, my desire to manipulate God. I created idols—a shakable kingdom, and God faithfully shook it and removed created things. In Leviticus 26, God opposes the stubborn heart—it is hostility toward God. He looks for confession of sin, payment for sin, and a humble heart. He punishes in increasing degrees of severity, giving the sinner the opportunity to repent, [but if he doesn't repent] then He turns up the heat. His goal is always restoration. He never punishes just to punish. That is how humans discipline.

God is who He is. Christians must come to know Him as He is, and not as they want Him to be. No amount of wishing God to be different than He is will matter. As the Psalmist wisely said, "Be still, and know that I am God" (Psalm 46:10). Let's briefly survey the character of the God who is.

GOD EXISTS

Most Big Bang cosmologists must be poor mathematicians, because their logic simply doesn't add up. Okay, let's agree for the moment that the world began with a "Big Bang." Genesis 1 certainly suggests a sudden beginning: "In the beginning God created the heavens and the earth . . . And God said, 'Let there be light,' and *there was light . . . the first day*" (Genesis 1:1, 3, 5, italics added). Boom! (perhaps).

Tell any reasonably alert elementary school child that the earth started with a Big Bang and they will immediately ask, "Who made it go bang?" I wonder why scientists with twenty years of education can't remember this simple rule: Every effect must have a cause.

Logic only leaves us two choices: First, every cause must also have a cause, which leads us into the bottomless pit of an "infinite regress" with no ultimate cause. Or, second, at some point a line is drawn, and there is what Aristotle called an "uncaused cause."

I believe there can be no rational doubt that at some point something with the power of being had to be self-existent (not created). Something or someone had to have the power to make it "go bang." The only question is whether or not this "uncaused cause" is *personal*.

Cosmologists who deny the existence of God search the outer reaches of the cosmos for some impersonal "cause" for the Big Bang. The question is not *what*, but *Who?* The Bible reveals a personal, self-existent, eternal Being who is "uncaused"—who has always been.

God is. God has "the power of being" within Himself—He is self-existent. There has never been a time when God did not exist.

You and I, on the other hand, are created. At one level we are created in His image, but this does not mean we are like God at *every* point, but, rather, at *many* points. Instead, it means there was nothing in man's pre-Fall nature that was *inconsistent* with the character of God. We are *like* God, but *less* than God. We are not part of His being, but are created and exist as a separate entity apart from His essence. We are not eternal; we have a beginning, while God has always been.

Even the term "eternal life" is something of a misnomer, for we have not existed forever. By His grace we, the creature, are gifted with everlasting life *to* eternity, but not *from* eternity. The Christian, a creature of God, receives by grace the incomprehensible gift of living for the *rest* of forever, but not forever.

No one doubts that God is—not really. Avowed atheists yell, "Oh, my God!" when they are terrified just like the rest of us. The question people struggle with is not *whether* God is, but *who* God is—and can He be known. Can He be known? Yes, because He revealed Himself to mankind.

The most awesome name of God is *Yahweh* (sometimes *Jehovah*), which means that He is self-existent and eternal. In times past the name "Yahweh" sent shudders of holy terror down the spines of faithful followers. In this name dwells the fullness and sum of all that God is, the totality of His being. In the Old Testament Yahweh is written LORD, all caps.

God was slow to reveal this most sacred name of His. Not until the time of Moses did God reveal Himself as LORD. He told Moses, "I am the LORD. I appeared to Abraham, to Isaac and to Jacob as God Almighty, but by my name the LORD I did not make myself known to them" (Exodus 6:3). Why did He not reveal His full identity sooner?

"LORD" is the memorial name God chose by which He wants to be remembered from generation to generation. Though He acted as the LORD from the beginning of creation, God waited until the singlemost miserable moment of human history—the prolonged slavery of His people in Egypt—to reveal His full identity. Why? One possible answer is so that when we think of Him we will always identify His memorial name, LORD, with His deep, very personal interest in people, and the awesome power He possesses to deliver us.

The LORD made a promise to His people that He would bring them out of misery in Egypt to a land flowing with milk and honey. To elevate the impact of the moment, God delivered Israel under the dark cloud of ten appalling plagues sent against Egypt and a hard-hearted Pharaoh. Culminating in the crossing at the Red Sea, Yahweh dramatically delivered Israel in such a miraculous way that His name LORD became the indelible autograph by which He is known to this day. He "divided the waters before them, to gain for himself everlasting renown" (Isaiah 63:12). What Christian has not heard about the plague of the frogs, the locusts, the Nile turning to blood, and the crossing of the Red Sea? What Christian doesn't know the LORD, who is God?

God exists. He "is," eternally. We know this about God because this is the way He chose to reveal Himself to us.

GOD IS INFINITE AND ETERNAL

Infinity often conjures up images of *space*. What we know so far about the stars, the galaxies, and the heavens staggers the mind. Some astronomers estimate the universe to be up to twenty billion light years across. In case you don't recall, a light year is the distance that light travels in a vacuum over a period of one year, or about 5.878 trillion miles. By contrast, our galaxy, the Milky Way, measures a mere 100,000 light years, or 587,800,000,000,000,000 miles. That's 23.5 trillion trips around the equator. Who can comprehend it?

It's really kind of humorous. Just about the time the cosmologists think they have built a paradigm to describe the universe, God mockingly enables an astronomer to build a bigger, better telescope. With this improved technology the astronomers discover a quasar from deep in space or a yet unknown collection of galaxies that smashes the old paradigm to bits.

Isn't it ironic? God uses the very same achievements that on one hand mark the apex of man's potential to, on the other hand, embarrassingly remind him of his limited powers of reason. Big Bang theories crumble right and left just as those gas cans imploded in chemistry class experiments. Science reaches out to touch the hem of infinity but cannot find it. Why? Simply because God is infinite. If infinity is not difficult enough to grasp, there is always eternity to ponder.

Eternity evokes thoughts of *time*. Who hasn't stepped off a curb to cross the street where a huge truck just rumbled by and shuddered thinking of the difference a few seconds makes. Where did that time

---

> ## "Science reaches out to touch the hem of infinity but cannot find it. Why? Simply because God is infinite."

---

go? Where is the time that has not yet happened? Eternity is time without beginning or end. Time is doubly difficult to comprehend because it is invisible. At least space has a visual reference point.

Christians are profoundly concerned about infinity and eternity because our God has invited us to join Him there and to bring along some others. How long is eternity?

Imagine a block of granite one hundred feet by one hundred feet by one hundred feet. Once every one thousand years a little bird comes along and sharpens its beak on the block of granite. However long it takes for the little bird to wear down the granite rock to powdery dust, that is the first blinking of eternity's eye.[1]

Such a specter of eternity sends chilling shivers down our spines. God is eternal, and if you know Him you will be able to celebrate every time that little bird drops by to sharpen its beak. But will our families, our friends, and our associates at work be watching with us? The reality of eternity demands that we think eternally about ourselves and the people God sovereignly places in the path of the rest of our lives.

GOD IS ONE: THE TRINITY

Driving alone up the Florida Turnpike toward northern Florida one day I was reviewing the remarks I would make at the luncheon where I would soon speak. While praying to God—Father, Son, and Holy Spirit—for a brief moment, no more than two or three seconds, an incredible, though thickly veiled, deeper understanding of the Trinity swept over me. Part of me felt as though I weighed a hundred tons, another part as though I was a helium balloon—simultaneously lead heavy and feather light.

In less than a minute the full veil returned and completely covered over that lucid, crystalline moment. No matter how hard I have tried I have never been able to find words to express the increased understanding of the Trinity I gained that morning (but it did happen; I promise).

God the Father, Jesus the Son, and the Holy Spirit: Three Persons, one essence. The Trinity is a deep and profound mystery. More than a few have ended up dizzy with a headache after thinking deeply about the triune God. The problem is that we have no human categories with which to compare the Trinity. Every analogy breaks down. How are the three Persons of the Godhead one essence? Here are some verses that speak of God's unity, and hint of the Trinity:

1. *The Father and Jesus are one.* Jesus said, "Anyone who has seen me has seen the Father" (John 14:9), "I and the Father are one" (John 10:30), and "All that belongs to the Father is mine" (John 16:15). Christ is the "Everlasting Father" (Isaiah 9:6). The Scriptures declare that Jesus is the image of the invisible God (Colossians 1:15), that Jesus is the exact representation of God's being (Hebrews 1:3), that Jesus is all of God in a human body (Colossians 2:9).

2. *The Father and the Holy Spirit are one.* "God is spirit, and his worshipers must worship in spirit and in truth" (John 4:24). "Now the Lord is the Spirit, and where the Spirit of the Lord is, there is freedom" (2 Corinthians 3:17).

3. *Jesus and the Holy Spirit are one.* "But you know him [the Spirit], for he lives with you and will be in you. I will not leave you as

orphans; I will come to you" (John 14:17–18). "The Spirit will take from what is mine and make it known to you" (John 16:15).

Because God is three Persons we ought to show interest in all of Him. When we ignore a Person of the Trinity we are not following the God who is, and we miss knowing the incredible promises and benefits the ignored Person of the Godhead offers. For example, the ministry of the Holy Spirit as Counselor, Comforter, Convicter, Guide, Empowerer, and Encourager is often overlooked by evangelicals. We often have an allergic reaction when it comes to the Spirit. I believe this comes from an overreaction to our charismatic brothers and sisters (who are also evangelicals). But to de-emphasize the Holy Spirit is to throw the baby out with the bathwater. Why? There are only two powers under which we can live: the power of the Spirit or the power of the flesh. The more closely we walk with the Spirit, the further we will walk from the flesh, but also vice versa.

Do you know the Holy Spirit as the personal *He* or as the impersonal *It*? Until we get to know the Person of the Holy Spirit—"He"—we don't yet know the God of the Bible, nor can we walk in His power. The only Christians I have ever met who are *consistently* leading victorious, joyful lives (whether in plenty or in want) are those who have gotten to know the Holy Spirit. More on the Holy Spirit in chapter 16, "How to Change."

GOD IS SOVEREIGN

Every day millions of Christians throughout the world repeat the Lord's Prayer, "Your kingdom come, your will be done on earth as it is in heaven" (Matthew 6:10). Some repeat it daily, others weekly, some only occasionally. How many might say it on a given Sunday? One hundred million? Five hundred million?

With so many of us praying, either God's will is, in fact, being done or God must not hear, or worse, not have the power to act.

While we equivocate about the sovereignty of God, the Bible does not: "Are not two sparrows sold for a penny? Yet not one of them will fall to the ground apart from the will of your Father" (Matthew 10:29). The Bible unambiguously claims that everything happens according to the will of God, "according to the plan of him who works out *everything* in conformity with the purpose of his will" (Ephesians 1:11, emphasis added).

The Bible claims without the slightest trace of hedging that God is completely, totally in control and that His will *is* being done in *everything*. No detail, no matter how minute, escapes the purpose of His sovereign will—not even the falling of a single sparrow.

He is God, and He is in charge. *Nothing* happens unless *caused* or actively *allowed* by God. Instead of despair, this should provide the most indescribable comfort to us. It means that even though *we* cannot make heads or tails out of our circumstances, God stands behind the stage engineering all things to work together "for the good of those who love him, who have been called according to his purpose" (Romans 8:28). There are no random, renegade molecules running loose. The comfort is this: If God were not sovereign He could not work the decay, the suffering, and the evil for good. Much more on this in chapter 10, "The Radical Effect of the Fall."

In those moments when you stand utterly bewildered at the foot of the Cross, remember: God is working out the purpose of His will. Our job is to be faithful.

GOD IS CREATOR

Not only does God sovereignly rule, everything He rules is something He made. "You are worthy, our Lord and God, to receive glory and honor and power, for you created all things, and by your will they were created and have their being" (Revelation 4:11).

> The God who *made the world* and *everything* in it is the Lord of heaven and earth and does not live in temples built by hands. And he is not served by human hands, as if he needed anything, because *he himself gives all men life and breath and everything else.* From one man he made every nation of men, that they should inhabit the whole earth; and *he determined the times set for them and the exact places where they should live.* God did this so that men would seek him and perhaps reach out for him and find him, though he is not far from each one of us. *"For in him we live and move and have our being."* (Acts 17:24–28, emphasis added)

He made the world and everything in it. He Himself gives life, breath and "everything else" to all men whether believer or non-believer. His common grace extends to all men. Without His quickening no man could draw a single breath. Without His air there would be nothing to breathe.

He "determines the times" which mark our birth and our death. Why were you born in this century and not the last? Or the next? He "determines . . . the exact places" where we will live—the country, the culture, the community.

God the Creator picked this time and place for you to live. He has a purpose and plan for your life. Our task is not to convince the Creator to get in step with our dreams and ambitions, but to gratefully acknowledge His gift of life to us; then wait quietly, patiently at His feet until He reveals His will, plan, and purpose for our lives.

GOD IS PERSONAL

Many believe in God, but they think that He is distant, aloof, and impersonal. This is deism—to believe that God exists, but that He wound up the world, and now we are on our own to make of it what we can. One popular example is the song "From a Distance," in which the deistic spirit is captured by Bette Midler. The song describes God watching "from a distance," and leaves the impression of an impersonal force looking out over the oceans, mountains, and man.

The Bible gives a markedly different report. We are personally and individually created by God. He is the First Cause who created each of us:

> For you created my inmost being; you knit me together in my mother's womb. I praise you because I am fearfully and wonderfully made; your works are wonderful, I know that full well. My frame was not hidden from you when I was made in the secret place. When I was woven together in the depths of the earth, your eyes saw my unformed body. All the days ordained for me were written in your book before one of them came to be. (Psalm 139:13–16)

God is not an impersonal being, but most personal. Not distant, He is involved with every detail, intimately. "I live in a high and holy place, but also with him who is contrite and lowly in spirit" (Isaiah 57:15).

I once had the honor of walking the Hall of Heroes at the Pentagon, which lists the names of Congressional Medal of Honor recipients. A deep, heavy sense of awe and admiration flooded my emotions as I walked by more than 900 faceless nameplates from WWI, WWII, the Korean War, and Vietnam. Of approximately 35,600,000 men and women who served, only one of every 38,500 were so decorated. What bravery! What patriots! You could almost see them charging an enemy bunker, filled with a strange admixture of fear and fortitude. All courageous, many sacrificed their very own lives for their comrades.

As inspiring as it is to know that someone would throw himself on a grenade to save a half dozen fellow soldiers, it does not begin to compare to God putting on skin and volitionally letting a half dozen soldiers pierce His body with nails and a spear. He shed His blood and died for people He had never even met—you and me. The Scriptures put it this way: "Very rarely will anyone die for a righteous man, though for a good man someone might possibly dare to die. But God demonstrates his own love for us in this: While we were still sinners, Christ died for us" (Romans 5:7–8).

Jesus Christ threw Himself on the grenade intended for you. That's personal.

GOD IS LOVE

God is 100 percent love. There is no time at which God is not love. Twenty-six times Psalm 136 repeats the refrain: "His love endures forever." Everything God does is motivated by His character, which always includes love (John 3:16). He has promised that no one can snatch us away from Him once we have believed (John 10:28). He is the Good Shepherd who lays down His life for His sheep (John 10:11). He died for our sins while we were still sinners (Romans 5:7–8).

Though God is many things, if He were not loving, His nature contains no other attribute sufficient to motivate Him to send Christ into the mainstream of human history and offer reconciliation to mankind. Said differently, if God did not love people, no one would be saved.

Think of God's other attributes for a moment: He is holy, eternal, immortal, omniscient, omnipotent, omnipresent, and self-existent, among many other things. Are any of these characteristics sufficient to offer salvation to men? The holiness of God sends us to our knees, but it is the love of God that sends us to heaven. Without love heaven is a canceled party.

That God always loves does not mean that He is maudlin or permissive. The great love He has for the world is part of His nature. It is the perpetual disposition of His heart. He is slow to anger because He abounds in love.

Personally, the most emotional private devotions I have ever had have been the times I have studied the passages which assure me that God loves *me*, personally, individually. Have you felt His great love for you lately? You can possess a complete assurance of your eternal security with God. Read these passages slowly, for they are wonderful reminders of His exquisite love:

> I am the good shepherd. The good shepherd lays down his life for the sheep. . . . I am the good shepherd; I know my sheep and my sheep know me. . . . My sheep listen to my voice; I know them, and they follow me. I give them eternal life, and they shall never perish; no one can snatch them out of my hand. (John 10:11, 14, 27–28)

> Not only so, but we also rejoice in our sufferings, because we know that suffering produces perseverance; perseverance, character; and character, hope. And hope does not disappoint us, because God has poured out his love into our hearts by the Holy Spirit, whom he has given us. (Romans 5:3–5)

> Who shall separate us from the love of Christ? Shall trouble or hardship or persecution or famine or nakedness or danger or sword? As it is written: "For your sake we face death all day long; we are considered as sheep to be slaughtered." No, in all these things we are more than conquerors through him who loved us. For I am convinced that neither death nor life, neither angels nor demons, neither the present nor the future, nor any powers, neither height nor depth, nor anything else in all creation, will be able to separate us from the love of God that is in Christ Jesus our Lord. (Romans 8:35–39)

> And I pray that you, being rooted and established in love, may have power, together with all the saints, to grasp how wide and long and high and deep is the love of Christ, and to know this love that surpasses knowledge—that you may be filled to the measure of all the fullness of God. (Ephesians 3:17–19)

Like a healing ointment the Word of love salves our wounds and heals our hurt. His love whispers, "Shhhh," and quiets our heart to a weak whisper in troubled moments when we need rest and revival. Like a shivering, shaken child held in our Father's loving arms our confidence slowly surges back. When the love of the Shepherd has at long last been revived, He releases in us the Spirit's incendiary, electric power to do overflowing works of love for others. As a friend says, "It's a great life."

GOD IS HOLY

God is 100 percent holy. God is 100 percent holy and 100 percent love 100 percent of the time. There is no time at which God is not holy. He is always simultaneously holy and loving.

Not only is God holy, He is "holy, holy, holy" (Isaiah 6:3). Words do not adequately capture the intensity of His holiness, but several Bible stories give us a glimpse of the beauty and awesomeness of His holiness.

One such experience was the vision Ezekiel had of Christ. The purpose of a wedding processional is to elevate the moment, to create anticipation. Like a wedding processional, the events of the first chapter of Ezekiel pique anticipation for what is to come. After first describing many of the heavenly mysteries Ezekiel wrote,

> Above the expanse over their heads was what looked like a throne of sapphire, and high above on the throne was a figure like that of a man. I saw that from what appeared to be his waist up he looked like glowing metal, as if full of fire, and that from there down he looked like fire; and brilliant light surrounded him. . . . This was the appearance of the likeness of the glory of the LORD. (Ezekiel 1:26–28)

When Ezekiel saw the glory of the Lord did he run to greet Him? No, rather, "When I saw it, I fell facedown" (Ezekiel 1:28).

Ezekiel is not the only man to have an encounter with the holiness of God and fall facedown, hide his face, or cry out in holy terror. Others include Moses, Isaiah, Gideon, Joshua, Elijah, Job, Daniel, Peter, James, John, and Paul.

When God spoke to Moses from the burning bush "Moses hid his face, because he was afraid to look at God" (Exodus 3:6).

Isaiah cried, "Woe to me! . . . I am ruined! For I am a man of unclean lips, and I live among a people of unclean lips, and my eyes have seen the King, the LORD Almighty" (Isaiah 6:5).

The gaze of God struck terror in Gideon: "'Ah, Sovereign LORD! I have seen the angel of the LORD face to face!' But the LORD said to him, 'Peace! Do not be afraid. You are not going to die'" (Judges 6:22–23).

When God's angel spoke, "Then Joshua fell facedown to the ground in reverence, and asked him, 'What message does my Lord have for his servant?'" (Joshua 5:14).

The fire of the LORD consumed the sacrifice of Elijah. "When all the people saw this, they fell prostrate and cried, 'The LORD—he is God! The LORD—he is God!'" (1 Kings 18:39).

The presence of the LORD passed by Elijah not in a fierce wind, not in an earthquake, not in a blazing fire, but as "a gentle whisper. When Elijah heard it, he pulled his cloak over his face" (1 Kings 19:12–13).

Job lamented, "My ears had heard of you but now my eyes have seen you. Therefore I despise myself and repent in dust and ashes" (Job 42:5–6).

"I, Daniel, was the only one who saw the vision; the men with me did not see it, but such terror overwhelmed them that they fled and hid themselves. So I was left alone, gazing at this great vision; I had no strength left, my face turned deathly pale and I was helpless. Then I heard him speaking, and as I listened to him, I fell into a deep sleep, my face to the ground. A hand touched me and set me trembling on my hands and knees" (Daniel 10:7–10).

What so repeatedly terrified these men when they found themselves in the presence of God? It was the awesome, dreadful presence of the holiness of God. It is said there are places in outer space where a tea-spoon of matter weighs as much as a dozen elephants. That is what the holiness of God is like. It is a compressed, leaden glimpse of the glory of God. It is a weighty, majestic presence that overwhelmed their emotions.

Until we have this same sense of God's holiness and majesty, we have more to learn of the God who is. Worse, when we purposely avoid His holiness, we as much as tell Him that we would rather be a cultural Christian than a biblical Christian. The passion for God we aspire to comes only after we have experienced the compressed, heavy, leaden glimpse. Ask God to reveal His holiness to you, but carefully, humbly, and with patience, perhaps even for many years. When the time is right, He will show this aspect of Himself to you.

GOD IS AWESOME

A great problem today is that many Christians still do not see how high and holy God is. If we desire to seek the God who is, we must examine His character. Who is God? What is He like? How is He different from what I first imagined? Have you taken this crucial step yet? If not, begin to study the character of God: His holiness, His sovereignty, His unchanging nature, His power, His love, His goodness, His grace, His mercy, His faithfulness, His justice. He is immutable, immortal, invisible, omnipotent, omniscient, and omnipresent.

When we increase our pursuit to understand the character of God an interesting thing begins to happen. It dawns on us that He is higher than we first thought. In fact, the more we learn about Him the higher He gets. There seems to be no limit to how high God is.

After a time of gazing at the character of God, after peering at how high He is, another interesting thing begins to happen. One day it occurs to us that we are not as high as we once thought. Our opinion of ourselves—our abilities, our goodness—begins to shrink. Not in the sense of our human dignity or worth, but the overwhelming sense of how high and holy God is causes us to retreat into humility. This is not a humility born of human intent, but from the overpowering presence that comes from gazing at the glory of God. It is self-abasement. It is genuine worship. It is the undoing of our spiritual pride.

Over time, the distance between the height of our understanding of God and the depth of our understanding of ourselves grows ever larger. Call it the awe gap. It is the fear of the Lord regained. It is a deep reverence for the God who is. It comes from a growing glimpse of God.

A glimpse of the glory of God reveals in an intense, compressed moment how high and holy God really is. When is the last time a glimpse of the glory of God has driven you down to your knees, or made you burst into tears? Don't be as high as you thought you were. And see God higher than you thought He was. As we look intently at the character of God the gap between His highness and our lowness will grow, for He is awesome.

Our response to the God who is, is holy fear, humility, contrition, repentance, worship, exultation, praise, joy, gratitude, and so much more.

Obviously, we cannot fully explore each attribute of God in this short space. I encourage you to make a life-long file on each attribute of

---

"The overwhelming sense of how high and holy God is causes us to retreat into humility. . . . It is the undoing of our spiritual pride."

God, study Him, listen to tapes, attend special conferences, make sermon notes, photostat meaningful quotes, scribble notes on napkins and put them all in your file. Make a life-long commitment to constantly learn and personally experience God's character and beauty. *Experience with God is the only way to move our understanding of Him from abstract to personal.*

When we do begin to plumb the depth and richness of each attribute or characteristic of God, that attribute will have a profound impact upon our beliefs, our doctrine, our faith, our practices, our motivations, and our daily lives—increasingly so as we move along the spectrum from the cold blues of abstract to the warm golden tones of personal experience.

Over the long haul God will draw each of us to know Him as He is. As a friend says, "We pursue God out of priority or pain." Don't wait until adversity strikes. Make knowing God a priority.

ぁ   ぁ   ぁ

DISCUSSION QUESTIONS

1. Do you ever feel a chill of doubt sweep over you about the reality of God? Describe a time when such a feeling crept in? Was it a crisis? Reread the section entitled, "God Is Love." Do you possess the assurance of your salvation? Why, or why not?

2. Do you refer to the Holy Spirit as "He" or "It"? Why is it important to know all three Persons of the Trinity intimately? What practical benefits come from knowing the Holy Spirit well?

3. Do you struggle with the concept that God is utterly sovereign, that nothing happens unless *caused* or *allowed* by God? Why do you think many people find this idea preposterous? What are the practical benefits in believing that God is sovereign?

4. Words often used to describe God include the following: immortal, invincible, immutable, omnipotent, omniscient, omnipresent. In everyday language describe what these words communicate about the character of God.

5. What is a problem buffeting you? In what ways are you wrestling with accepting that God is sovereign over your circumstances?

6. What practical steps can you take to learn more about the character of the God who is? Will you?

THE RADICAL EFFECT OF THE FALL

*D*ear Journal,

I see so much suffering, brokenness, and evil in the world. If God is all-powerful, then how could He be good? If He is good, then how could He be all-powerful? I've learned how loving God is. And I know that He is holy. Since He is so loving why does He allow such pain? And since He is so holy why doesn't He just use His power to put an end to this place and bring us all home? The world was an interesting experiment, but I don't think it's working. It seems like a confused situation to me. It seems like such a waste.

Robert

CHAPTER 10

A WORLD OF CONTRASTS

"Bill, this is Robert," he said to his Bible study discussion leader. "Remember how you mentioned that any time I got stuck to give you a call? Well, I'm calling . . . ."

Imagine that you are in a plane at 35,000 feet, high up in the sky on the way home from a trip. From the window seat of your plane the sparkling majesty of the heavens stretches endlessly out toward the gentle curvature of a hazy horizon. Below, an eye-pleasing quiltwork of farmlands covers the earth like a warm blanket.

As you approach your destination the green patchwork yields to a pulsating checkerboard of urban ingenuity. Sitting in that chair high above the face of the earth gives you a lofty perspective. You can't help but reflect on the beauty and magnificence of the created world and the amazing accomplishments of mankind.

Once you've landed, however, the drive down Main Street jars you back to one of life's other, less pleasant realities. The more up close and personal we get, the more blemishes we see. Almost anything looks beautiful from a distance.

The glitter and gloss flaunted by human hucksters are raunchy reminders of a world deeply influenced by the Fall. Unconsciously, a twinge of disappointment turns the dimmer switch on those majestic, ecstatic feelings you had while soaring through the air. It is a long way back down to earth in more ways than one.

Your mind wanders across the world of issues: poverty, crime, drugs, gangs, homelessness, pornography, abortion, the Federal deficit, the education system, government graft, aging, AIDS, homosexuality, sexual promiscuity, nuclear weapons, war, and racism. So much wrong, so much evil, is in the world—you don't like to think about it often. You cannot and remain sane.

Finally the moment you longed for arrives. You turn on your blinker, signaling your retreat from the world of glaring neon lights you eagerly leave behind. Abruptly, like a chameleon, the world changes once again to the secure, familiar reminders of neighborhood, family, and friends. Yet even the sight of certain homes along this familiar road you call "home" reminds you that the world's problems first belonged to individual families.

As you pull into your driveway, your happy children squeal as they rush out to meet you. A tingly feeling quickly dispatches the nettlesome thoughts of two such contrasting worlds.

FALLEN MAN

No dividing line between humanists and Christians looms larger than the debate over the basic nature of man. When the pendulum is not swinging, is man *essentially* good, or not? In other words, are the wicked, hurtful, hateful things we do simply a mistake, an aberration, the exception? Or are they a more fundamental part of our character than mere pockmarks on the skin of humanity?

The Bible teaches at a specific moment in history there existed an independent man and woman who made a moral choice and rebelled against God. This is the Fall.

No mere blemish on the edge of human life, the Fall diseases the very core of the human heart. The Fall is a complete Fall, not a partial one.

By the time of Noah, "The LORD saw how great man's wickedness on the earth had become, and that every inclination of the thoughts of his heart was only evil all the time" (Genesis 6:5).

Later Jeremiah wrote, "The heart is deceitful above all things and beyond cure" (Jeremiah 17:9). Yet later Paul penned, "There is no one righteous, not even one" (Romans 3:10).

Jesus understood the radical effect of the Fall on the human heart: "But Jesus would not entrust himself to them, for he knew all men. He did not need man's testimony about man, for he knew what was in a man" (John 2:24–25).

Today we would simply say that everyone has a little larceny in their heart.

Is man basically good? I can't help but chuckle when someone suggests he is. If so, why won't the car salesman let you test drive a new car by yourself? (But man is basically good.) As a friend observed, "Why do we need a dozen keys on a ring?" (But man is basically good.) Why do they have metal detectors at airports? (But man is basically good.) Would you leave your purse or briefcase unattended in a public place? (But man is basically good.) Have you been for a drive in rush hour traffic lately? (But man is basically good.) The other day I saw an American flag—with a lock-box on the pole so no one could steal it. But man is basically good. Right.

This radical effect the Fall has had on man is sometimes called *the doctrine of the total depravity of man*. Personally, I do not believe in the total depravity of man—whatever it is, it's much worse than that!

Though fallen, man is not without value. As Francis Schaeffer said, "Man is not nothing." Here is his entire idea:

The Bible teaches that, though man is hopelessly lost, he is not nothing. Man is lost because he is separated from God, his true reference point, by true moral guilt. But he will never be nothing. Therein lies the horror of his lostness. For man to be lost, in all his uniqueness and wonder, is tragic.[1]

FALLEN "ME"

The difficulty with the Fall is not so much that man fell (we can see that plainly enough), but that "I" fell. Some rebel against this idea, but few over forty. After that age, we see all too clearly the imprint of the Fall on our attitudes, our ambitions, our motives, our relationships, our lusts, our emotions, our wills, our bodies, and our minds.

The Fall of Adam and Eve was *representative*—they were not freelancing. Their choice to rebel was not the crime of two mavericks acting alone, but a proxy for every living person—you and me. In other words, none of us are so different from Adam and Eve that we would have somehow heroically not succumbed to the temptation from Satan. Is there anyone among us so naive to think that he, on his own, could have overcome Satan and not rebelled against God?

What did the Fall do to us, really? The Fall exposed our sinful nature and removed our ability to keep God's standard and live without sinning in our own strength. The spiritual giant Paul himself said, "I have the desire to do what is good, but I cannot carry it out. For what I do is not the good I want to do; no, the evil I do not want to do—this I keep on doing" (Romans 7:18–19).

Let's be honest. We often (*very* often) find we lack the *ability* to keep from sinning. But worse, if we are completely transparent with ourselves, unlike Paul we sometimes don't even *desire* to keep from sinning. Peter Marshall put it this way: "Most of us know perfectly well what we ought to do; our trouble is that we do not want to do it."[2] This is the radical effect of the Fall, and the problem Jesus came to fix.

Why do we lack the ability (or power) and sometimes the desire (or motivation) to follow God rightly? The Fall created a "gap" between *God's standard* (perfection) and *man's performance*. There are two ways to look at this "gap." If we concentrate (legalistically) on what is *lacking* for our beginning point, then our view will always point toward our defeat:

GOD'S STANDARD

— **MAN'S PERFORMANCE**

SIN AND GUILT

If, on the other hand, we focus on *God's provision for man's sin* instead of *man's lacking of God's standard* we arrive at a totally different schema:

MAN'S PERFORMANCE

+ **GOD'S GRACE BY THE SPIRIT**

GOD'S STANDARD

Simply, to focus on man's performance leads to the "minus," but to focus on God's empowering grace to us through the Holy Spirit leads to the "plus." One is negative; the other, positive.

Because of the Fall when things are left to themselves they atrophy, rust, and rot. Weeds take over, paint peels, bodies deteriorate, memories fade. The vector of the Fall is negative. Our natural disposition, not positive, is to sin. We must acknowledge this about ourselves. We are *not* good. Paul was humble about his own nature. "I know that nothing good lives in me, that is, in my sinful nature" (Romans 7:18). Have you been this honest with yourself?

And what is the solution? Fallen people like us have two choices: to walk in the power of the Spirit or the power of the flesh (the sinful nature). It is our choice. The flesh wars against the Spirit, and the Spirit also wars against the flesh. "So I say, live by the Spirit, and you will not gratify the desires of the sinful nature" (Galatians 5:16). How to live in the power of the Spirit is taken up more fully in chapter 16, "How to Change."

A FALLEN WORLD

Do you remember in art class how you were taught the principle of perspective? To draw a road you would begin with a single point and then draw two lines from that single point toward the distance. The farther from the original point, the wider the road. That is exactly how the Fall has worked into the world. From the single point of the original sin, sin has widened, expanded, and multiplied by cause and effect into all of life. Original sin was the first domino; once it fell, it set off a chain reaction.

When man fell, the world fell with him: "Cursed is the ground because of you" (Genesis 3:17). After the Fall the world wears these three faces: glory, evil, and frustration.

1. *Glory*. If you travel much then you know that God is at work in every corner of the world. Everywhere His glories are on display like a fireworks extravaganza on the Fourth of July:

   - snow covered mountain peaks soaring toward the heavens
   - delicate, brightly colored flowers with pleasing fragrance
   - the breathtaking changes in the hues of a sunrise
   - fascinating animal, bird, and insect kingdoms to watch in amazement
   - the mystery of how a fish can breathe underwater
   - the softness of a baby's skin

2. *Evil*. Similarly, everywhere we can see the distinct imprint of the Fall in depraved deeds done by malicious men. Child abuse, pornography, abortion, crime, drugs, gangs, government corruption, white collar crime, and on and on. Satan reigns as the progenitor of all evil deeds.

3. *Frustration*. Then there is a third category, perhaps the most difficult to accept and deal with, humanly speaking. When the world fell, the ground was cursed. "It will produce thorns and thistles for you" (Genesis 3:18). It is a thorny world, a world full of thistles, a frustrating world.

The Fall explains why we must gaze at the brilliant beauty of a blazing sunrise through thick glasses that grace the bridge of a runny nose.

How is it possible for glory, evil, and frustration to all co-exist at the same time?

A VEILED GLORY

Though the world is fallen, it is at the same time full of God's glory. One time Isaiah had a most remarkable experience. He saw celestial beings praising God and they were calling to each other with the words, "Holy, holy, holy is the LORD Almighty; the whole earth is full of his glory" (Isaiah 6:3). Is that true? Is the whole earth full of God's glory?

Based on the evil and the tragedy, how can we say that "the whole earth is full of his glory"? The explanation is simple. The earth *is* full of God's glory, but it is not *only* full of God's glory.

The earth is a creation *of* God, but the earth is *not* God. Earth is a creation, but not part of the essence or being of God. The earth exists apart from His being as a separate creation. If the earth *was* God, then no impure thing could exist. But because the earth is created and stands apart from the essence of God, we can make an allowance for something other than God's glory to also exist.

Because of the Fall the earth is *also* full of moral depravity: Sin, evil, and wickedness. "The Scripture declares that the whole world is a prisoner of sin" (Galatians 3:22). In the same way that a cup of tea is at the same time full of water and tea, the whole earth is at the same time "full" of His glory and sin.

When we survey all the suffering and evil in the world we must say, if we are completely honest with ourselves, that it doesn't look like God is very powerful. If "the whole earth is full of his glory" then why doesn't His glory crowd out all pain?

We have shown how the earth is full of God's glory but not *only* His glory. Now we must see exactly what kind of glory it is that does fill the earth. The earth is not full of God's *unveiled* glory. The kind of glory that fills the earth is a *veiled* glory. Edith Schaeffer calls this *leftover beauty* from before the Fall.

The Bible teaches that no man may see God and live. That is to say, no earthbound man may see the unveiled glory—the essence—of God and live. Like the smog over Los Angeles, the whole earth stands enshrouded with a thick haze that protects us from the brilliance of God's unveiled glory. Why? Because of the Fall. Christians no longer live in darkness, but neither are we yet in the full light of His presence.

Why isn't the earth filled with God's glory all the time? The question begs the larger issue of God's power to rule the earth. God is not blocked from revealing His glory, but He chooses to because of the Fall. The awesome, holy sight of God in His unveiled glory is not seen by His design, not because God is somehow thwarted in breaking through. And what else is in the design of God for the earth?

FRUSTRATION

The Bible teaches that it is God's will for creation to be subjected to *frustration*. "For the creation was subjected to frustration, not by its own choice, but by the will of the one who subjected it" (Romans 8:20).

Why would God do that? Why would He actively allow suffering, frustration, and pain? Paul put it best: "In hope that the creation [creature] itself will be liberated from its bondage to decay and brought into the glorious freedom of the children of God" (Romans 8:20–21). It is not for our defeat but our victory that God allows the pain. In other words, the purpose of the Fall's thorns and thistles is good, not evil.

Our Father's chief desire is for rebellious men to turn to Him. When we are not with Him, we strive to have our own way. In response to our rebellion, He has put a path of frustration before us so that in our pains and toils we will look for Him and call out to Him to save us, though He is not far from any of us. The Bible teaches that if God did not "frustrate" us we would never seek Him.

Here is an interesting nuance: The word "frustration" used by Paul is the same word used by Solomon and translated "meaningless." "'Meaningless! Meaningless!' says the Teacher. 'Utterly meaningless! Everything is meaningless'" (Ecclesiastes 1:2).

Recall that Solomon experimented with every earthly avenue to find the purpose and meaning of life. But he found in every pursuit overwhelming "frustration" (synonyms include *vanity* and *futility*). He concluded that apart from God life has no meaning. Exactly! God has "frustrated" the world (made it meaningless, futile, and vain) with thorns and thistles so that men would find life apart from Him "meaningless!" This, then, is God's method of getting man's attention.

"It is not for our defeat but our victory that God allows the pain."

This frustration is not voluntary; it is by His will. But it is purposeful—it is for a reason. And for what reason? The "expectation" or "confidence" that we will be liberated and delivered from our bondage to decay and made part of the family of God. In other words, *the meaninglessness, vanity, frustration, and futility of life is the catalyst God employs to draw us toward Him*. Grace gets us home, but not until frustration gets our attention.

The Bible teaches that frustration has a good result for those who believe. Frustration produces humbling; humbling produces believing; and by believing we will be "brought into the glorious freedom of the children of God" (Romans 8:21).

So, the earth is full of God's glory, but not *only* His glory; it is *also* full of frustration. This, then, explains the verse, "The whole earth is full of his glory." It explains the co-existence of God's glory and the effect of the Fall.

The effect of the Fall is very deep and very radical. It touches every area of life: the body, the mind, the will, the emotions, the earth, and our relationships. Yet it is all purposeful—to bring us into the glorious freedom of the children of God.

It is with this understanding that Peter wrote to us: "Dear friends, do not be surprised at the painful trial you are suffering, as though something strange were happening to you" (1 Peter 4:12).

Paul, too, understood the radical effect of the Fall and the redemptive quality of frustration. "We must go through many hardships to enter the kingdom of God" (Acts 14:22).

WEAKNESS, PAIN, AND TRAGEDY

Probably the single most difficult question in life is this: "Why do bad things happen to good people?"

Certainly the Fall introduced sin into the world, but it also introduced weaknesses, limitations, and imperfections. Sure, sometimes we suffer as a consequence of our sins, but sometimes it's just life: "There I was standing around minding my own business and, all of a sudden, life happened." As a mother told her little girl, "Everyone gets the flu, dear. That's just the way life is."

Because of the Fall:

- the world is broken
- people have weaknesses
- having babies hurts
- work is toil
- our bodies break and wear out
- the world is imperfect
- people have limitations
- tragedies occur
- life has many frustrations

The ripples of the Fall lap against every life. Because of the Fall everyone has at least one major weakness, be it in the mind, the emotions, the will, or the body. Jesus put it this way when the disciples couldn't stay awake at Gethsemane: "The spirit is willing, but the body is weak" (Mark 14:38).

Memories go bad. So we forget birthdays and anniversaries. Our minds betray us. You have a thought sitting right there on the tip of your tongue, but you simply can't form the words to express it.

Bodies give way to age. You can't bend over as far as you once did and your hair is falling out. Skin spots, bone spurs, glasses, heartburn, aches and pains, and aspirin. Your aging dad fell asleep at the wheel and knocked down the neighbor's mailbox.

Before the Fall there was time for everything. Now time is limited and you can't seem to satisfy everyone's demands. An unemployed friend is upset because you didn't call to encourage him. That was because your boss had you on overtime, and your wife's unhappy about it, too.

Our weaknesses sometimes bring out the worst in others. A teen-aged boy born with cerebral palsy weeps himself to sleep almost every day over the taunts of boys from school who mock his slurred speech and spastic walk.

We suffer from other people's errors in judgment. A young man swerves to miss hitting an oncoming car, slams into a tree, and spends the rest of his life in a wheelchair.

We are born with weaknesses in our minds and bodies. A young woman deep in debt learns her spending sprees are linked to the manic-depressive disorder with which she must learn to cope. Daily headaches prompt a man to squirrel pain pills in his coat pockets, his glove compartment, his desk, his briefcase, as well as keep a stockpile at home.

Tragedies strike at seeming random and without respect. A middle-aged man dies suddenly of a heart attack leaving a wife and three school-aged children alone in the world. A retired man loses most of his capital in the Black Monday stock market crash and must go back to work.

Perhaps the most difficult to accept and most distressing of all the effects of the Fall are those tragedies that sort of just happen. Recently a father took his eighteen-year-old son on his very first hunting trip, then accidentally killed him with a shotgun blast after mistaking him for a deer. In utter despair, the father then killed himself with the same gun.

How can such tragedies be explained?

GOD NEVER WASTES ANYTHING

The call came without warning. Leighton Ford's twenty-one-year-old son, Sandy, was in the hospital with a heart problem. The surgery began at 7:15 A.M. The morning gave way to afternoon as the hours ticked slowly away. Finally, at 6:50 P.M. the doctor came to tell this dear family that the surgery had been successful, but they could not get their son off the heart-lung machine. His heart wouldn't start. The doctors frantically kept working. Sometime after 8:00 P.M. the doors opened and the doctor solemnly walked into the waiting room. "We never got him off the table."

Just days later a newspaper headline asked, "When a good man dies; what a waste, who can explain it?" Among the many loving expressions of sympathy which came, one stood out. It came from a missionary with whom Sandy Ford had worked one summer in France. Among the other things said in his letter, he wrote: "God never wastes anything."[3]

God never wastes anything. I believe this is the true meaning of Romans 8:28: "And we know that in all things God works for the good of those who love him, who have been called according to his purpose." In other words, in supernatural ways we do not know of or understand, God sovereignly engineers our circumstances for our good—even when they seem bad—because He never wastes anything.

One day at L'Abri a young girl was to make some cakes but ended up, instead, with a big bowl of goo. It seemed the only thing to do was throw it out but, since money was so scarce, Edith Schaeffer sat down and figured out all the ingredients the girl had dumped into the bowl to end up with this goo. By adding another ingredient she was able to turn the goo into what Francis Schaeffer described as some of the most marvelous noodles you ever tasted.[4]

This is how God works. What is to the non-believer "scrap" to be thrown on the pile of human waste is to God the "ingredients" of His recipe to make us whole. He takes the goo we are in, then adds the necessary ingredients to work it for good, because He never wastes anything.

Christians have no inoculation against suffering. Crushing blows are felt by the believer and non-believer alike. That is because the radical effect of the Fall touches the same points of humanity in the believer as the non-believer. We all ache from the flu, bleed when we are cut, and sneeze when we catch a cold. Christians have financial catastrophes, broken relationships, die from cancer, and live with multiple sclerosis.

But there are differences at the spiritual level. Several times I have heard Steve Brown pastorally encourage believers, "I believe that every time a non-Christian gets cancer God allows a Christian to get cancer, too, just so that the world can see the difference." In other words, God uses calamities for higher purposes—He makes them work for good; they are not scrap; God never wastes anything.

"Though outwardly we are wasting away, yet inwardly we are being renewed day by day. For our light and momentary troubles are achieving for us an eternal glory that far outweighs them all" (2 Corinthians 4:16–17).

Don't panic at the struggles another person is going through. You never know what God is doing in a man's life.

The non-believer, sadly, cannot say that all things work together for good. He cannot say that God never wastes anything. For him, life's adversities become scrap. They are spiritual rubble destined for the waste dump of defeat, despair, and disillusionment.

"In supernatural ways
we do not know of or understand,
God sovereignly engineers our
circumstances for our good—even
when they seem bad—because
He never wastes anything."

Christians, though, profit from disease and disaster because God molds all Christian tragedy into spiritual good. For the believer nothing is wasted. Everything contributes to God's plan and purpose. For the believer, tragedies are "ingredients" our Father spiritually forges into strength, peace, joy, and good—"in all things."

                       è   è   è

DISCUSSION QUESTIONS

1. Everyone sometimes falls into a dark mood over the state of the world. What puts you in one of those moods?

2. Everyone sometimes experiences an elevated mood over the joy, kindness, and love seen in the world. What puts you in one of those moods?

3. The world is simultaneously full of God's glory and full of tragedy and evil. Explain how this can be.

4. Read Romans 8:18. Compare our present sufferings with our future glory.

5. Read Romans 8:20–21. Who has subjected creation to frustration? Why? Can you explain frustration in terms of the Fall?

6. Read Romans 8:28. This may be the most beloved, yet hardest to believe, passage in the Bible. What does the passage mean? Why is the meaning so hard to believe? What can happen in a Christian's life when he finally comes to the point at which he *really, truly believes* that "God never wastes anything"?

7. Describe an effect the Fall has had on your life. Do you believe that the hardship, pain, struggle, or evil you have faced is an ingredient for good and not merely scrap? Why or why not?

THE CONTENT
OF THE GOSPEL

CHAPTER 11

D*ear Journal,*

*Yesterday I had a frightening experience at the
office. I have been trying to live for the Lord there,
but I have "hedged" by not actually telling anyone
about what Christ means to me. I guess I don't want
to be ridiculed or have it held against me. Besides, I
had figured that what someone else wants to believe
is their business, not mine. But yesterday Steve said
he admired the meaning I seemed to find out of life.
He asked me why. I am scared to death. It's
difficult. I do believe—I have faith—but I can't
express it. I don't understand the gospel well enough
to express it. So, anyway, I accidentally muttered
something about having lunch today to talk about it.
I guess I'll have to go through with it. God, help me!*

Robert

THE DUTY OF A CHRISTIAN

When I was a skinny young teenaged soldier in the
U. S. Army I started attending a local church in the
town next to the post where I was stationed. During a
protracted period of feeling lonely and isolated I made
an appointment with the minister. I was warm toward
the idea of God, but I did not have much personal
knowledge of God or the Bible. Buckets of tears
streamed down my face as I wrestled to find the right

words to describe my feelings of isolation and loneliness. He looked on sympathetically, his mouth progressively curling into a restrained-but-knowing smile as I rattled on.

"I'm really sorry you're going through this," he finally offered. "But you have to understand. This is just the sort of thing everyone has to go through from time to time." That was it.

As I left his office the tears kept rolling down from behind my sunglasses. In my heart of hearts I knew that God was there—that He was the answer. I was looking for God. And I was looking for Him in the most logical place for a young man who didn't know where else to look. But I did not find Him that day. It would be six more years before I understood the gospel.

The man couldn't help—what a tragedy. Every believer is called to be a witness of the gospel—the "good news"—of Jesus Christ. "Always be prepared to give an answer to everyone who asks you to give the reason for the hope that you have" (1 Peter 3:15). If someone asked you to explain the reason for the hope you have, could you? Could you assist someone in understanding what it means to have a personal relationship with the living Christ? A firm understanding of what we believe is a first step to "give the reason for the hope that you have." We cannot express as clear ideas what we don't clearly understand.

What is the gospel, actually? One of the most respected evangelists of the twentieth century, Dr. Billy Graham, in the opening remarks of a sermon he preached at the *Conference for Itinerant Evangelists* in Amsterdam, 1983, asked this question: "How do we communicate the gospel with power and effect in this materialistic, scientific, rebellious, secular, immoral, humanistic age?"[1] (I think that about sums it up, don't you?)

Wisely, Dr. Graham answered his own question with the Apostle Paul's own conclusion as he entered Corinth, a city then much like our country now. Paul said, "For I resolved to know nothing while I was with you except Jesus Christ and him crucified" (1 Corinthians 2:2).

"For I resolved to know *nothing* except . . . ." The pressure is always on to add other requirements to salvation: Jesus Christ plus *good deeds*. Jesus Christ plus man-made *rules and regulations*. The gospel, however, is Jesus Christ plus *nothing*.

The most excellent, productive worker in any field has mastered his subject. Few experiences in life equal the pleasure of watching the deceptive simplicity and ease with which a skilled craftsman plies his trade: the bold strokes of the master carpenter's hammer . . . the wisdom of a mother guiding her children . . . the skillful orchestrations of the seasoned administrator. Competence is beauty; it is aesthetic. Yet we know the easier a thing is made to look, the greater the sacrifice of study and years of hard work that stand behind it.

How can we become skilled in communicating the simple, profound message of the gospel? We do so by knowing its content. What are the facts surrounding Christ? How do we lay Him as our foundation? Let's review the gospel of Jesus Christ. For all of us this will be a reminder and, if not already done so, the content of the gospel should be probed and penetrated until completely understood, and the concepts committed to memory. This is the most joyful news ever announced.

UNIVERSAL OPPORTUNITY

Four hundred faces stare at the speaker. There are no distinguishing features, few cues to signal who knows Jesus and who does not. After explaining the gospel, the speaker gives the invitation: "If any would like to receive Jesus Christ as their Lord and Savior, please come now to the front of the auditorium so that we can pray together."

It is a universal offer. The speaker has labored to tell of his own relationship with Jesus, how it came about, and how each of those in the auditorium can also receive Jesus and begin a personal relationship with the living Lord.

Thirty faces stand and begin edging through the audience to the front of the building. Some virtually dart to the podium; others seem reluctant, almost embarrassed. As one man starts forward a slight gasp is heard, and a muffled murmur titters across the crowd. This tough customer was surely the big surprise of the day. No one ever gave him a chance of coming to Christ.

Nothing could be more clear in Scripture than this idea: *Everyone who believes in Jesus will be saved.* Consider these verses:

> "For my Father's will is that *everyone* who looks to the Son and believes in him shall have eternal life, and I will raise him up at the last day." (John 6:40, emphasis added)

> For God so loved the world that he gave his one and only Son, that *whoever* believes in him shall not perish but have eternal life. (John 3:16, emphasis added)

> He is the atoning sacrifice for our sins, and not only for ours but also for the sins of the *whole world.* (1 John 2:2, emphasis added)

> This is good, and pleases God our Savior, who wants *all men* to be saved and to come to a knowledge of the truth. (1 Timothy 2:3–4, emphasis added)

What are the common threads in these passages? First, God has a will. God's will is that *everyone* who looks to Jesus for eternal life shall receive it; *whoever* believes in the Son will not perish but have everlasting life.

Second, though the offer is universally *made*—"Everyone who calls on the name of the LORD will be saved" (Joel 2:32)—the offer is not universally *accepted.* Many reject Christ as the Savior.

The sixty-four thousand dollar question, of course, is: Who is "everyone" and "whoever"? Since not "everyone" *does* look to Him, what is meant by everyone? Who will be part of the "everyone" and "whoever" who will look to Him? What determined which thirty of four hundred attendees *looked to the Son and believed?* Why do some receive the Savior while others reject Him?

THE NATURE OF GOD AND MAN

God is holy. Because God is holy His principal requirement for men and women to be in His presence is to be innocent of sin.

Fortunately, God is loving. Because God is loving He provides sinful people with a way to be counted as innocent in His presence. Why? Because the great, great desire of God is to be reconciled with people, personally, individually. In the heart of God He longs to have an eternal relationship with people. "God our Savior . . . wants all men to be saved and to come to a knowledge of the truth" (1 Timothy 2:3–4).

Men and women are God's image bearers, the finest work of God's creation. Man has intrinsic worth and dignity directly from God. "Man is not nothing." Men and women truly have enormous potential for human good.

At the same time, because of the Fall, men love themselves; they are self-lovers. We are born selfish and time only teaches us to disguise our selfishness. Man is rebellious. Left to his own devices, he would rather be a god than serve God. Men are not satisfied with the God

---

"We are born selfish and time only teaches us to disguise our selfishness."

---

who is. No matter how God has provided for man in the past, man forgets and rebels against the rule of God. Men deceive themselves, thinking they will draw a circle big enough to explain the meaning of life without God.

People want to give the impression they are strong and independent. The truth is that we are weak and frail. I can't remember my office mailing address; I forgot the name of the lady I met in church yesterday; recently I was daydreaming and ran a stop sign; I wanted to thank my son's coach but couldn't remember his name; and today I ran into the door frame and hurt my shoulder. We are not strong, but weak and dependent.

People love to make idols. By nature we are friendly toward the god(s) we want, but hostile toward the God who is. Only after God graciously turns our heart of stone into a heart of flesh do we become friendly and reverent toward the God who is.

UNIVERSAL SIN AND OUR DILEMMA

The effect of the Fall, as we have seen, is very deep and very radical. As we have said, sin is no mere blemish on the skin, but a failed heart— not skin cancer, but heart disease. The very core of the human heart is diseased unto spiritual death—"As for you, you were dead in your transgressions and sins" (Ephesians 2:1). Not exhausted. Dead.

It is sad to contemplate. God is not willing that any would perish. Yet the hearts of men are so darkened by sin that we were (or are) dead in our trangressions (Ephesians 2:5). Without Christ we are limp, lifeless, and void of any desire for the God who is, preferring our idols. Our "everyone" turns out to be a hopelessly lost sinner. "There is no one righteous, not even one. . . . All have turned away. . . . for all have sinned. . . . For the wages of sin is death" (Romans 3:10, 12, 23; 6:23).

Do you feel the weight of our dilemma? God has issued a universal opportunity for salvation—"everyone" who believes will be saved. Yet at the same time "everyone" turns out to be one and the very same "no one" who is dead because of sin. *Everyone* who can be saved is the same *all* that have turned away. It turns out that though He is willing, we are not.

On the one hand, God has issued a universal offer for all mankind to join Him at the table of His eternal banquet. On the other hand, the very people to whom He has made this generous offer are all steeped in sin—*all* have turned away, according to the Bible. Now what? Enter Jesus.

JESUS: GOD'S PLAN

Jesus healed the sick, raised the dead, cast out demons, and performed those one-of-a-kind miracles like calming the raging seas and multiplying fishes and loaves. He was the greatest moral teacher in history. He was the most righteous man to ever live. All of these make Jesus peerless, but all of these good deeds are not why men and women are willing to give their lives in His service two thousand years later.

What distinguishes the life of Jesus from other great men is that He claimed to be God. "Anyone who has seen me has seen the Father" (John 14:9). "I and the Father are one" (John 10:30). "The Father is in me, and I in the Father" (John 10:38). As J. B. Phillips has said, "It is impossible to avoid the conclusion that He believed Himself to be God."[2]

A comment from C. S. Lewis seems appropriate here:

> A man who was merely a man and said the sort of things Jesus said would not be a great moral teacher. He would either be a lunatic—on a level with the man who says he is a poached egg—or else he would be the Devil of Hell. You must make your choice. Either this man was, and is, the Son of God; or else a madman or something worse.

You can shut Him up for a fool, you can spit at Him and kill Him as a demon; or you can fall at His feet and call Him Lord and God. But let us not come with any patronizing nonsense about His being a great human teacher. He has not left that open to us. He did not intend to.[3]

The plan of God was simple. Brilliant. Pure genius, really. He is holy and unapproachable by anything which is unrighteous. But we were mired down in the sinfulness of our sin. It was an impasse. God decided, because He so loved the world, to send His Son, Jesus Christ, into the world.

Why did Jesus come? Jesus became a man for one overarching purpose. He came to seek and to save the lost. Jesus is the Messiah, the Savior: "I who speak to you am he" (John 4:26).

Jesus came for two principal tasks. First, to live a sinless life of perfect obedience to the Father. Second, to voluntarily substitute Himself in our place to die for our sins, the just for the unjust, the obedient for the disobedient. "God made him who had no sin to be sin for us" (2 Corinthians 5:21).

He would take on the sin of the whole world. He would die as a *sacrifice* so that we would not have to die spiritually. He would *substitute* Himself for us. He would make an *atonement* for our sins. He would shed His blood for the remission of our sins. He is the lamb of God that takes away the sins of the world. "Though he was rich, yet for your sakes he became poor, so that you through his poverty might become rich" (2 Corinthians 8:9). Pure genius.

Jesus did die for our sins according to the historical narrative of the Scriptures; He was buried; and He was raised from the dead on the third day. He appeared to Peter, then to the Twelve, then to over five hundred witnesses. He appeared to James. He appeared to all the apostles. He appeared to Paul (1 Corinthians 15:3–8). As important as the substitutionary death of Jesus was, it is His resurrection that proves that He was more than a merely good but deluded man.

God's part was to make a plan, to give us a way out of our lostness. Our part is simply to repent of our sins and believe in the One He has sent—"everyone" who believes will be saved.

Yet, only thirty out of four hundred come to confess and believe on this particular day. We are now back to our dilemma. Men know the solution, but they do not choose it. They do not take advantage of his universal offer. The Father has sent the Redeemer yet men still do not want to be redeemed, even after He has made it so abundantly clear, simple, and easy. Something else must be required. How can *anyone* become part of the *everyone?*

At first glance, it seems God only has two options. First, He can change the condition precedent for eternal life. He could determine that people don't have to believe in the Son of God after all. He could modify the criteria.

Second, He could hold fast and leave us all dead in our sins. He is, after all, perfectly holy and just. It would be difficult to blame God for sticking to His terms after making us such a kind, gracious offer on such easy-to-understand terms.

Instead, God chose a *tertium quid*—a third option.

THE GRACE OF GOD

Pascal comprehended how God reconciles men to Himself when he understood Jesus to say, "Thou wouldst not be searching for me hadst I not already found thee."[4]

Here is the crux of the matter: Even though God is willing that all who believe will be saved, we are not willing. We are dead in our trespasses. Our free will, as St. Augustine said, is merely the free will by which we choose to sin. He said it is not a free will, but a slave will. Martin Luther used stronger language. He said free will is Satan's kingdom in all men, and to sin is to die spiritually.

So, if God is to have *anyone* in His Kingdom, then He will necessarily have to add another ingredient, another component, another factor. What is that factor? *Grace.* Grace leads to faith in Christ.

We are saved by *grace* (the kindness, mercy, and compassion of God) *through faith.* "For it is by *grace* you have been saved, *through faith*—and this not from yourselves, it is *the gift of God*—not by works, so that no one can boast" (Ephesians 2:8–9, italics added).

Not only is faith a gracious gift of God, but we play no part in it. We have no merit with which to negotiate. After all, we are spiritually dead in our sins—lifeless and unable to help. Any contribution we claim to make on our own behalf in our salvation would amount to salvation by works, not by faith. As the Scriptures say: "not by works" (Ephesians 2:9).

"While 'everyone' and 'whoever' does believe will be saved, 'no one' can believe unless drawn to Christ by the Father."

Everyone who believes will inherit eternal life by faith in Jesus Christ. We are saved—or justified—by faith, and this justifying faith comes by the grace of God. "All have sinned and fall short of the glory of God, and are justified freely by his grace through the redemption that came by Christ Jesus" (Romans 3:23–24).

While "everyone" and "whoever" *does* believe will be saved, "no one" *can* believe unless *drawn* to Christ by the Father. As Jesus Himself succinctly put it, "everyone who looks to the Son and believes in him shall have eternal life. . . . No one can come to me unless the Father who sent me draws him" (John 6:40, 44).

There we have it. *"Everyone* who looks to the Son and believes" will be saved, *but* the only way *anyone* does "look" to Him is to be *drawn* into *faith* by the Father. The faith that results from this gracious drawing is His gift; "and this not from yourselves, it is the gift of God" (Ephesians 2:8).

God's grace through the quickening of the Holy Spirit is the *everything* of our salvation. Grace does the drawing. Grace draws thirty people to come forward to believe and receive everlasting life. This is why some come and some do not: Some are that day being drawn by grace, others are not.

God's *justice* is the catalyst that offers "everyone" the equal, universal opportunity to inherit eternal life. God's *grace* is the catalyst that results in "anyone" actually believing.

THE MYSTERY OF SALVATION

Why some and not others? Why do these thirty people receive the grace of God and not the others? We don't know. We don't know if they will ever receive Christ by God's grace or not. But we can be sure of one thing: God knows. In His secret counsel He makes these determinations. Our focus must remain upon what we can know, not what we can't know. Martin Luther wisely said, "We must keep in view His Word and leave alone His inscrutable will; for it is by His Word, and not by His inscrutable will, that we must be guided."[5]

He is good and kind and gracious and compassionate and merciful. That He would choose us to be part of His kingdom should be more mysterious to us than why He would not choose someone else. Do you remember what you were like? Have you recently recalled your former utter sinfulness, the incredible lostness of your soul? The bitterness, pride, lusts, anger, envy, jealousies, negative attitudes, malicious thoughts? "All of us also lived among them at one time, gratifying the cravings of our sinful nature and following its desires and thoughts" (Ephesians 2:3).

We do not find Christ, He finds us. We were hopelessly confused and lost. "As for you, you were dead in your transgressions and sins" (Ephesians 2:1). And He came to redeem us. And the Father has drawn us to Him. Yes, He was willing, but we were not. So God has given us His grace. "It is because of him that you are in Christ Jesus" (1 Corinthians 1:30). Praise be to God for the wonderful, mysterious gift of His salvation through Christ Jesus our Lord.

A SUMMARY OF THE GOSPEL

Here are the key points of the gospel's content in summary:

1. The nature of God is holy and loving.

2. The great, great desire of God is to be personally reconciled with each man and woman.

3. God provides a universal opportunity to receive salvation.

4. Though they bear the image of God, because of the Fall the nature of men and women is to rebel against God.

5. Through their rebellion all men and women are sinners, and the wages of that sin is spiritual death.

6. God's holy, loving solution was to send His Son to be the Savior for the people, to die in their place, and to pay the penalty for their sins so that through faith in the Savior they may receive forgiveness of sins and everlasting life.

7. The dilemma is: How will God reconcile men to Himself if they are sinners "dead in their trespasses"? The grace of God through the Holy Spirit quickens the hearts of people who would otherwise continue to rebel against God to have faith in Jesus Christ.

If you have received Christ but cannot give the reason for the hope you have, studying this chapter can help you get your facts straight. However, to develop practical skills on how to discuss these truths with someone you will need training. I believe every Christian should take at least one training class on how to share their faith. Ask your pastor for recommendations.

HOW TO RECEIVE SALVATION

Now let's turn our attention specifically to "how" someone can be reconciled with God, receive Christ, and gain eternal life. Remember, the great, great desire of God is to be reconciled with us, personally. Yet until we personally and individually receive salvation, our sins separate us from Him, leaving us unreconciled. To gain the gift of eternal life we must do two things.

First, we must acknowledge and confess our sins, purposing in our minds to repent, which means "to think differently." It is a change of disposition toward God. "If we claim to be without sin, we deceive ourselves and the truth is not in us. If we confess our sins, he is faithful and just and will forgive us our sins and purify us from all unrighteousness" (1 John 1:8–9).

Second, we must receive Jesus Christ by faith as both Savior and Lord. We must receive Him: "Yet to all who received him, to those who believed in his name, he gave the right to become children of God" (John 1:12). The Spirit of Christ literally enters our life when we receive Him. He is the way to God. Jesus said, "I am the way and the truth and the life. No one comes to the Father except through me" (John 14:6).

How does one receive Him? By faith: "For it is by grace you have been saved, through faith—and this not from yourselves, it is the gift of God—not by works, so that no one can boast" (Ephesians 2:8–9). Faith is trusting God. Faith is believing that Jesus is who He says He is—the Savior; that He did what He says He did—paid the penalty for our sins; and that He will do for us what He says He will do—forgive our sins and give us eternal life.

What if after reading this chapter you realize you have never received Christ by faith? Perhaps you have been wrongly "working" your way toward heaven. Are you sensing a desire to receive Jesus Christ now? If you are, that is the Holy Spirit working in you—"quickening" you—to give you the desire. "Flesh gives birth to flesh, but the Spirit gives birth to spirit" (John 3:6).

If you have never actually received Christ you may be thinking, "Okay, I'm interested. But *how*? How do I actually express this faith?" We can express faith and receive Christ by willfully surrendering our lives to Him. Jesus said, "Here I am! I stand at the door and knock. If anyone hears my voice and opens the door, I will go in and eat with him, and he with me" (Revelation 3:20).

How does one make such a willful surrender? You can make a willful surrender of your life and receive Jesus Christ by faith through prayer. Prayer is simply expressing your thoughts to God. Here is a suggested prayer to receive Him by faith into your life:

Lord Jesus, I need You. Thank You for dying on the cross for my sins, which I acknowledge and confess. I open the door of my life and invite You to come in. By faith, I believe, and I receive You as my Savior and Lord. Thank You for forgiving my sins and for giving me eternal life. Take control of my life and make me into the kind of person You want me to be. Amen.

Does this prayer express the desire of your heart, mind, and will? If it does and you have never received Christ, let me encourage you to kneel, pray to God, and settle the issue of your eternal destiny this very moment.

☙ ☙ ☙

DISCUSSION QUESTIONS

1. If you can, describe an experience when you wanted to tell someone about your faith but couldn't or didn't.

2. If you can, describe an experience when you did share your faith with someone and what happened.

3. Why do we need a Savior?

4. Are the lost *really* lost? If so, how does (or should) it make a difference in the way you live?

5. Read Acts 4:12. Is this true? Is there any other way for people to be saved? What practical relevance does this have to the philosophy of "live and let live"?

6. Do you believe you could give an answer for the hope that is in you if asked? If not, what would you be willing to do to become equipped to do so?

THE RELATIONSHIP
OF FAITH AND
WORKS

Dear Journal,

I am having great difficulty understanding the relationship of faith and works. On one hand, some verses say we are saved by faith alone apart from works. On the other hand, some Scriptures say that faith without works is dead. Which is it—faith or works? Or is it some combination? I can't explain this disparity. Why would God be so cryptic? Why is this so mysterious? Is this a contradiction?

Robert

CHAPTER 12

ASSURANCE OF SALVATION

A young businessman assumes that because he is honest in business he will go to heaven when he dies. Another older man believes he will not go to heaven because, even though he believes in Christ, he has not been as righteous as the Bible commands. A young mother struggles to be "good enough" to be accepted by God.

Few doctrines are as misunderstood and controversial as the relationship between faith and works. It cuts through to the very core of the gospel: How is a man saved? By faith or works or both? In this chapter we will put each in its proper perspective. Again, this is not meant to be comprehensive. We have compressed an enormous topic into a few pages. So wrestle with it, study the Scriptures for yourself, read books, ask your pastor, and pray for wisdom.

One of the great tragedies in every era is that many Christians lack a confidence that they belong to the family of God and will be with Him in the afterlife. At the same time others unwittingly place their confidence in their church membership and good deeds rather than faith in Jesus Christ. Understanding the role and relationship of faith and works also helps answer the question: How can I be sure I am saved?

I can think of few other principles which have such far reaching, and often devastating, consequences. A wrong view of the role and relationship of faith and works causes immeasurable damage to both Christians and non-Christians. A wrong understanding can rob us of an assurance of our salvation, cause us to judgmentally think others are not true believers when they are, and turn us into legalists. We can be deceived into performing for God instead of loving and trusting Him in personal faith. A wrong understanding hamstrings the gospel. When people wrongly believe they must perform to merit God's salvation, they become sentenced to a prison of unmet expectations and false guilt.

Until we trust and know God well enough that we possess a deep, abiding assurance of our salvation, we will not enjoy and serve Him to the full. Our doubts will keep us from growing spiritually, reaching out to others, and trusting Him in the daily details. Others are wrongly confident that attending church qualifies them for eternal life. Such false confidence of salvation can be like eternal poison.

The enigmatic relationship of faith and works has caused many a believer to throw up his hands in despair of ever understanding it, much less explaining it to someone else. Is there an explanation a layman can understand? And repeat?

Jesus said, "Not everyone who says to me, 'Lord, Lord,' will enter the kingdom of heaven, but only he who does the will of my Father who is in heaven" (Matthew 7:21). What is the will of God to enter the kingdom of heaven? How is a man saved? Is it by faith, by works, or by both?

Much of the biblical record emphasizes the importance of good works. But no passage seems more poignant than the parable of the sheep and the goats. In this parable Jesus invites one group to take their inheritance in the kingdom of God, while condemning another group to "the eternal fire."

Those rewarded did good works: "For I was hungry and you gave me something to eat, I was thirsty and you gave me something to drink, I was a stranger and you invited me in, I needed clothes and you clothed

---

"Until we trust and know God well enough that we possess a deep, abiding assurance of our salvation, we will not enjoy and serve Him to the full."

---

me, I was sick and you looked after me, I was in prison and you came to visit me" (Matthew 25:35–36).

The damned did not do good works: "I tell you the truth, whatever you did not do for one of the least of these, you did not do for me" (Matthew 25:45).

Does this not sound like salvation by works? It would if the passage was about salvation, but it is not. The text does not answer the question, "How can a man be saved?" but "How will men be judged?" The Bible distinguishes between how men are saved and how they are judged.

HOW CAN A MAN BE SAVED?

Man is saved by faith alone. "For no one can lay any foundation other than the one already laid, which is Jesus Christ" (1 Corinthians 3:11).

A man is saved by faith alone apart from works. "For it is by grace you have been saved, through faith—and this not from yourselves, it is the gift of God—not by works, so that no one can boast" (Ephesians 2:8–9).

There is one and only one basis upon which a man may be saved: faith in the finished work of Jesus Christ on the cross. Here is the heart of the gospel:

For what I received I passed on to you as of first importance: that Christ died for our sins according to the Scriptures, that he was buried, that he was raised on the third day according to the Scriptures, and that he appeared to Peter, and then to the Twelve. After that, he appeared to more than five hundred of the brothers at the same time. (1 Corinthians 15:3–5)

In one sense we *are* saved by works—Christ's work on the Cross; but they are *His* works, not our works.

This is the gospel: Jesus died to atone for our sins, He was buried and resurrected, and by faith in Him we, too, may gain everlasting life. That's it. Faith alone. Nothing *need* be nor *can* be added to it.

THE ROLE OF WORKS

Does this mean, then, that works are not important? Not at all. Philipp Melanchthon, Martin Luther's close associate, put it best: *"Justification is by faith alone, but not by a faith that is alone."* In other words, faith alone leads to salvation, but out of the abundance of a heart filled with gratitude good works will overflow.

What kind of faith is it that has no works? Why, it is no faith at all. The Apostle James observed:

What good is it, my brothers, if a man claims to have faith but has no deeds? Can such faith save him? Suppose a brother or sister is without clothes and daily food. If one of you says to him, "Go, I wish you well; keep warm and well fed," but does nothing about his physical needs, what good is it? In the same way, faith by itself, if it is not accompanied by action, is dead. (James 2:14–17)

Saving faith *necessarily* produces good works. In his lectures, Dr. R. C. Sproul uses three equations that summarize aptly:

1. *Faith + Works = Justification*. Right or wrong? Wrong. It is not our faith *plus* our works that saves a man. We are saved, or justified, by faith alone.

2. *Faith = Justification − Works*. Right or wrong? Wrong. Faith *without* works is really not faith at all. The Bible says clearly that a faith without works is an indication that the faith is not *genuine*.

3. *Faith = Justification + Works.* Right or wrong? Right. It is faith *alone* that saves a man, but out of an abundance of gratitude he will *voluntarily* add works and live a life of service. Works don't save, but they do demonstrate that a man is saved. "Justification is by faith alone, but not by a faith that is alone," as Melanchthon wrote.

HOW IS A MAN JUDGED?

While man is not saved by works, he will be judged by them. We are saved by faith alone, but good works are the evidence of that faith. Works are not sufficient to *gain* the Cross, but works are the necessary evidence that prove we *have* the Cross.

In Matthew 25:37 Jesus referred to those who fed the hungry, invited strangers in (and so on) as "the righteous." He called them righteous not because of their good works, but because of their faith. "For in the gospel a righteousness from God is revealed, a righteousness that is by *faith*" (Romans 1:17, italics added). And a few paragraphs later Paul writes, "This righteousness from God comes through *faith* in Jesus Christ

> ## "The presence of good works doesn't necessarily indicate the presence of faith, but the absence of good works does necessarily indicate the absence of faith."

to all who believe" (Romans 3:22, italics added).

They were not righteous because they did good works; they did good works because they were righteous. As Chester Pennington put it, "No amount of good deeds can make us good persons. We must be good before we can do good."

Are those assigned to eternal fire cursed because they lack good works or because they lack faith? It is lack of faith. The presence of good works doesn't necessarily indicate the presence of faith, but the absence of good works does necessarily indicate the absence of faith. Where there never are any works there is no faith.

Can the unrighteous do good works? Yes, but not in such a way as to give them any merit for salvation. "Many will say to me on that day, 'Lord, Lord, did we not prophesy in your name, and in your name drive out demons and perform many miracles?'" (Matthew 7:22). What are these except good works? Jesus continues, "Then I will tell them plainly, 'I never knew you. Away from me, you evildoers'" (Matthew 7:23).

Simply put, Jesus disqualifies good works as a basis for salvation. Good works have nothing to do with salvation, but everything to do with judgment. You don't need good works to *become* a Christian, but you will have good works if you *are* a Christian.

The Man with No Works

Three groups of people will be present on Judgment Day:

1. The Righteous Who Did Good Works (Matthew 25:34–40).

2. The Unrighteous Who Did Not Do Good Works (Matthew 25:41–46).

3. The Unrighteous Who Thought They Did Good Works (Matthew 7:22–23).

But won't there be a fourth group there, too? How about "The Righteous Who Did Not Do Good Works." Sorry, there is no such group. Again from James, "As the body without the spirit is dead, so faith without deeds is dead" (James 2:26).

What about a death-bed conversion? The thief on the cross was the first death-bed conversion. Though he had no opportunity to do good works he was freely justified by his faith. The appropriate conclusion for those who had no opportunity to do good works after the beginning of genuine faith is that they would have if they had been able, and Christ knows their hearts.

As we have said, saving faith necessarily produces good works. A house built on sand will not stand; it has no foundation. Salvation is by faith alone, but not by a faith that is alone. The man who *never* has good works is without hope (remember, however, that we *all* have *temporary* lapses into backsliding).

The Man with Low Works

"If any man builds on this foundation . . . his work will be shown for what it is" (1 Corinthians 3:12–13).

Although no one can claim to be a true believer and have no works, it is possible to be a believer and have low quality works. Here is where many of us let out a sigh of relief. Among the righteous who do good works, some are better than others based upon spiritual gifts, natural ability, and other strengths and weaknesses. There is a continuum of good works ranging from gold and silver on the high end to hay and straw on the low end.

While a man with *no* works cannot be saved—he has no faith, a man with *low* works will be saved—but barely.

> If any man builds on this foundation [Christ] using gold, silver, costly stones, wood, hay or straw, his work will be shown for what it is, because the Day will bring it to light. It will be revealed with fire, and the fire will test the quality of each man's work. If what he has built survives, he will receive his reward. If it is burned up, he will suffer loss; *he himself will be saved, but only as one escaping through the flames.* (1 Corinthians 3:12–15, italics added)

A "defeated" cultural Christian—one who has faith but is living in temporary defeat—has the same assurance of salvation as one whose faith is strong. God's salvation of the person with "low" works is as complete as the one whose walk is completely faithful in every respect. It is not our salvation that is at stake when our works are few, but our judgment.

WORKS LEAD FROM THE CROSS

If you have been relying on works instead of faith, consider that Christianity is not a *task* we perform but a *relationship* with Jesus. Our good works are merely the natural consequence of that relationship. Works lead from the Cross in gratitude, not to the Cross in duty.

If you have been relying on faith to the exclusion of works, know that there is no such doctrine upon which we can rely. It is self-deceit. It is seeking the God we want instead of the God who is.

Don't live on the borderline of faith, "as one escaping through the flames." Produce fruit in keeping with repentance. Why take a chance?

From this chapter you can see that if you believe in Jesus Christ you can be absolutely assured of your salvation. With that confidence you can be filled to the overflow with thanksgiving. And out of the overflow of your gratitude you can grow, serve, and trust Him more each day. Your increased understanding will give you a deeper affection for the lost.

ॐ   ॐ   ॐ

DISCUSSION QUESTIONS

1. What would you say to each of the following people?

   - Someone who believes they are saved because they are good.
   - Someone who doesn't believe they are saved because they are not good enough.
   - Someone who doesn't know whether or not they are saved because they don't understand how salvation comes about.

2. What does the "outward sign" of your works say about the "inward seal" of your faith?

3. "Justification is by faith alone, but not by a faith that is alone."

   ☐ Agree   ☐ Disagree

   Explain why.

4. Which formula best symbolizes the truth, and why? Why are each of the other formulas wrong?

   - Works = Salvation (Matthew 7:21–23)
   - Faith = Salvation (James 2:24)
   - Faith + Works = Salvation (Ephesians 2:8–9)
   - Faith = Salvation + Works (Matthew 25:34–40)
   - Faith = Salvation – Works (James 2:14–17)

5. On Judgment Day the evidence of our faith will be the works we have done because we took the time to see needs and satisfy them. What are the unmet needs in your discussion group right now? Develop a complete listing of them. How can you help each other meet those needs?

CULTIVATING AN AUTHENTIC CHRISTIAN LIFESTYLE

PART FOUR

THE MOST
IMPORTANT THING

CHAPTER 13

D*ear Journal,*

*The Christian faith embodies the most noble ideas
ever considered about how men and women might
attain a righteous life. Subjects like justice, mercy,
love, forgiveness, faithfulness, wisdom, truth, and
humility—which of these is the greatest? Or is it
something else? Is there one idea which is to be the
overarching, central focus of Christian living—sort of
the point of departure for all the rest? I need an
umbrella concept or some sort of unifying idea to put
this all into perspective. In short, I need an
organizing principle so that I will know where to
start. What is the most important thing?*

Robert

THE ULTIMATE STANDARD

Men and women spend their lives for the ideas in
which they believe. Many ideas have great worth,
merit, and value. Mortimer Adler's book, *Six Great
Ideas*, discussed and filmed with Bill Moyers for public
television, narrows the list to truth, goodness, beauty,
liberty, equality, and justice.

In the temporal realm is any one idea more worthy,
meritorious, and valuable than all the others? Is there
an idea that stands alone? The Christian does not ask
this question to empty wind, but instead turns to God
for the answer.

Christ could have stressed any point He wanted. He could have said the most important thing (the overarching idea, the guiding principle) is obedience or truth or trust or gratitude or gentleness or goodness.

He might have chosen beauty, equality, justice, mercy, forgiveness, fellowship, faith, or family. Or He could have said hope or holiness or heaven or hell. Maybe joy, peace, patience, kindness, or faithfulness. What if He had picked courage or self-control or service or works? Would He have been wrong to do so? His options included money or career or pride or power or pleasure or fame or reputation or reward.

Jesus foreknew that hundreds of millions of people would follow Him, that all of the world would judge His teaching by the cornerstone concept He picked. Whatever Jesus laid down as our guiding principle would set the tone, the texture, the tension, the tenor, and the timbre for every aspect of human life for evermore. It would reach into the privacy of every dining room, every board room, every bedroom, and set the ultimate standard by which everything is judged.

Do you see the profound implications of what Jesus would name the most important thing? This was destined to become the organizing principle for all human affairs, for both those who follow Him and those who don't. He picked love.

Even card-carrying humanists make a concession to love. Aldous Huxley said:

> Of all the worn, smudged, dog-eared words in our vocabulary, "love" is surely the grubbiest, smelliest, slimiest. Bawled from a million pulpits, lasciviously crooned through hundreds of millions of loudspeakers, it has become an outrage to good taste and decent feeling, an obscenity which one hesitates to pronounce. And yet it has to be pronounced, for after all, love is the last word.[1]

The Bible discusses three kinds of love in particular: God's love for man, man's love for God, and man's love for man.

GOD'S LOVE FOR MAN

God loves men. He cannot help it. It is part of His nature. Bearing His image we, too, love the sons and daughters we "create." As mentioned in chapter 9, "The God Who Is," God is 100 percent love. And it's a good thing, since His nature contains no other attribute sufficient to motivate Him to offer reconciliation and redemption to mankind. If you are a Christian, He loves you with redemptive love. If you are not, He invites you to believe in His Son and enter into the corridors of His eternal love.

MAN'S LOVE FOR GOD

Recently I served on jury duty. One thing that struck me was the number of questions the attorneys asked for which they already knew the answer. An expert in the law once similarly asked Jesus a question:

> "Teacher," he asked, "what must I do to inherit eternal life?"
>
> "What is written in the Law?" [Jesus] replied. "How do you read it?"
>
> He answered: "'Love the Lord your God with all your heart and with all your soul and with all your strength and with all your mind'; and, 'Love your neighbor as yourself.'"
>
> "You have answered correctly," Jesus replied. "Do this and you will live." (Luke 10:25–28)

To love God this completely we must come apart from the daily press of life and spend time alone with God, reading His Word, meditating upon it, and praying to Him. We are to love God with the total-

---

"We are to love God with the totality of our being, and this cannot be done on the run."

---

ity of our being, and this cannot be done on the run. We must pause, quiet our hearts, and listen for the "still small voice of God." If we will love God in our private watch with all our heart, soul, and mind, then we will be able to go into the marketplace and love Him there, also, with all of our strength.

Love God and love people. The Living Bible says, "Keep only these and you will find that you are obeying all the others" (Matthew 22:40, TLB). The Bible says that loving God and people is a proxy statement for how we are doing with all the other commandments. These two are ultimate; everything else is less ultimate, if you will.

If we are loving God then we will not make idols, we will not misuse His name. If we are loving people we will not lie, steal, or covet. The first and most important thing is love. Everything depends on love; love is the organizing principle for all of human life. In this chapter we will give special attention to loving one another.

MAN'S LOVE FOR MAN

Love is the law of Christ. "A new command I give you: Love one another. As I have loved you, so you must love one another" (John 13:34). And elsewhere, "My command is this: Love each other as I have loved you" (John 15:12).

The Law of Love

What is a command? A command is an order that comes from a superior. Consider these synonyms for command: law, order, rule, statute, regulation, fiat, injunction, edict, dictate, charge, decree, demand, mandate, and directive. If Jesus is the ruler of our hearts, then He has the right to issue commands, and we must obey. To issue a command one must have authority. Jesus said that all authority in heaven and on earth was given to Him. If Jesus is our authority, then must we not become fervent, passionate lovers of mankind?

Whether or not we obey the commands of Jesus (not merely mouthing empty words) is the principal way He determines if we truly love Him. "If you love me, you will obey what I command" (John 14:15). He commands us to love other people. Loving them is how we prove we love Jesus. We do not obey in servile fear to a tyrannous taskmaster, but we obey out of the gratitude of a heart filled to overflow. When we love Jesus we must unavoidably learn to love other people.

Love prevails as the only law we need. The Living Bible captures the idea with unexcelled clarity. "All ten [commandments] are wrapped up in this one, to love your neighbor as you love yourself. Love does no wrong to anyone. That's why *it fully satisfies all of God's requirements. It is the only law you need*" (Romans 13:9–10, TLB, italics added).

Jesus attached enormous significance to the law of love. He made love the most important thing—the overarching, guiding principle. He rested the full weight of His teaching, life, and ministry on love. By this, "All men will know that you are my disciples if you love one another" (John 13:35). If love fails, Jesus fails. And Jesus never fails.

So what should we make of this "law of love"? Under the supreme authority of the law of love we should strive to make our first thought of, discussion about, or encounter with another person be guided by this notion: *By the command of Christ and the power of the Holy Spirit I choose to love this person as an act of my will.*

Clearly, then, love is what we are to do, but what is love?

The Definition of Love

To define what love is taxes our powers of reason; it overloads our circuits. In the end, we cannot actually define what love *is*, but we can add on layers of meaning by describing over and over again what love *does*.

Some men on a fishing trip off the coast of Costa Rica sat in a circle at the back of their chartered trawler and traded stories. From a distance one of the Spanish-speaking crew kept eying them curiously, skeptically. About halfway through the day he approached one of the men, with an English-speaking crewman in tow to translate.

"I have been watching you today," he said through his translator. "I don't know what is the bond that you men share, but this is the thing I have been looking for all of my life. Can you tell me? What is the thing that you men share together?"

Love is the internationally understood language. Love is the thread of continuity woven into the fabric of every authentic Christian life. Under the umbrella of love all other spiritual ideas find their shelter. Love is the ligament that holds the tendons of truth to the muscles of faith to the bones of belief to the hope of heaven.

Love is the *glue* that holds us together and the *oil* that keeps us from rubbing each other the wrong way. When the world tries to pull families apart and smash them into little fractured pieces, love alone can cement us together. Can you think of any other bonding agent that unites like love?

But when people come together they often rub each other the wrong way. So love also towers above all else as the oil that keeps down the friction between us. Can you think of any other ingredient that lubricates relationships like love? In human relations love stands alone as the overarching principle, idea, and concept which holds life together and keeps it running smoothly.

One way to throw the meaning of a term into sharper relief is to describe what it is *not*. This story borrowed from Jim Dobson and *American Girl*, the Girl Scouts magazine, explains what love is not:

That's the Way Life Goes Sometimes

When I was ten, my parents got a divorce. Naturally, my father told me about it, because he was my favorite.

"Honey, I know it's been kind of bad for you these past few days, and I don't want to make it worse. But there's something I have to tell you. Honey, your mother and I got a divorce."

"But, Daddy—"

"I know you don't want this, but it has to be done. Your mother and I just don't get along like we used to. I'm already packed and my plane is leaving in half an hour."

"But, Daddy, why do you have to leave?"

"Well, honey, your mother and I can't live together anymore."

"I know that, but I mean why do you have to leave town?"

"Oh. Well, I've got someone waiting for me in New Jersey."

"But, Daddy, will I ever see you again?"

"Sure you will, honey. We'll work something out."

"But what? I mean, you'll be living in New Jersey, and I'll be living here in Washington."

"Maybe your mother will agree to you spending two weeks in the summer and two weeks in the winter with me."

"Why not more often?"

"I don't think she'll agree to two weeks in the summer and two in the winter, much less more."

"Well, it can't hurt to try."

"I know, honey, but we'll have to work it out later. My plane leaves in twenty minutes and I've got to get to the airport. Now I'm going to get my luggage, and I want you to go to your room so you don't have to watch me. And no long goodbyes either."

"Okay, Daddy. Goodbye. Don't forget to write."

"I won't. Goodbye. Now go to your room."

"Okay. Daddy, I don't want you to go!"

"I know, honey. But I have to."

"Why?"

"You wouldn't understand, honey."

"Yes, I would."

"No, you wouldn't."

"Oh well, Goodbye."

"Goodbye. Now go to your room. Hurry up."

"Okay. Well I guess that's the way life goes sometimes."

"Yes, honey. That's the way life goes sometimes."

After my father walked out that door, I never heard from him again.[2]

Relationships create responsibilities. Time is everything to a relationship. We must each give time to whom time is due.

Bible love is *agape* love; it is a decision to love as a matter of duty, principle, or propriety. *Agape* love is a chain: God *agape*-loves us, then

---

"Love is the glue that holds us together and the oil that keeps us from rubbing each other the wrong way."

---

we *agape*-love Him, then we *agape*-love our neighbor. It's all the same kind of love—a volitional decision, an act of the will. *Agape* love is not an emotion but a commitment to love others because God first loved us.

So we see that love is the most important thing, and we learn what love *is* by what love *does*. But the question remains, *how* do we love?

JESUS: OUR ROLE MODEL

The world is a touchy place. If someone accidentally cuts me off in traffic I become irritated. A perceived slight might set your ego on fire.

The world is a petty place. After a great message on love one Sunday morning, the first person I met griped about how the children were wearing out the grass: "And why can't they stay on the sidewalk, anyway?"

The world is an ungrateful place. You will often be met with indifference. One evening when our children said thank you at dinner, the waitress commented how unusual it was for children to express appreciation these days.

How do we move the idea—the command—to love one another from the realm of abstract to personal? The secret is in the wording of what Jesus calls a *new* command. "A new command I give you . . . ." Why does Jesus call this a "new" command? After all, Moses gave us the law of love long before Jesus, way back in 1400 B.C.: "Love your neighbor as yourself " (Leviticus 19:18).

The "new" in Christ's command is that Christ had put on skin, permanently changing love into a living, personal example. The "new" part of Christ's command is, "Love each other *as I have loved you.*" We love people by following the perfect example of Christ's love toward us. He wore human flesh and loved mankind with a perfect love, leaving a perfect example to follow—"as I have loved you."

If this is how we are to love one another, then exactly how did He love us? I suppose we could fill multiplied volumes to answer this question, but I will list three especially important ways.

1. Jesus Loves Us as We Are

In *Rocky*, voted best movie of 1976, the central character, Rocky, is a dull-witted neighborhood pug who operates just beyond the fringe of the real world. He falls in love with Adrian, a pale, homely petstore clerk who repeatedly deflects his romantic interest. Finally, Adrian's brother Paulie, Rocky's friend, virtually forces them together and, at long last, Adrian returns Rocky's affections.

Later, Paulie is astonished that his sister and Rocky really got together and asks Rocky,

> "How are you getting along together? What's the story? What's happening? You really like her?" [he asked.]
> "Sure I like her."
> "I don't see it. What's the attraction?"
> "I don't know. I guess it fills in gaps."

"What's gaps?"

"I don't know—gaps. She's got gaps. I've got gaps. Together we fill gaps."

Everyone has gaps. There are no perfect people—people without gaps. Everyone is looking for someone to help fill their gaps. We live in a love-hungry world, a world full of unfilled gaps and unloved hearts: lonely hearts, broken hearts, hurt hearts, wounded hearts, empty hearts, sad hearts—in short, a world of gaps.

Many people don't have a single person who even *knows* their gaps, much less *fills* them. Do you have someone who knows your gaps?

Jesus knows our gaps and loves us just as we are. Jesus loved beggars, thieves, and prostitutes. He loved blind people, lame people, and sinful people. He loved tax collectors—even Pharisees. He loved broken people, hurting people, tired people, afraid people. He loved people just as they were. Jesus doesn't say, "Change and I will love you," but "I love you, now change." He says, "I love you so much I died for you—just as you are." Jesus says, "Love each other as I have loved you."

Who are the people you are struggling to accept as they are? An acquaintance, a friend, a family member? Love people just as they are. *God gives people with gaps to other people with gaps to fill each other's gaps.* Love people, not in spite of, but because of their gaps. After all, we all have them.

2. Jesus Overlooks Our Offenses

One day I phoned an 800 number to make a motel reservation. The depressingly disinterested reservations clerk who answered the phone tempted me to think the worst of her. *Who does she think she is. I'm the customer. I don't have to put up with this. I don't have to do business with these people. Does she have any idea how many motel chains there are? I can go anywhere I want,* I thought. But I was in a good mood. "You must be having a bad day," I said cheerfully.

"Oh, yes, sir, I am. My last customer kept yelling at me, and I am a little rattled right now. Thank you for understanding." Of course, I had not understood a thing. I simply stumbled into the principle of letting the little ones go. What came within a whisker of ruining my day and making this nice young girl want to quit her job turned into an uplifting, encouraging ten-minute opportunity to glorify God. She even found a room for me at an extraordinarily low rate.

The secret of loving others is to let the little ones go. "A man's wisdom gives him patience; it is to his glory to overlook an offense" (Proverbs 19:11). Don't adjudicate the little ones. Christ did not set the record straight on every little matter. He simply loved people. He set the example in love, not in law. He did not adjudicate their petty offenses; He loved them.

Here is the test for letting the little ones go. Ask yourself, *As badly as I feel, as wrongly as I have been treated, can I still love this person?* Hear the echo of the Master's words: "As I have loved you, so you must love one another."

Who is someone with habits that annoy you? Perhaps your wife, your husband, a child, an associate, a friend, a boss, an employee? Learn to overlook the offense. Don't set the record straight. Let the little ones go. Constantly work to let increasingly bigger offenses go.

3. Jesus Forgives Our Sins

Jesus forgave the sins of all who sought His forgiveness, and of some who did not. Once some men brought a paralytic to Christ to be healed. On the basis of *their* faith, *not* the paralytic's, Jesus not only healed the man, but forgave his sins (Matthew 9:2–8). Because of His unconditional love Jesus forgives our sins, and in the same way we must unconditionally love one another and forgive their sins.

Jesus said we must forgive someone who sins against us seventy times seven, or 490 times. Then what? We start over again. How serious is forgiving others? Jesus said, "If you do not forgive men their sins, your Father will not forgive your sins" (Matthew 6:15). Very serious. "*Above all*, love each other deeply, because love covers over a multitude of sins" (1 Peter 4:8, italics added).

Six hours after starting our family vacation we pulled into a hamburger chain parking lot somewhere in south Georgia. Tired minds, stiff muscles, and low blood sugar apparently caught up with us all at once because my daughter and I started to fuss over whether she could drive the car. "Well, I don't understand why I can't drive," she said.

"Because I said so, that's why."

"Well, I don't understand . . . ."

Within sixty seconds World War III erupted as I screamed at the top of my lungs, "If you say one more word I'm going to unscrew your head!"

This was not a very wise choice of words. My wife gasped, my daughter burst into tears, and my eleven-year-old son screamed back at me, "Dad, I can't believe you said this. That's not right, and it's not a very nice thing to say."

"Forgiven. The offense is overlooked. The offense occurred, but it is overlooked. The relationship is restored."

An hour later, after many tears and too many words, when all the emotions had leveled out, I called a family meeting as we drove up the interstate highway. "I'm sorry. It's all my fault. Will you forgive me?" What a release to confess and unload the weight of true guilt.

What a blessing to be forgiven by my wife and son and to hear my daughter say, "That's okay, Dad. I forgive you. Will you forgive me, too?"

"Of course I will. It's forgiven."

Forgiven. The offense is overlooked. The offense occurred, but it is overlooked. The relationship is restored. Who is someone against whom you have sinned? Always ask to be forgiven. It will make your burden light.

Who is someone who has sinned against you? They may be seeking your forgiveness but you have withheld it. Or they may not be seeking your forgiveness and couldn't care less. It doesn't matter. Jesus forgave your sins. Forgive them, too. Since Jesus forgave our sins we ought to also forgive others their sins.

Would you like to take this principle of forgiveness to a full and final conclusion? If so, first prayerfully make a list of every sin you can think of which you have committed or which has been committed against you no matter how long ago. Second, confess your sins and ask God to restore you to fellowship with Him. Third, ask God to forgive those who have sinned against you. Fourth, forgive those who have sinned against you. Finally, where practical and wise, personally meet with those you need to forgive and to ask for forgiveness. This is love in action, and it will set you free.

THE SUPREMACY OF LOVE

Can you remember one of those incredibly lucid moments when the understanding of a Bible verse virtually leaped off the page? A moment of such condensed, crystalline clarity that you thought you would burst with joy? A brief instant of such precise, pure essence that you were irrevocably a changed person?

In more than a dozen letters, the Holy Spirit divinely inspired the Apostle Paul to capture with pen and parchment the most compact, distilled essences of divine truth. Among his writings, though, perhaps the most pregnant, poignant, and perfectly packaged thoughts are the riveting, razor-sharp sentences Paul wrote on love. They must have exploded in his mind like booming cannons.

The Apostle Paul charted love as the highest road to travel. He began, "And now I will show you the most excellent way" (1 Corinthians 12:31). His next divinely drafted words have never been exceeded:

> If I speak in the tongues of men and of angels, but have not love, I am only a resounding gong or a clanging cymbal. If I have the gift of prophecy and can fathom all mysteries and all knowledge, and if I have a faith that can move mountains, but have not love, I am nothing. If I give all I possess to the poor and surrender my body to the flames, but have not love, I gain nothing.
>
> Love is patient, love is kind. It does not envy, it does not boast, it is not proud. It is not rude, it is not self-seeking, it is not easily angered, it keeps no record of wrongs. Love does not delight in evil but rejoices with the truth. It always protects, always trusts, always hopes, always perseveres.
>
> Love never fails. . . . And now these three remain: faith, hope and love. But the greatest of these is love. (1 Corinthians 13:1–8, 13)

Great thunderbolts! What compression! There must easily be ten thousand sermons in these few lines of verse. Each weighty word is a bar of gold bullion. That Paul could attain this perfection is beyond my comprehension; it could only be the work of God. Every writer knows the indescribable agony of seeking just the right word. Mark Twain said it well: "The difference between the right word and the almost right word is the difference between lightning and the lightning bug." Paul penned the most electric words on love ever contemplated.

Peruse these again slowly, quizzing yourself with a mental love scorecard. In the first paragraph: What is a man without love? What is a woman without love? In the second and third paragraphs: Can you find the eight "is's" of love? Can you spot the eight "is nots" of love?

The most important thing is love. It is the guiding principle for all of life. Love for one another is how we demonstrate to Jesus that we love Him. Here are the key phrases one more time:

Love does no wrong to anyone.

Love fully satisfies all of God's requirements.

"A new command I give you: Love one another."

"Love one another as I have loved you."

Love is the only law you need.

Love is the most excellent way.

The greatest of these is love. . . .

Above all, love each other deeply.

Love covers a multitude of sins.

Love people the way they are.

Overlook offenses.

Let the little ones go.

Forgive people their sins.

Love is in such limited supply. You will not always reap love where you have sown it. Instead, your love will often be met with ingratitude (90 percent of the time if you use the parable of the ten lepers as a guideline). Unless you know how to replenish the love you give out, you will soon be emptied out and become weary, bitter, and empty of love.

The law of love can only be satisfied by so filling ourselves up with the love of Christ that we not only have love enough for ourselves, but love left over to give away. People will not replenish our love supply. So many people burn out on the law of love because they look for love in return. Look to Jesus for love, and then out of the overflow of His love, love others.

Love is not easy, for people can make life miserable. But we do need each other, and love is our best hope for healthy relationships. Love helps us to fill in each other's gaps, empowers us to let the little ones go, and motivates us to restore broken relationships.

Love is the most important thing. And although love is the most important thing, it is not the only thing. From this foundational point let's examine the other pieces of a life devoted to God.

ら   ら   ら

DISCUSSION QUESTIONS

1. Love is a most difficult idea to communicate. Can you think of an experience that illustrates what love is? If not, is there something in this chapter that you can recall to illustrate love?

2. Do you agree that love is the most important thing? Why or why not?

3. The greatest commandment is to love God. What are the practical ways you demonstrate your love for God? Are there any additional ways you would like to express your love to Him?

4. Jesus said, "A new command I give you: Love one another. As I have loved you, so you must love one another" (John 13:34). How has He loved you? How can you love others in the same way?

5. Read 1 Corinthians 13:1–8, 13. Develop a working definition of how to love people. It is easier to tell what love *does* than to describe what love *is*. Why is this so?

GOD'S BLUEPRINT FOR LIVING

D*ear Journal,*

How are we to view the brief time we will live on earth? Are we like bored little children waiting for the school bell to ring? Are we merely worn-out workers waiting for the whistle to blow? Are we passive pilgrims lounging in the station house until the train comes to take us home? What are we supposed to do? How should I invest the rest of my earthly life?

Robert

A SELF-APPRAISAL

When someone asks "How are you doing?" what is the first thing that comes to your mind? The line along which we answer reveals the driving force of our lives, the thing that keeps us going.

In a culture dominated by performance, many of us would answer in terms of our production. If our sales are up, we're up. If our sales are down, we're embarrassed; we even avoid giving a straight answer. If the kids are turning out well, we're proud. If the kids are struggling, we say they're great anyway. In the world, the spoils go to the strong.

In a world filled with ambition and pride we tend to constantly compare ourselves—and hence, our self-worth—to other people. We rank ourselves on an un-

CHAPTER 14

193

spoken-but-universally-understood pecking order based on beauty, brains, bucks, and brawn. Culture teaches us to evaluate how we are doing—hence, our value as a person—on the basis of performance, production, position, prestige, status, and acceptance by others.

Is it any wonder people are so disillusioned with life? When Christians unwittingly adopt the values of their culture they, too, wake up one day to the embarrassing realization that they suffer from the same empty values.

This begs the question: "How *should* I decide how I am doing?" This is the question we should ask ourselves in our private watch before God. And we should have our answer ready when someone wants to know, "What makes you tick? What gets you out of bed in the morning? Why are you the way you are?" Mull over these questions in your private watch:

- Am I seeking to love God with all my heart?
- Is Jesus my first love?
- Am I seeking first the kingdom and His righteousness?
- Am I in the center of God's will? Am I following His will?
- Am I the husband/father or wife/mother I should be?
- Am I a faithful, diligent, honest employee/employer?
- Am I striving to be financially responsible?

These questions are not the obscure, mysterious imponderables probed only by spiritual contemplatives sequestered in dark rooms lit by dim, flickering candles. Rather, these questions are the core essentials for everyday Christian living. These questions both lift our gaze to the eternal horizon and concretely address the practical needs of the moment.

The fallen world wants to ask you a decidedly different set of questions to learn who you are and what makes you tick:

- What do you do? (Meaning: "Who are you? Oh, I see. You are just a housewife and mother?")
- How much money do you make?
- Do you have any petty honors to impress me?
- Where should I fit you on the social pecking order?
- Can you tell any witty stories?
- Will you agree with me and give me what I want? If you do I will like you.

- Don't I know you? Are you somebody important?
- Do you know who I am? I'm a very important person.
- Do those clothes you're wearing have the proper labels?
- Are you pretty or handsome? I like beautiful people.
- Are you smart? I like to associate with intellectuals.
- Are you famous? If so, I would like your autograph.

At the very moment the world asks if we can meet its shallow expectations, it writhes in the predictable pain such expectations produce:

- My marriage isn't working.
- Life has no meaning and purpose.
- My children hate me.
- My job is oppressing.
- I hate my boss. And he hates me.
- I may have to declare bankruptcy.
- If there were a God, these things wouldn't happen to me.

For the Christian the way of the world will never do. Someone once said, "You only have time for one passion in life. Pick your passion." We must each make our choice—to live by a distinctly Christian set of philosophies, values, and beliefs. Only then will we achieve the authentic, passionate, life-changing, difference-making life of a genuine biblical Christian. To pull this off we must each understand God's blueprint for Christian living.

Someone whose life was missing the mark said, "I guess I need a new paradigm." The Bible presents God's blueprint—or paradigm—for how to live. His graphically detailed blueprint applies to every Christian in every way and reveals a plan for building a successful, satisfying life. Before we study the blueprint, though, let's explore the intentions of the Architect.

THE INTENTIONS OF THE ARCHITECT

God's intention is that we live as called people. First, God graciously calls us *to the Cross,* and then He calls us to live and work *from the*

Cross. Dwight L. Moody once said, "Before my conversion I worked toward the Cross, but since then I have worked from the Cross; then I worked to be saved, now I work because I am saved."[1]

The concept of *calling* is rich and diverse in its meaning. The Bible uses calling three ways:

- Calling—Type 1: God's summons to salvation.
- Calling—Type 2: God's blueprint for how to live.
- Calling—Type 3: God's task for your life.

Since we have already discussed salvation, this chapter will focus on God's blueprint for living, and His tasks for your life.

God calls us both to *be* and to *do*. First, He is profoundly concerned about our being. He wants us to be a certain kind of person in character. He wants to shape a new identity in us. He helps us answer the question, "Who am I now that I am a Christian?" He molds our philosophies, our values, our beliefs, and our doctrines. He gives us the indescribable privilege of having a personal, private walk with God. He helps us build a Christian base.

Second, He is profoundly concerned about our doing. God also wants us to be a certain kind of person in conduct. He wants to shape a new purpose in us. He helps us answer the question, "Why do I exist now that I am a Christian?" He molds our behavior, our lifestyle, and our practices. He gives us the indescribable privilege of doing specific, predetermined work for God—not only in our occupation, but all of life. He helps us live a Christian life.

As we move from the cross we will both *work for God* and *walk with God*. Our work, or service, for God is the *task* we do for Him and our walk with God is our *relationship* with Him. The concept of calling captures the idea of both relationship and task, both a walk with God and a work for God.

The Bible teaches us to make no distinction between secular and sacred in the world, work, and life. To understand and follow the calling of God is to know and do His good, pleasing, and perfect will. It is to live by biblical priorities. It is to find in Christianity a circle big enough to embrace all of life and give it meaning, purpose, and direction.

THE MASTER'S BLUEPRINT

How can we draw God's blueprint for living without listing every other verse of the Bible? And on the other hand, how can we reduce the listing without missing something important? Here we have an almost impossible challenge.

The solution is to search out those commands, callings, and responsibilities of *first importance* for all Christians. With this approach we can identify several categories of Christian calling summarized in figure 14.1 as *God's Blueprint for Living*. You should review this before reading further.

Two flexibilities will make this blueprint a useful working tool and something more than a fool's errand. First, realize there will be some overlap and, second, allow for important-but-secondary-or-subordinate threads of our calling to go unlisted. Perhaps we could think of those secondary callings as threads twisted into larger strands which are further twisted into the whole calling.

If we can reasonably fit any secondary calling under a heading already on the list, then we can rightly say that our chart is comprehensive. If that is the case, then this chart captures the biblical blueprint of how to live out the rest of our earthly lives for God's will and glory. Let me encourage you to make a copy of this chart and put it in your Bible for further study.

Now let's look over the blueprint itself. To fully amplify each point is beyond the scope of this book, but let us venture a thought about each aspect of God's blueprint.

1. Two Great Commandments

To *love God* with all of our heart, soul, mind, and strength—the totality of our being—stands supreme and alone as the greatest commandment and greatest aspiration of every true believer. To *love one another*, Jesus said, is how men will know that we are His disciples—or not.

2. Four Principal Callings

Every Christian is called to become *a disciple*, or learner, of Christ—the name He most frequently used for His followers. The name "Christian" actually came later, after Christ's death and resurrection. The greatest

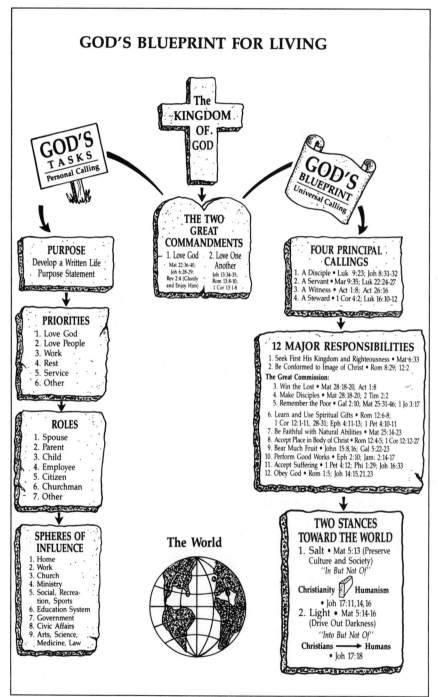

GOD'S BLUEPRINT FOR LIVING

The KINGDOM OF. GOD

GOD'S TASKS Personal Calling

GOD'S BLUEPRINT Universal Calling

THE TWO GREAT COMMANDMENTS
1. Love God
   Mat 22:36-40;
   Joh 6:28-29;
   Rev 2:4 (Glorify and Enjoy Him)
2. Love One Another
   Joh 13:34-35;
   Rom 13:8-10;
   1 Cor 13:1-8

PURPOSE
Develop a Written Life Purpose Statement

FOUR PRINCIPAL CALLINGS
1. A Disciple • Luk 9:23; Joh 8:31-32
2. A Servant • Mar 9:35; Luk 22:24-27
3. A Witness • Act 1:8; Act 26:16
4. A Steward • 1 Cor 4:2; Luk 16:10-12

PRIORITIES
1. Love God
2. Love People
3. Work
4. Rest
5. Service
6. Other

12 MAJOR RESPONSIBILITIES
1. Seek First His Kingdom and Righteousness • Mat 6:33
2. Be Conformed to Image of Christ • Rom 8:29; 12:2
The Great Commission:
3. Win the Lost • Mat 28:18-20, Act 1:8
4. Make Disciples • Mat 28:18-20; 2 Tim 2:2
5. Remember the Poor • Gal 2:10; Mat 25:31-46; 1 Jo 3:17
6. Learn and Use Spiritual Gifts • Rom 12:6-8;
   1 Cor 12:1-11, 28-31; Eph 4:11-13; 1 Pet 4:10-11
7. Be Faithful with Natural Abilities • Mat 25:14-23
8. Accept Place in Body of Christ • Rom 12:4-5; 1 Cor 12:12-27
9. Bear Much Fruit • John 15:8,16; Gal 5:22-23
10. Perform Good Works • Eph 2:10; Jam: 2:14-17
11. Accept Suffering • 1 Pet 4:12; Phi 1:29; Joh 16:33
12. Obey God • Rom 1:5; Joh 14:15,21,23

ROLES
1. Spouse
2. Parent
3. Child
4. Employee
5. Citizen
6. Churchman
7. Other

SPHERES OF INFLUENCE
1. Home
2. Work
3. Church
4. Ministry
5. Social, Recreation, Sports
6. Education System
7. Government
8. Civic Affairs
9. Arts, Science, Medicine, Law

The World

TWO STANCES TOWARD THE WORLD
1. Salt • Mat 5:13 (Preserve Culture and Society)
   "In But Not Of"
   Christianity Humanism
   • Joh 17:11,14,16
2. Light • Mat 5:14-16 (Drive Out Darkness)
   "Into But Not Of"
   Christians ⟶ Humans
   • Joh 17:18

Figure 14.1: Categories of Christian Calling

Christian is *a servant* (sometimes *doulas*—"a slave" and sometimes *diako-nos*—"an attendant or waiter" from which we get "deacon") who denies himself and takes up his cross daily, seeking to serve others and not to be served. A *witness* gives testimony four ways: to the God who is, to that which we know to be true, to that which we have experienced, and to everyone God sovereignly places in our lives. The call to be *a steward* means we are to manage whatever form of God's grace is entrusted to our care, whether gifts, ability, or prosperity—and carefully manage that part of His creation where we have been sovereignly placed.

3. Twelve Major Responsibilities

When we faithfully *seek first His kingdom and His righteousness*, then He will supply all of our material needs as well. A first goal, priority, desire, and ambition of every Christian life is to *be conformed to the image of Christ.*

The Great Commission means that we are to *win the lost* by bearing witness to the world with the gospel. We are not only to win new converts, but also to *make disciples* of them, teaching them to obey all that Christ commanded. We are exhorted to *remember the poor* through the examples of Jesus, Peter, and Paul, and as a basis of our future judgment (see chapter 17, "Becoming a Great Commission Christian").

Part of every Christian's calling is to learn and put into service the *spiritual gifts* received from the Holy Spirit which He gives to equip us for good works (see chapter 18, "Developing a Personal Ministry"). Success in spiritual service is not how much we accomplish but how faithful we are with both the gifts and the *natural abilities* with which God entrusts us. Every Christian is called to a specific place in *the body of Christ*, where we are to serve quietly, humbly, and faithfully, doing our part to build the kingdom of God.

We are appointed to *bear much fruit*, fruit that will last, including all the fruit of the Spirit. We are created to do *good works* which God prepared for us to do before we even knew Him. We have been given the privilege of not only believing in Christ but also of *suffering* for Him, for which we should not be surprised: "We must go through many hardships to enter the kingdom of God" (Acts 14:2). Paul's ministry was to call people "to the *obedience* that comes from faith," and Jesus said,

"If you love me, you will obey what I command," making obedience the trademark of the biblical Christian.

4. Two Stances Toward the World

Christians are called to be the *salt* of the earth, both flavoring and preserving culture and society. We each are called to be *"in but not of "* the *world* as strangers and aliens resolved to not syncretize, but to maintain the purity of our life and worldview:

"IN BUT NOT OF"

Christianity  Humanism

But we are also the *light* of the world, illuminating the Truth of the gospel through our good deeds and driving out darkness. We are to be *"into but not of "* the *world*, which relates to our ministry, works, and service to a dying planet on behalf of Christ:

"INTO BUT NOT OF"

Christians $\longrightarrow$ Humans

To grasp these universal callings is to understand the proportioned, balanced way God calls us to live the rest of our lives. They are for every Christian in every way. Every Christian is exactly alike in some respects—and universally called. In other respects, though, we each are unique, created differently for a specific, distinct, personal calling or vocation.

GOD'S TASK FOR YOUR LIFE

However you are wired, no pain is more excruciating than feeling set aside by God—benched and not useful. Reflect on the pain you have felt or now feel when one or more of these thoughts rule your mood:

- I have no vision for my life.
- My life has no purpose.
- I don't feel called to any task.
- I don't have a mission in life.
- My life has no direction.
- I have no goal in life.
- My life is without a passion.
- I have no sense of destiny.
- There is no driving force in my life.
- I have no guiding principle.
- I feel as if God has put me on a shelf.
- I am equipped but with nowhere to go, nothing to do.

This story has a happy ending. God has a personal, unique calling for your life. He has a unique, one-of-a-kind life planned for you. Our unique calling is how we work out the details of the already mentioned universals which apply to us all. The following figure illustrates:

UNIVERSAL CALLING
Every Christian in Every Way

PERSONAL CALLING
Every Christian in Unique Ways

How do we find it? There are four issues to settle to find and implement God's personal calling or task(s) for your life. They are our purpose, our priorities, our roles, and our spheres of influence. Let's briefly discuss each issue.

1. Purpose

A man or woman can undertake no assignment that is more important than to understand and settle the question: "What is the *purpose* of my life?" This, then, can become the organizing principle for your life. It becomes the thread of continuity in all you do; it helps you *aim* and *focus* your life. It is sort of like a personal mission statement.

This subject was more fully developed in chapter 5 of *The Man in the Mirror*, "Purpose: Why Do I Exist?" If you have not settled the issue of your own life purpose I would encourage you to work through the *Developing a Written Life Purpose Statement* worksheet in that chapter (women, too).

2. Priorities

Once you have settled your purpose you then have a basis upon which to pick your *priorities*. If you know "why" you exist, you then have a basis upon which to decide in advance "what" you will focus and con-centrate upon.

To set priorities simply means to decide in advance what is import-ant to you. It is "pre" -deciding which possible uses of time and money have greatest value to you. In this way, when you must make a choice, you already have some set guidelines in place through which to filter your decisions.

Early in His public ministry in Galilee, a crowd of people tried to pressure Jesus to stay with them. "The people were looking for him and when they came to where he was, they tried to keep him from leaving" (Luke 4:42).

How did Jesus decide whether or not to stay with them? Because Jesus knew His purpose—the reason for His life—He was able to set priorities in advance that helped Him decide what to do. "But he said, 'I must preach the good news of the kingdom of God to the other towns also, *because that is why I was sent'*" (Luke 4:43, italics added).

Jesus' purpose was to preach the good news of the kingdom of God to all the towns throughout Palestine. Knowing His purpose, He could then set priorities. He decided in advance what was important to Him, so He had some guidelines already in place when a specific decision had to be made. Jesus decided in advance on the priority of visiting "the other towns also." So when they pressured Him to stay, He didn't have to waver back and forth about what to do. Jesus decided how to spend His time based upon priorities, not pressures.

"Decide how to spend your time on the basis of your priorities, not your pressures."

And that is the lesson for us: *Decide how to spend your time on the basis of your priorities, not your pressures.*

Here are five areas of priority to think through and settle. Why not take a sheet of paper for each area and "pre"-decide how much time, money, and ability you will devote to each of these and any other priorities God may be leading you to set.

Love God. How much time do you want to spend in private devotions? How can you maintain your "first love"? What distracts you from giving God first place? What practical steps can you take to remove those distractions? How can you live in the overflow of a vital personal relationship with Jesus?

Love People. Relationships create responsibilities. When we say "I do" or bring children into the world, these relationships need time. Time is everything to a relationship. How much time do you want to spend on your relationships? How much time do you want to give strangers at the expense of those in your immediate family and circle of friends?

Work. Right or wrong, work is the outlet most of us have for finding much of our identity and significance. We should find work we love and pursue excellence. Frances Schaeffer said, "If you do your work well you will have a chance to speak." What is the proper amount of time and mental energy God wants you to give to your work? Decide this in advance.

Rest. In a culture that requires more energy than people have to give, the individual must pace himself and guard against burn-out. A good friend once said, "Try to take a 'mini' vacation every day." Even if it's only ten minutes invested in a good novel just before turning out the light, I have found this practice invaluable. If you haven't dipped into a Tom Clancy novel, you haven't lived! If you haven't spontaneously piled the family into the car after dinner and gone out for ice cream, you've missed one of life's great moments.

Service. How much time, money, and ability is God leading you to devote to serving Him in personal ministry? The only service that we will continue to perform comes out of the overflow of a heart filled with gratitude for all Christ has done in our lives. How grateful are you? As an expression of that gratitude, what kind of service should you decide in advance to perform for God? In chapter 18, "Developing a Personal Ministry," a number of ways are suggested for you to identify your spiritual gifts and possible outlets for service.

3. Roles

Once we know our purpose and have set some priorities, we need an outlet for the personal calling, or tasks, we sense. One helpful way to think about our calling is to consider the *roles* we have in our family, our society, and the world. The principle roles Christians occupy are: *spouse, parent, child, employee, citizen, and churchman.* These follow the four main authority structures of society: the family, the government, the church, and the employer.

God calls us personally and specifically to marry or not to marry, to have children or not, to be born in a certain country, to work for a certain employer or work for yourself or work in the home, to have a personal ministry, and to be part of a church body. Our calling *includes* our occupation, but it is not *limited* to our occupation. Said differently, our occupation is *part* of our calling, but our calling includes all of life.

Our roles in life are not transparent, and which roles to choose become some of the most difficult decisions to make. In the next chapter we will discuss ways to find the will of God for difficult decisions.

4. Spheres of Influence

In addition to our roles, we all have spheres of influence in which we move about. The primary spheres in which we fulfill our roles, and thus our calling, are home, work, the church, ministry, social life, recreation, sports affiliations, education, government, civic affairs, the arts, science, medicine, and law.

We should *probably* remain in the roles and spheres of influence we are in when we receive Christ. Using three different settings as examples, the Apostle Paul instructs us to "remain in the situation" we were in when Christ found us as a matter of calling. "Each one should retain the place in life that the Lord assigned to him and to which God has called him" (1 Corinthians 7:17, see also 7:20, 24). This doesn't mean we never change jobs or move and the like. It does mean that God has called us to be "in the world" for His purposes and we should not chafe and withdraw from culture, but rather, we should represent Him there.

God orchestrates our personal calling according to His good purpose, or will. "For it is God who works in you to will and to act according to his good purpose" (Philippians 2:13). God works in us to shape our purpose, our priorities, our roles, and our spheres of influence to reflect His personal call.

GOD'S SCHEDULE

God is working everything out in conformity with the purpose of His will. Since we are not privy to His schedule, our job is to follow His

> "God has called us to be
> 'in the world' for His purposes
> and we should not chafe and
> withdraw from culture, but rather,
> we should represent Him there."

universal blueprint and perform the personal tasks He gives us. We are to be faithful stewards of the world and also to be disciples, servants, and witnesses of the kingdom of God in the family, job, country, ministry, and church to which we are called. We are connected together in a body, and every member must do their part.

The concept of calling is not a stiff, wooden, brittle idea, but one that flows naturally when we walk closely with the Lord. The different parts of our calling are not separate compartments we move in and out of, but they are all part and parcel of the full-orbed Christian life.

The challenge is for every true believer to find their personal niche in culture, commerce, the home, the community, law, medicine, science, education, the arts, government, and/or religion. There we must walk with God and work for Him and represent Him to broken, hurting people.

How do we discover the particulars of our purpose, what our priorities should be, the roles we ought to fill, and the spheres of influence in which God wants us to move? These choices are not specifically spelled out in Scripture, yet God has a will for each. In the next chapter we will delve into seven ways to discover the will of God for these and other issues.

ﻚ   ﻚ   ﻚ

DISCUSSION QUESTIONS

1. What gets you out of bed in the morning? Is your passion a call from God? Why, or why not?

2. If applicable, how have you lived as though God has a call on your life in the past? How has His call influenced your purpose, priorities, roles, and the spheres of influence in which you move?

3. Review the chapter subheading, "The Intentions of the Architect." Pick two or three distinctions that strike you as interesting and explain why.

4. Review the figure, *God's Blueprint for Living.* Where have your strengths been? Your weaknesses? Which issues have you not previously considered? What adjustments would you like to make?

5. From this figure, put a check mark by the three areas at which you have most excelled. Now put an asterisk next to the three areas you would most like to work on. Explain the reasons for your choices.

6. Can you think of any sphere of society and culture today in which the dominant influence is biblical Christianity? If not, why do you think that's the case? What can we do to turn things around? Do you think it will happen quickly, and why or why not? What would be your strategy for Christendom? . . . for yourself?

7. What do you think could happen if every true Christian thought seriously about implementing their universal and personal callings at the level we have discussed in this chapter? What would happen if you did?

SEVEN WAYS TO FIND GOD'S WILL

D*ear Journal,*

I now have a better understanding of the call God has placed upon my life. I think I understand the blueprint He has laid out for all Christians. But there are several aspects of His personal calling on my life that are still fuzzy. My biggest problem right now is finding guidance to settle on my purpose, my priorities, my roles, and the spheres with which I should associate. I am eager to do whatever it takes to find God's will. What are the means of guidance to finding the will of God?

Robert

CHAPTER 15

THE WILL OF GOD

In Bristol, England, George Mueller cared for ten thousand orphans over a span of sixty years, relying only on faith and prayer to feed and house the children. He never once asked for money, though he regularly asked for more orphans.

One morning with no food or milk on hand Mueller seated his orphans around the breakfast table and prayed, "Father, we thank Thee for the food Thou art going to give us."

Just then a knock came at the door. A baker told Mueller, "I was awakened at 2:00 A.M. and felt I should bake some bread for you."

Within minutes came another knock. A milkman said, "My milk wagon just broke down in front of your place. I must get rid of these cans of milk before I can take the wagon for repairs. Can you use this milk?"

Mueller meticulously recorded thousands of similar instances in his journals. To what did Mueller attribute God's continual provision? He always satisfied himself that He was doing God's will before he started a project. Then he stood on the promises of the Bible and continued to ask God for help in prayer.[1]

What is the will of God? The will of God is the sum of the choices and determinations God has made in His mind from an infinite number of possible choices. God's will is the confluence of those choices into an order of things, into a system. God's will is what God wants to do. He is God. He can do whatever He wants.

The picture of a single life must necessarily fit into the big picture of God's character (what He is like) and purpose (what He wants to do). Finding the will of God is not a matter of persuading God to our way of thinking, but of coming to a complete, total surrender of our will to His will—His good, pleasing, and perfect will.

The overarching will of God for every Christian is this: "For those God foreknew he also predestined to be conformed to the likeness of his Son, that he might be the firstborn among many brothers" (Romans 8:29). Whatever happens, and however it happens, the reason *why* it happens is to conform us to the image of His dear Son and our Savior, Christ Jesus.

While the Bible is clear about God's will for our *character*, it is virtually silent about His will for our *circumstances*. How much education do we pursue and where? Who do we marry? What kind of work do we seek? Where do we live? How many children should we have? Should we change jobs? Where should we worship? What kind of ministry should we have? And on and on.

"What is God's will for my life?" Few words occupy so much of our thinking or burn up so much of our energy. J. I. Packer said, "To many Christians, guidance is a chronic problem. Why? Not because they doubt that divine guidance is a fact, but because they are sure it is."[2] How do we go about finding the will of God for our lives?

Our main job is to get our hearts right. George Mueller captured the idea when he said, "I seek at the beginning to get my heart into such a state that it has no will of its own in regard to a given matter.

Nine-tenths of the trouble with people is just here. Nine-tenths of the difficulties are overcome when our hearts are ready to do the Lord's will, whatever it may be."[3]

If getting our heart right is nine-tenths of finding God's will, what's the other one-tenth? Bill Gothard printed this on a card: "God's will: Exactly what I would choose if I knew all the facts." God has provided us with ample means to discern His will. Whether you are walking

---

"Whatever happens, and however it happens, the reason why it happens is to conform us to the image of His dear Son and our Savior, Christ Jesus."

---

closely with Christ or have been doing your own thing, a better understanding of how to find the will of God will help you grasp a clear picture of His plan for the rest of your life. In this chapter we will address the guidance we gain from: the Bible, prayer, the Holy Spirit, conscience, circumstances, counsel, and fasting. The means of guidance to discern God's will do not act separately but are like several tributaries that merge to form a great river. Supreme, first, and most dependable among our means of guidance is the Bible.

1. THE BIBLE

George Mueller attributed much of the success of his life to the Bible:

> I believe that one of the chief reasons that I have been kept in happy useful service is that I have been a lover of Holy Scripture. It has been my habit to read the Bible through four times a year; in a prayerful spirit, to apply it to my heart, and practice what I find there. I have been for sixty-nine years a happy man; happy, happy, happy.[4]

Happy, happy, happy. Can you say that of your own life? Would that not be a wonderful direction in which to aim the rest of your life? Few of us will feel led to read the Bible through four times a year, but how about a page a day? No matter what your current level of Bible reading, almost all of us would benefit by devoting more time to daily Bible reading. The Bible contains the big picture of God's will.

The Bible also contains many specific principles of daily living. "Should I sue a fellow Christian? Can I divorce my spouse for abandoning me? Can I marry a divorced person? What should be my attitude toward an unethical employer?" These are not easy questions, but they do have answers—answers which are the will of God, and found in the Bible.

The first step in finding the will of God is to simply ask, "Has God already spoken on this matter?" Where the Word of God has already spoken, the obedient child of God will immediately submit.

A man decided to try an experiment with the next ten decisions he would have to make. He resolved to first develop the most carefully thought-out human solutions he could forge. Then he would study the Bible to find out what God's Word said. In nine of the ten situations the biblical solution was the exact opposite of the solution he had developed from his human logic.

The crinkly pages of the Bible span from history to doctrine, from poetry to parables. The Word is the most comprehensive blueprint for successful living ever written. Guidance for living out the will of God comes from both the *commands* and the *principles* of God.

First, what God *commands* is *duty*. For example, "Honor your father and mother," "Love one another," and "Pray for your enemies" are not suggestions, but commands—therefore, duty. Once you have heard them your life can never be the same again. They are obligations, and all believers are bound by them. They are not only what we *ought* to do; to not do them breaks with the known will of God. It would be an act of open rebellion against God. If we don't obey, then we sin. Obedience to the known will of God is the trademark of a biblical Christian.

Obviously, a distinction can be drawn between *what* we are to do and *how* we are to do it. *That* we must honor our father and mother is certain. *How* we show them honor leaves room for creativity, logic, and wisdom.

Second, what God establishes as a *principle* we must follow *wisely*. Consider, for example, this passage: "Folly is bound up in the heart of a child, but the rod of discipline will drive it far from him" (Proverbs

22:15). Few passages have led to more abuse than this "principle." It is not a *command* to spank, but a vein of thinking. The principle is that disciplining your children is important because they are foolish, and

---

"To learn the Bible is to learn the mind of God. To be willfully ignorant of the Bible is to invite disaster."

---

spanking helps them overcome that foolishness. Without wisdom the principles of God's will in the Bible can be distorted to fit our preconceived notions.

Do you think biblically? In other words, when you develop a *plan*, set a *priority*, solve a *problem*, or make a *decision* do you think in biblical categories? This is central. It is not possible to know the will of God apart from the Bible.

The people who make the greatest shipwreck of their faith are the people who don't think biblically—even though they are Christian. To learn the Bible is to learn the mind of God. To be willfully ignorant of the Bible is to invite disaster.

Learn the will of God first from the Bible. "Do not go beyond what is written" (1 Corinthians 4:6). Follow the *letter* and *spirit* of God's Word from a heart filled with gratitude.

---

2. PRAYER

When Abraham learned that God was considering the destruction of Sodom he said to God, "Will you sweep away the righteous with the wicked? What if there are fifty righteous people in the city? Will you really sweep it away and not spare the place for the sake of the fifty righteous people in it?" (Genesis 18:23–24). The unusual dialogue which follows stands without peer anywhere else in the Bible:

> The LORD said, "If I find fifty righteous people in the city of Sodom, I will spare the whole place for their sake."

Then Abraham spoke up again, " . . . what if the number of the righteous is five less than fifty? Will you destroy the whole city because of five people?"

"If I find forty-five there," he said, "I will not destroy it."

Once again, he spoke to him, "What if only forty are found there?"

[God] said, "For the sake of forty, I will not do it."

Then [Abraham] said, "May the Lord not be angry, but let me speak. What if only thirty can be found there?"

He answered, "I will not do it if I find thirty there."

[Abraham followed up,] " . . . what if only twenty can be found?"

[God] said, "For the sake of twenty, I will not destroy it."

Then Abraham said, "May the Lord not be angry, but let me speak just once more. What if only ten can be found there?"

God answered, "For the sake of ten, I will not destroy it." (Genesis 18:26–33)

What happened in this unusual exchange? Did Abraham persuade God to change His mind? No, Abraham did not persuade God to change His mind. Instead, God used this exchange to guide Abraham into an understanding of His will.

For us, the broader question is, "Can we use prayer to change God's mind?" The purpose of prayer is not to get God in sync with us, but to get us in sync with God. Prayer doesn't change God; it changes us. The value of prayer is that it helps us discover and get in tune with God's will.

When we are in tune with God's will, our prayers release the will of God: "He listens to the godly man who does his will" (John 9:31). Prayer is the most effective means possible to release the will of God. Our Father hears every prayer made in accordance with His will. "This is the assurance we have in approaching God: that if we ask anything according to his will, he hears us" (1 John 5:14).

Our God "hears" everything, of course. But He doesn't hear prayer outside His will in the sense that He doesn't *act* on it. He does act on everything in line with His will, however, releasing His power on our behalf. "And if we know that he hears us—whatever we ask—we know that we have what we asked of him" (1 John 5:15).

The greatest prayers ever prayed were for the purpose of seeing the will of God done. Jesus taught us, "Your kingdom come, your will be done" (Matthew 6:10). And, "Father, if you are willing, take this cup from me; yet not my will, but yours be done" (Luke 22:42). To submit our requests to the will of God is the essence of what we mean when we pray, "in Jesus' name, Amen."

> **"Prayer doesn't change God; it changes us. The value of prayer is that it helps us discover and get in tune with God's will."**

We likely will pray two kinds of prayers to discern the will of God: One when we know what we would like to happen and another when we don't know.

The Prayer for a Specific Outcome

When God firmly gives us the desire for a specific outcome, then we should pray for it with all our heart. On the other hand, we must allow that the desire may not be from God, but born of our own desires. It is possible for us to pray against the hidden will of our Father. Hence, it is important to approach prayer for a specific outcome praying "in His name," meaning "according to Your will, whatever You think best." This is the consummate act of submission of our will to His will. Then, if perchance we have prayed in error, we still bring it under the mantle of the Cross.

What specific outcome are you praying for? Bring it "in His name" to the foot of the Cross and lay it there.

The Prayer for Guidance

You stand at the fork in the road. Traffic is backed up. Everyone is waiting for you to make a decision. Which way do you go? Or do you do nothing? The prayer for guidance comes when a need surfaces, but we do not yet sense God's definite leading.

Our prayers for God's will to be done are being answered in the private chambers of God, a place He invites us to come. "Let us then approach the throne of grace with confidence, so that we may receive mercy and find grace to help us in our time of need" (Hebrews 4:16).

We can be sure He hears us when we pray in His name and according to His will, and we can have confidence He will meet all of our needs and many of our wants. He will cause everything to work together for good because we are called according to the purpose of His will.

If you are waiting for guidance and you don't sense it coming, wait for Him. Don't force the issue. Don't take matters into your own hands. God will supply the answer if you wait patiently for Him to act. Someone has said, "God is frequently early but never late." Someone else said, "God is *rarely* early but never late." The point is this: whether God is frequently or rarely early, He is *never* late.

The Attitudes of Pleasing Prayer

What should be our attitude in prayer? Three of the chief characteristics of pleasing prayer are humility, submission, and patience.

Prayer stands alone as the consummate act of humility. The next time you pray, spend a moment talking to God about your posture. Tell Him why you have bowed your head, why you have folded your hands, why you have assumed the posture you have chosen. I think you will be surprised over what you tell Him.

Prayer ranks as the ultimate act of submission. After we cry out with our feelings, our indignation, and our hurt, we begin to calm down. Reason sets in. We begin to soften, to listen. Before God can speak to us, the proud strutting rooster in us must become the little chick beneath the wing of the hen. We, like Jesus, must say, "Lord, if I can't have what I want, then let me have what You want."

To wait patiently for the Lord to act is at once the most difficult but most rewarding aspect of prayer. Impatience often leads to heartache. "But they soon forgot what he had done and did not wait for his counsel" (Psalm 106:13). *The single greatest time waster is the time we spend undoing that which ought not to have been done in the first place.* What percentage of your time do you have to spend sorting out the consequences of hasty choices? Patience brings great reward.

3. THE HOLY SPIRIT

The Holy Spirit intercedes with the Father to help us discern and do the will of God. "The Spirit intercedes for the saints in accordance with God's will" (Romans 8:27).

The principal means by which the Spirit speaks is the Bible. "The sword of the Spirit, which is the word of God" (Ephesians 6:17). The Spirit will never contradict the Word. Still, not all leading of the Spirit is through the Word.

The Holy Spirit also speaks to our hearts. The Spirit whispers the assurance of salvation to our hearts. "The Spirit himself testifies with our spirit that we are God's children" (Romans 8:16).

The Holy Spirit teaches us everything we need to know and also reminds us of everything we have already learned when we need it. Jesus said, "But the Counselor, the Holy Spirit . . . will teach you all things and will remind you of everything I have said to you" (John 14:26). Can you recall a single instance of already knowing but not remembering Christ's teaching on a subject? The Holy Spirit always reminds us, though we do not always obey Him.

The Spirit is our counselor both now and forever. Jesus said, "The Father . . . will give you another Counselor to be with you forever—the Spirit of truth" (John 14:16–17).

We must be extremely cautious in listening for leading from the Holy Spirit. Scott ministered to a prisoner over a period of one year. This death row inmate knew the Bible inside out. One day when Scott went to visit him he learned the inmate had been placed in solitary confinement. After being led deep into the bowels of the prison, Scott finally found his friend.

"What did you do?" Scott asked him. "Why are you in here?"

"This guy was on my case and the Holy Spirit told me to stab him so I did." As bizarre as it may seem, every day Christians respond to the "voices" in their brain and give undue "credit" to the Holy Spirit.

As the prophet Samuel finished anointing Saul as the first king over Israel he told Saul to go to Gilgal and wait there seven days for him to come. When Samuel did not arrive right on the button, King Saul felt "compelled" to perform the priestly duty and make the offerings. He heard a little inner voice, but it was not the voice of the Lord.

When Samuel arrived he told Saul, "You have not kept the command the LORD your God gave you" (1 Samuel 13:13). In the end it cost him his kingdom.

Paul also spoke of being "compelled," but "by the Spirit" (Acts 20:22). His leading was very different from King Saul's. Paul was led by the Spirit; King Saul was led by his own flesh. The strong leading of the Spirit must never be confused with the strong natural inclinations of our own flesh.

Do not be surprised if the Spirit's guidance only comes partially before it comes entirely. God rarely unfolds the whole field of vision before our eyes. The stage curtain is often (usually) partially drawn. God said to Abraham, "Leave your country, your people and your father's household and go to the land I *will* show you" (Genesis 12:1, italics added). Abraham obeyed, but he was "going, not knowing."

And don't be surprised if the Spirit's guidance leads you into a storm rather than out of one. After feeding the five thousand, "Immediately Jesus made the disciples get into the boat and go on ahead of him to the other side" (Matthew 14:22). Then Jesus dismissed the crowd and went up into the hills to pray. When the boat was in the middle of the Sea of Galilee, about three miles from shore, a fierce squall came up out of nowhere. Though not expected, such sudden storms were not that uncommon on this fresh water lake so much a part of everyday life in Galilee. When it seemed their oars would snap and their hearts would melt like wax, Jesus finally came to them in the middle of the storm.

Here's the curious point: Jesus only saved them *from* the storm after He had sent them *into* the storm. Storms are part of life. Sometimes storms just happen. Other times the Spirit leads us into storms. They are opportunities for us to rely upon Him, and for Him to bring glory and honor to the Father when He delivers us. If the Spirit leads you to cross a lake and halfway over it storms, know that He will sovereignly and lovingly guide you the rest of the way, too.

We must each make countless choices regularly for which we find no specific guidance in the Bible. In these cases we rely upon the leading of the Spirit, subordinated to everything we have mentioned. Even when the Spirit leads us, however, we can never know we have heard God with the same certainty that we can know from his Word. So we

---

"Here's the curious point: Jesus only saved them from the storm after He had sent them into the storm."

---

should always be on guard against self-deceit, and check our progress regularly.

---

4. CONSCIENCE

A bad conscience is like static on a radio; it garbles the communication. A biblically developed conscience led by the Holy Spirit removes the static in our communication to and from God. "Dear friends, if our hearts do not condemn us, we have confidence before God and receive from him anything we ask, because we obey his commands and do what pleases him" (1 John 3:21).

Who can live with such confidence before God? When you seek the kingdom and the righteousness of God with all of your heart, keep short accounts with Him, sift your thoughts, and surrender your life daily at the foot of the cross, you can.

The surrendered conscience is dependable, though it always requires an alert sentinel posted to watch for attacks of self-deceit. In our fallen nature all of our ways seemed innocent to us. Through Christ we, too, have risen from the dead, but we are not yet glorified. We still have the stain of the fallen world as a temporary blemish until God perfects us through our own physical death. So although we can rely upon our conscience, we must be on guard.

Paul wrote, "I speak the truth in Christ—I am not lying, my conscience confirms it in the Holy Spirit" (Romans 9:1). Elsewhere he says, "Our conscience testifies that we have conducted ourselves . . . in the holiness and sincerity that are from God" (2 Corinthians 1:12). Hebrews 13:18 says, "We are sure that we have a clear conscience and desire to live honorably in every way."

But just so we don't *overly* depend upon the conscience, Paul also writes, "My conscience is clear, but that does not make me innocent" (1 Corinthians 4:4). We should live by the pledge of a good conscience, but always keep in mind our human fallibility.

5. CIRCUMSTANCES

In times past I took great pride in telling people, "I always go through the open door." But I left out one minor detail. I neglected to add that many of those doors opened only after I had blown off the hinges.

We can walk with confidence through the door that God opens. If the door is stuck, shut, or locked, however, don't force it open—pray it open. If it still doesn't shake free, put some oil on the hinges. If it still won't jar loose, then go ahead and picket. Maybe do a sit-in. And if you have to extend your vigil late into winter—go ahead, do it. That's fine. But whatever you do, never, never, never break through the door God has left closed. Think of the hundreds of hours we spend trying to undo the damage of the doors we have forced open.

God is at work in your circumstances. "For it is God who works in you to will and to act according to his good purpose" (Philippians 2:13). He is up to something good, kind, and holy.

Our circumstances are the portrait of our life. Sometimes life goes our way; sometimes it doesn't. Consider two Christian women. One is a haggard, bent woman waiting serenely at a bus stop bench to get home to her doting husband of forty-two years. Every day she is dropped off there by a lonely, middle-aged woman whose husband can think to buy her a big house and car, but never flowers.

When God circumstantially opens a pleasant door and gives you the desire to go through it, this is His doing. Receive the blessing of God, whether humble or exalted, with reverent gratitude.

If your circumstances are a bed of nails, you should try to improve them. If you cannot, then you can trust in your loving, holy Father to work it out for good in the end. Where we can exert no influence, we should accept whatever God sovereignly allows or causes to happen.

We should ask God to guide us to success in our circumstances. We can ask Him to help us in our priorities, our relationships, and our finances. It is honorable to consider what the likelihood of success will be. It is not likely to be God's will for you to undertake a job, a marriage, or a ministry that seems doomed to failure from the outset.

> **"God . . . will never sacrifice the quality of our character to increase the quantity of our circumstances. God puts character ahead of stuff."**

Though God's message about material blessings has been distorted by the manic teachings of the "health and wealth" gospel, let's not throw the baby out with the bathwater. The Scriptures do say that God wants to give material blessings to His children. But He will never sacrifice the *quality of our character* to increase the *quantity of our circumstances*. God puts character ahead of stuff.

God is more interested in the success of your character than the success of your circumstances. Don't misunderstand. God is vitally interested in your circumstances. But He will never *sacrifice* your character to *improve* your circumstances. Instead, He frequently reengineers our circumstances to get at our character.

6. COUNSEL

Why seek counsel? We seek counsel because we genuinely want to uncover what God wants us to do. We really do want what He wants.

We seek advice because we want our plans to succeed. Only a fool wants to fail. Often, though, our thoughts become jumbled together by the intense, constant grind of the daily routine. We begin to see wheels inside wheels, and we lose our focus on the big picture. We need help: "Plans fail for lack of counsel, but with many advisors they succeed" (Proverbs 15:22).

"Counselor" Counsel

There are two types of counsel. Sadly, nearly all advice flows from the perspective of *"counselor" counsel.* In this type of counsel your advisor tells you what *he* would do if he were *you.* Of course, he isn't you and while his advice may help, it often merely reflects the hasty opinion of one who doesn't understand where you are coming from, what you are trying to accomplish, or how far along your thinking has already developed.

Here is an axiom for seeking counsel: Beware the person who has more answers than questions. Weigh cautiously advice that comes from someone who makes you feel rushed to explain yourself, then interrupts you halfway through your explanation by saying, "I understand. What you need to do is . . . ."

Think twice about accepting the quick answer. Better is the counselor who asks, "Well, I'm not sure. What do you think God is trying to say to you about this?" It is important to do what *God* is calling you to do, *not what someone else thinks God is calling you to do.* No one can tell another person what God's will is for his life. No one.

"Counselee" Counsel

Every now and then you meet someone who can give you *"counselee" counsel.* They hear you out, they are not impatient to draw a hurried, impulsive conclusion. They ask you questions before they offer bold solutions. You sense they are not trying to tell you what they would do, but to help you think through God's will for the matter.

What is the problem that seeking counsel solves? Far and away the easiest temptation we fall into when seeking God's will is self-deceit. Self-deceit means deciding what we want, then looking for evidence to support the decision we have already made. As noted in an earlier chapter, this leads to creating a fifth gospel—good news "made to order." Invariably, however, when we deceive ourselves we do it alone, without counsel. Counsel exposes self-deceit.

There are two ways we can take advice. Many times we are not looking for the way to go, but permission to act. When Ahab, the wicked king of Israel, asked Jehoshaphat, the king of Judah, to be his ally against an enemy of Israel, he replied, "'I am as you are, my people as your people, my horses as your horses.' But . . . 'First seek the counsel of the LORD'" (1 Kings 22:4–5).

Ahab's four hundred cringing prophets instead said, "Go." But Jehoshaphat asked the essential question, "Is there not a prophet of the LORD here whom we can inquire of?" (1 Kings 22:7).

Ahab surrounded himself with quaking, cowering advisors who trembled at his voice. They would tell him anything he wanted to hear. When we explode over (or pout or put down) the advice our spouse or a friend offers, the other person soon learns the rules of our game. He knows we don't want advice, but someone to baptize our "already made" decisions. It is permission, not counsel we seek. The best way to get bad advice is to repeatedly chafe at good advice.

Even the most well-meaning friends can counsel in earnest against God's purpose. When the brothers in Caesarea learned Paul was destined for prison in Jerusalem they pleaded with him not to go. Yet Paul resisted this earnest advice and set his course in the direction he was sure God was leading. "When he would not be dissuaded, we gave up and said, 'The Lord's will be done'" (Acts 21:14). Remember to seek counsel, but always subordinate it to the Word and the distinct leading of the Spirit.

The Voice of Passion Versus the Voice of Reason

It is crucial to distinguish among your counselors. When we need to be motivated to do *what we already know should be done*, we need a counselor who will be *the voice of passion*. He motivates, enthuses, and encourages us. But when we *don't* know which way to go we need a counselor who will be *the voice of reason*. At the point of our indecision we need the wisdom of calm, not the daring of confidence.

The consistent counselor speaks the word of wisdom. You go back to him because his counsel is for *you*, not for any specific *outcome*. His agenda is simply you.

Good counsel is recognized by the impression the Spirit leaves, confirmed by the seal of the Scriptures. If counsel "feels" right, "thinks" right, and "reads" right, the counselee can conclude, at least provisionally, that the counsel *is* right. When peace grips your heart and the Scriptures are in accord, the transfer of wise counsel has been made. As someone has said well, "Peace is the umpire."

7. FASTING

"But when you fast, put oil on your head and wash your face, so that it will not be obvious to men that you are fasting . . . and your Father, who sees what is done in secret, will reward you" (Matthew 6:17–18). I will probably lose my reward for telling this story, but I do so with the high hope that you will be encouraged in your pilgrimage, and do so willingly for the point it makes.

It was 2:00 P.M. on a Monday afternoon. I had just returned to the office after eating lunch at home, my usual practice. While usually refreshed, on this day a heavy, suffocating blanket of fatigue enveloped me. This was not a physical fatigue, but a deep, saturating spiritual languor.

For months on end I had been calling out for a word from the Lord, to feel His presence. *Just a touch, Lord, just a little itsy, bitsy touch,* I prayed. Utterly paralyzed, I did not know which way to turn. My emotions were raw from the ups and downs. Waves of exhaustion swept over me. I simply could not bear another minute of the problems. I was more than burned out; I was incinerated.

As I sat at my desk and considered the weariness I felt in my bones, I couldn't help but wonder if my Lord had forsaken me, abandoned me for some unknown reason. I had lost my bearing; I feared I would lose my grip.

In the preceding weeks my thoughts had occasionally drifted to times when God met with men during times of fasting. A friend sent me an unsolicited letter in which he chronicled a fast he had undertaken and the effect it had on him. His transparency surprised me. Frankly, I was a little offended that he thought I might have enough problems to warrant the advice. *Boy, is he ever an assuming person,* I thought. Of course, I had a barrel-full of problems.

Almost on impulse, I decided to begin a fast as an act of faith, believing that God would honor it and reveal His will to me. I didn't actually have a clue how I would know when the fast should end. I couldn't name any specific thing I was seeking from the Lord. I only knew I could not go on another instant without a word from Him. I decided I would fast until God came to me personally and spiritually, or until I died.

I called Patsy, my wife, to tell her what I was up to. Patsy has always been careful to listen for the voice of the Lord in her own life. She has been equally perceptive to hear His voice in mine. This particular day she seemed discreetly quiet when I announced my intentions.

The next several days I fasted and went about business and life as usual. Nothing. Then, on the morning of the fourth day, the peace of God came over me quietly without fanfare. I called Patsy and together

---

"We must never fast for our own purposes, but to discover God's plan and purpose."

---

we ended the fast by having lunch together. Nothing externally had changed. All the problems were the same. But I sensed a new closeness with God, a deeper fellowship with the Holy Spirit, a renewed resolve, and a strong leading to press on. I have fasted since, but never has God done so much in me in so short a time, and so inexplicably.

In tough cases when discerning the will of the Lord seems hidden deeply from our sight, fasting will bring us in touch with our Lord. We must never fast for our own purposes, but to discover God's plan and purpose. Fasting is an expression of our humility. We can fast to petition God, to mourn, when we sin, or when we need His special touch. Oh, for that special touch!

SOME PRACTICAL IDEAS

Here are five practical ideas to employ when we feel stumped or blocked in our pursuit of God's will. First, we should examine the stresses in our lives. When someone mentions to me they can't find God's will, the first questions I ask focus on their emotional and physical life, not their spiritual life. The Scriptures say, "Don't you know that you yourselves are God's temple and that God's Spirit lives in you?" (1

Corinthians 3:16). A few simple questions can identify whether the blockage is not more physical and/or emotional stress than lack of divine guidance:

- When was the last time you had a vacation? Some time off?
- How many hours per week are you working?
- How are you sleeping?
- How are your eating habits?
- How much exercise are you getting?

Quite frequently the blockage is right at this point. We must care for the temple of the Spirit so we can hear and discern what the Spirit says. Often the best path to find God's will is to pile in the car and head to the beach for a long weekend.

Second, we may need visual clarity. Often our decisions are complex and multi-faceted. When so, it is difficult to keep the facts straight in our minds. One practical idea (attributed to Benjamin Franklin) is to simply take a sheet of paper and make two columns—one listing "the advantages" and the other "the disadvantages." Writing down our thoughts uniquely clarifies most decisions. As Francis Bacon said, "Writing maketh an exact man."

Third, we should examine our motives. The Bible says, "All a man's ways seem innocent to him, but motives are weighed by the Lord" (Proverbs 16:2). We all have motive problems from time to time. Ask yourself these illuminating questions:

- What am I trying to accomplish, and why?
- What is my objective and my purpose?
- What are my expectations, and why?
- Am I considering this from a sense of calling, or duty?
- What would Jesus do if He were me?

Fourth, filter your decision through Figure 14.1, *God's Blueprint for Living*. Where do your natural abilities and your spiritual gifts lie? Where do you fit into the body of Christ? What kinds of roles best suit you? These and similar questions, when united with prayer, can bring you closer to knowing the will of God in both general and specific matters.

Fifth, what do we do about that unsettled feeling we sometimes have? We often underestimate the effect of "other influences" on our choices. Pressures from our *culture*, errors in our *life view*, desires to *please people*, *temptations* from the enemy, and our own selfish *ambitions* cause us to twist facts in ways virtually unknown to us. The whisper of the Holy Spirit must be heard above the din of this horrific competition.

A man interviewed for and was offered a new job. The money, the hours, the challenge, the people, and everything else looked right. He decided he would really like that job. Then he and his wife began to pray about it. They prayed and prayed. The more they prayed, the more unsettled they felt, but everything about the job seemed perfect. Where does that unsettled feeling come from, and what should we do when we get it?

"Anytime your 'gut' leaves you feeling unsettled you can be 100 percent certain it is not God. The Holy Spirit is not the author of confusion. Satan, however, is."

Anytime your "gut" leaves you feeling unsettled you can be 100 percent certain it is not God. *The Holy Spirit is not the author of confusion.* Satan, however, is. Whenever you think you know what you want to do but you have the unsettled feeling, then wait.

Unfortunately, most of us decide what we want and then look for evidence to support the decision already made. Then our minds, caught in the sticky web of self-deceit, will wage *the war of rationalization*. But until you have *peace* you have not heard from God. Listen to your "gut." Peace is the umpire.

WHEN ANSWERS STILL WON'T COME

You may be at a point in your life where you don't have a clue about what God is doing in your life. Perhaps you have been living by your own ideas and have slowly awakened to a life that is not very satisfying.

Maybe you have always had a vision for the future, but now can say with confidence that you have no idea what you should be doing with your life. Perhaps you face a foreboding decision that could irrevocably alter the course of your life for the worse.

As I write these words I can honestly say I have little idea what God is doing in my life right now. There is no plan, no vision, no mission, no overarching goal, no focusing challenge, no compelling task. God simply won't tell me where He is taking me (though I have pleaded to know). I've wanted to know for so long that sometimes I have given up wanting to know. Have you ever felt like that?

For most of my life I always had a plan (not necessarily a good plan, but at least a plan). For several years, though, God has seen fit to keep me on a short tether without a plan. Until recently I did not think it was possible to live without a long term plan, yet I have lived quite well without one for several years. I think one of the things God is trying to teach me is that I will not wither away and die if I don't have a plan. I think He is saying, "I am the plan."

Through this I am learning what it means to depend upon Him. A caring friend keeps telling me, "You will never know Jesus is all you need until Jesus is all you have." In some strange way I know that I am right where God wants me to be. I know that I am squarely in the middle of His will, though sometimes it feels more like *stuck* in the middle of His will. I don't have the first clue about what I'll be doing a year from now, but I believe, from both the Bible and experience, that He cares.

It's not that I don't want a vision and a plan. I do. But I have this growing sense that God is sovereignly in control of my life and I don't have to wear myself out to make it. Sometimes God offers us content-ment *in* our circumstances, rather than escape *from* our circumstances.

Truth be known, it's pure, undiluted joy to be so broken, so depen-dent, that all the smugness gets squeezed out the pores. Over and over again the Bible explains how we become smug, and how God responds to smugness: "When I fed them, they were satisfied; when they were satisfied, they became proud; then they forgot me. So I will come upon them like a lion" (Hosea 13:6–7). It's an interesting progression: Fed, satisfied, proud, independent, disciplined, humbled, healed, dependent. It's a progression motivated by His love, grace, and mercy. God tests us to *make* us, not *break* us.

If you are struggling to find His will and the answers still won't come, simply continue in the faith. Where else would you go, anyway? Because we live on this side of the Cross we have the full measure of His joy. Because we live on this side of the Fall we suffer. Those two

---

> *"It's an interesting progression: Fed, satisfied, proud, independent, disciplined, humbled, healed, dependent. It's a progression motivated by His love, grace, and mercy. God tests us to make us, not break us."*

---

tracks—joy and suffering—are the realistic expectations of the disciple of the Lord Jesus. The answer we get may not be what we want, but we can trust Him.

To discern the leading of God we must faithfully employ all of the means for guidance which He graciously provides. The wise Christian will be open to God's leading through different means at different times. Through the leading of the Spirit, through prayer, and the study of the Word we can find God's will. Our odyssey is aided by our conscience, circumstances, seeking counsel, and fasting. And nothing helps more than to have our minds and bodies clear, to write out our thoughts, and to pay attention to any unsettled feeling.

A final reminder: Do what God calls you to do, not what someone else thinks God is calling you to do. No one but God can tell you what His will is for your life.

ช   ช   ช

DISCUSSION QUESTIONS

1. What is something in your life right now over which you have struggled to find God's will?

2. What means to discern His will have you been using?

3. Describe an experience or decision in which you sought the will of God and found it. By what means did God reveal His will to you? At the time how certain were you that you had found His will?

4. Put a number between 1 and 5 next to each means of guidance to indicate the frequency with which you put them into use:

   1 represents little or not at all

   3 represents sometimes

   5 represents regularly

   ☐ The Bible

   ☐ Prayer

   ☐ The Holy Spirit

   ☐ Conscience

   ☐ Circumstances

   ☐ Seeking Counsel

   ☐ Fasting

5. Which of these areas would you like to make more use of? What can you do to make the areas you selected a more integral part of your daily spiritual pilgrimage?

6. Which of the five ideas in the section subtitled "Some Practical Ideas" are you currently using? How can the ideas not currently used be of value to you?

HOW TO CHANGE

Dear Journal,

My life has been slower to change than I had originally expected. I had hoped to be further along by now. What can I do to accelerate the way I'm living my life for God? I would really like to grow spiritually, to become more sanctified, to become a kingdom person. Why does it take so long? What should I be working on? Where do I get the power and strength?

Robert

CHAPTER 16

IT TAKES TIME

Bruce Wilkinson once began a retreat by asking the attendees, "How many years was it before you really started to do business with God?" Not before he counted up to eight, nine, even ten years did a majority of hands go up. I obtained a similar result at a weekly men's Bible study I teach.

We *become* a Christian in one brilliant, sparkling instant when God massages our heart to life, but then we spend years, even decades, laboring to work out the details of what it means to *be* a Christian. Why does it take so long?

Some changes do take place rapidly, even dramatically. For the majority of us, though, most changes come slowly, often painfully slowly. Personally, I have always found the changes in my own life come so slowly that they make molasses look like a flash flood.

Jesus hints at why it takes so long in this familiar parable: "The kingdom of heaven is like a mustard seed, which a man took and planted in his field. Though it is the smallest seed of all your seeds, yet when it grows, it is the largest of garden plants and becomes a tree, so that the birds of the air come and perch in its branches" (Matthew 13:31–32).

Why does it take so long? It takes time to grow a tree.

John Calvin always emphasized the gradualness rather than the suddenness of conversion. He observed, "We are converted little by little to God, and by stages."[1] Even in his own life he found it difficult to make progress in the Christian life. So how do we grow in the things of the kingdom?

A CASE STUDY IN SPIRITUAL GROWTH

An elite handful of leaders run every community. It's a fraternity, and membership is guarded carefully. For every member there are hundreds who don't make it. Many aspire, but only a privileged few are hand-picked to join the club.

An unusually gifted, educated, and articulate young man, Paul was obsessed with leaving his mark on the world. He became one of those talented few who break into the rarefied ranks of the power elite. Once admitted in, his career took off like a rocket and he became the bright young star on the scene.

The Apostle Paul's own conversion fell upon him like a fireball out of heaven on a dusty ribbon of road leading to Damascus. Paul never had any illusions that his own efforts had anything to do with his salvation:

> As he neared Damascus on his journey, suddenly a light from heaven flashed around him. He fell to the ground and heard a voice say to him, "Saul, Saul, why do you persecute me?"
> "Who are you, Lord?" Saul asked.
> "I am Jesus, whom you are persecuting," he replied. (Acts 9:3–5)

What was Paul (a/k/a Saul) doing out there, anyway? Paul was on his way to persecute the believers. If experience was to be any indicator, he would drag some women from their homes, separate them from their children, throw the men in prison, try to torture the leaders until they would blaspheme Jesus, and, if that didn't work, cast his vote to put them to death.

Interesting. Jesus said to Paul, "I am Jesus, whom you are persecuting." In other words, "Don't you know that when you do that to them, you do that to me? Why do you persecute us like that, Saul?"

As dramatic as that day was, it was not the end of Paul's conversion, but the beginning of a process that would convert his *tasks*, his *relationships*, his *thinking*, and his *plans*. Let's examine what happened to him.

In a single mind-boggling moment God radically changed Paul's heart. Because God so radically changed Paul's heart, Paul consecrated himself to radically change his life. But it didn't all happen overnight. Paul didn't fully convert to an obedient life of fruitful service in that one imperial instant. Why? Because he needed to work some things "in" to his life and some things "out" of his life. It takes time to get to know the God who is. Let's look at the four areas upon which Paul concentrated.

1. Conversion Means a Change in Tasks

> At once he began to preach in the synagogues that Jesus is the Son of God. All those who heard him were astonished and asked, "Isn't he the man who raised havoc in Jerusalem among those who call on this name?" (Acts 9:20–21)

The first thing Paul changed was his tasks. He redirected his tasks, reoriented his zeal, and refocused his energy. It is important to see that Paul stayed in the same line of work—religion. Most of us will be called to remain in our present vocation. No vocation is intrinsically a higher calling than any other. Whether a businessman, homemaker, doctor, or plumber—all work is consecrated when done for the glory of God. What are the tasks we should change?

Tasks that take away from important family time, distract from devotion to Christ, or cause you to not give your employer a fair day's labor are tasks to be subtracted. On the other hand, priorities that go begging for attention point out tasks to be added.

There are some things we are doing which are questionable. There are some things we are *not* doing that need to be done. What are they? In your own walk with Christ, what tasks should you do that you are not doing? What tasks should you not do that you are doing?

2. Conversion Means a Change in Relationships

> The Jews conspired to kill him, but Saul [Paul] learned of their plan.
> Day and night they kept close watch on the city gates in order to kill
> him. But his followers took him by night and lowered him in a basket
> through an opening in the wall. (Acts 9:23–25)

Paul's second change was in his relationships. When Paul became a
follower of Christ his friends became his enemies, and his enemies became his friends. The Jews tried to kill him, but his former foes became
his new accountability group—"his *followers* took him by night . . . ." In
the same way a wary Senator Harold Hughes hugged a newly converted
Chuck Colson, the disciples took Paul in.

Why don't we simply segregate from our enemies? After all, we are
supposed to have no fellowship with darkness. We each have three
groups of people in our lives: friends, enemies, and the undecided. The
reason we don't segregate is for the sake of the undecided. Because we
often can't tell the difference between an enemy and an undecided, we
mingle among them so that some of them may see our changed life and
believe in Christ.

"Half the people in the world are not going to like you anyway, so they may as well not like you for the right reason."

It would be easier to segregate, of course, but we are sent "into" the
world. So don't be afraid to make some enemies; do it for the sake of
the undecided. Remember this: Half the people in the world are not
going to like you anyway, so they may as well not like you for the right
reason. And make some new friends along the way, too, for personal
encouragement.

3. Conversion Means a Change in Thinking

> I went immediately into Arabia and later returned to Damascus. Then after three years, I went up to Jerusalem to get acquainted with Peter. (Galatians 1:17–18)

The third change Paul made was in his thinking. Paul must have been thoroughly confused. His calling was so high, so profound, so dramatic, yet they tried to kill him. So he went off to think it over, spending three years in Arabia and, later, in Damascus. Paul would not be a ninety-day-wonder. He moved from the power elite to fugitive.

It makes sense. Paul was educated, smart, and ambitious. To alter the success system he had built up in his mind would take time. It couldn't happen overnight. He needed time to change his thinking—radically. So he went off to Arabia.

While we don't know exactly what Paul did there, I'm sure he perused his parchments in the dim light of a flickering lamp during those lonely Arabian nights. He probably would sit for hours pouring over his ancient scrolls to see where he had missed the Truth, twisted the Scriptures, and become a counterfeit.

If Paul lived today what would he do? Perhaps he would join a church, attend a home Bible study, join an accountability group, and maybe even take a few seminary classes. While we don't really know when or where, we do know that at some point Paul radically changed his thinking. We, too, must radically change our thinking.

4. Conversion Means a Change in Plans

> When he came to Jerusalem, he tried to join the disciples, but they were afraid of him. . . . [After they finally accepted him, Paul] stayed with them and moved about freely in Jerusalem, speaking boldly in the name of the Lord. He talked and debated with the Grecian Jews, but they tried to kill him. When the brothers learned of this, they took him down to Caesarea and sent him off to Tarsus. (Acts 9:26–30)

The irony must have been suffocating. Instead of storming the world with the gospel, he was being shipped off to a remote outpost. Once famous as an enemy of Christ, Paul was rapidly becoming an unknown spokesman for Christ. His new accountability group sent him back to his hometown, Tarsus, where he lived in obscurity for another ten years before we hear from him again. Paul did something many of us don't do: He surrendered his plans to the sovereign plan of God.

God has a plan for the rest of your life—call it God's will for your life. It may be the same as the plan you have thought, but it may be different. For some of us, God's plan may mean a period of relative obscurity. He wants to convert and sanctify our lives, radically. Are you ready to resign your great plans to God? Are you willing to live in obscurity if that is God's will for your life?

Paul's conversion and sanctification radically altered his life, but it took time. Though the process was lifelong, Paul made some significant changes in the early years that every believer also ought to make: He converted his tasks, his relationships, his thinking, and his plans to a Christian base. After that he was able to serve God rightly.

Conversion to faith in Christ takes place instantly, but conversion to obedience takes time. We did not become the way we are overnight. We will not change overnight. And sometimes we are simply obstinate about the whole affair. Said Oswald Chambers:

> The hindrance in our spiritual life is that we will not be continually converted, there are wedges of obstinacy where our pride spits at the throne of God and says—I won't. . . . There are whole tracts of our lives which have not yet been brought into subjection, and it can only be done by this continuous conversion. Slowly but surely we can claim the whole territory for the Spirit of God.[2]

If we are going to lead lives of significance for the kingdom of God we are going to have to make some radical changes. In which areas do you need to make some changes, even radical changes?

Do not be at all discouraged if change comes slowly. Slow is normative. Do what you can and trust God to make up the difference. William Temple said, "Conversion is to give as much of yourself as you can to as much of God as you can understand, and to do so every day."

The conversion that leads to the cross brings salvation, while the conversion that leads from the cross brings sanctification. Let's look at God's part and our part in sanctification.

GOD'S PART: SANCTIFICATION

God is holy, and He makes us holy. Christians are a people whom God is making holy, conforming us to the image of His dear Son, Jesus. Sanctification is this process by which God "sets us apart" for Himself and makes us holy. If we belong to Him, God is sanctifying us— whether we know it or not, whether we cooperate or not. Of course, a close look at our lives may not yield much evidence. It takes time to work Christ into the details of our daily lives.

Imagine a father with two sons to whom he desires to teach good manners. One son seems eager to learn. Every time his father advises or corrects him he thanks his father for teaching him good manners. But the other son kicks, screams, fusses, and fumes against his father's counsel. He rebels and rejects his father's instruction. One resists while the other cooperates.

Do you think the father will be any less committed to teaching both sons good manners simply because they respond differently? No, the father will continue to be equally committed to teaching both children the same good manners. What loving father would so easily give up on his child?

The difference: For one child the experience is entirely pleasant, but for the other it is pain and torture. We, too, can cooperate with the Father's plan of sanctification, or we can resist. Sanctification *always* produces the intended result. If we cooperate the results come more quickly and with considerably less pain. No matter, He will sanctify one way or the other. Wouldn't it be more pleasant to cooperate than resist? But how do we cooperate with God's sanctification?

OUR PART: SANCTIFICATION

Dwight L. Moody was the Billy Graham of the nineteenth century. On his first trip to England a young Moody heard these challenging words which would radically alter his life: "The world has yet to see what God will do, with, and for, and through, and in, and by, the man who is fully and wholly consecrated to Him."

"He said 'a man,'" thought Moody; "he did not say a great man, nor a learned man, nor a rich man, nor a wise man, nor an eloquent man, nor a 'smart' man, but simply 'a man.' I am a man, and it lies with the man himself whether he will, or will not, make that entire and full consecration. I will try my utmost to be that man."[3]

To cooperate with God is to consecrate ourselves to Him. Consecration is another word for sanctification. God sanctifies us and, in return, we are exhorted to sanctify ourselves to Him. "But sanctify the Lord God in your hearts" (1 Peter 3:15, KJV). "Offer your bodies as living sacrifices, holy, and pleasing to God" (Romans 12:1). Our part is to set ourselves apart to cooperate with what God is going to accomplish anyway. Our consecration *to* God is our cooperation *with* God for our sanctification *by* God.

One in a Hundred

Have you burned those boats yet? Have you eliminated the option of turning back? Do something radical. Make the commitment to consecrate the rest of your life to know and do the will of God. But, alas, few do.

Great men of God have observed the rarity of men and women who have made that entire and full consecration to God. Oswald Chambers said, "One life wholly devoted to God is of more value to God than one hundred lives simply awakened by His Spirit."[4]

John Wesley put it this way: "Give me one hundred preachers who fear nothing but sin and desire nothing but God . . . such will shake the gates of hell and set up the kingdom of heaven on earth."[5] And Calvin noted, "God has sown a seed of religion in all men. But scarcely one man in a hundred is met with who fosters it."[6]

Solomon surpassed the "one-in-a-hundred" school of thought. He lamented, "I found one upright man among a thousand. . . . Men have gone in search of many schemes" (Ecclesiastes 7:28–29).

Has the world seen yet what God will do, with, and for, and through, and in, and by you? The world needs you. Your family needs you. And God wants to make you holy.

Make that entire and full consecration. Set yourself apart to obey God out of the abundance of a heart filled with gratitude. Let the Father sanctify you—make you holy. And be sure to cooperate with Him. It is the logical next step of our spiritual growth.

Our Guide: The Holy Spirit

Where does the power come from to make that entire and full consecration and then to convert our lives to kingdom values? If we make
the full and entire consecration, how will we keep it up? The answer,
quite simply, is that we cannot. Only the Holy Spirit can empower us
to do our part.

Who has the Holy Spirit? Every Christian has the Holy Spirit.
"Having believed, you were marked in him with a seal, the promised
Holy Spirit, who is a deposit guaranteeing our inheritance until the
redemption of those who are God's possession—to the praise of his
glory" (Ephesians 1:13–14).

> ## "Though the Holy Spirit indwells every Christian, not every Christian depends upon the Holy Spirit to empower him/her to live the life of a biblical Christian."

We are told to live by the Spirit. "So I say, live by the Spirit, and
you will not gratify the desires of the sinful nature" (Galatians 5:16). If
we don't live by the Spirit we cannot please God. "Those controlled by
the sinful nature cannot please God" (Romans 8:8).

Unfortunately, our sinful nature is at war with the Spirit, and the
Spirit with the sinful nature. "For the sinful nature desires what is contrary to the Spirit, and the Spirit what is contrary to the sinful nature"
(Galatians 5:17). Regrettably, the sinful nature often wins. Why? Because living by the Holy Spirit is a choice we make.

Though the Holy Spirit indwells every Christian, not every Christian depends upon the Holy Spirit to empower him/her to live the life of
a biblical Christian. Cultural Christians live in defeat because they don't
choose to live filled with the Spirit but instead allow the desires of the
sinful nature to entice them and drag them away into sin (James 1:14).

So what is the solution? "Instead, be filled with the Spirit" (Ephesians 5:18). Once we make that entire and full consecration, how can we walk in the power of the Holy Spirit? The answer is to keep short accounts with God: to immediately confess any area of your life that becomes displeasing to God. Then ask Him to again take control of your life and live by the power of His Spirit.

Does this make sense? The Holy Spirit is the source of power to enable us to live out the consecration we make and to radically turn our lives toward the kingdom of God.

Here is a prayer you may want to clip out or copy. Anytime you become aware that you are not walking in the Spirit, pause and talk it over with Christ.

> Lord Jesus, I need You in my life right now. I acknowledge that I have succumbed to the sinful nature and I have sinned. I have not been living by the Spirit. I desire to be reconciled with You and to again experience the joy of Your love and forgiveness. I confess my sins to You and ask You to forgive me (Note: confess specific sins to Him). Thank You for forgiving all of my sins. I invite You to again take control of my life and continue making me into the kind of person You want me to become. Help me live in moment-by-moment fellowship with You through the power of Your Holy Spirit. Empower me to be a biblical Christian. Amen.

> (Note: Keep this prayer handy. Pray it anytime you discover you have sinned and are not living by the Spirit and not enjoying fellowship with God.)

          ❧   ❧   ❧

What this chapter boils down to is growing spiritually through a commitment to "change." If we belong to Christ we will change, because God will convert our lives and sanctify us.

One day, the story goes, a group of small children went on a field trip to the studio of a great sculptor. The chiseled stone figures fired the imaginations of the children. But by far the most imposing statue was that of a fierce, stately lion which stared stonily down at the boys and girls.

Awed by the precise detail of this life-like lion, one little boy asked the sculptor, "How did you make such a realistic lion?"

"It was easy," came the reply. "I chipped away everything that didn't look like a lion."

Growing spiritually is chipping away everything that doesn't look like Christ. How are you doing?

ᴈ   ᴈ   ᴈ

DISCUSSION QUESTIONS

1. What are some things you have chipped away from your life that didn't look like a Christian? How has this made you feel about yourself?

2. The Apostle Paul's conversion to faith in Christ came in one explosive moment, but then he spent the next several years converting his tasks, relationships, thinking, and plans. How has your pilgrimage been similar to Paul's? How has it been different?

3. To which of the four areas listed below do you need to give attention? Write down some specific actions you would like to take in the coming days. Now put an asterisk by the one that needs the most attention.

   My tasks _____

   My relationships _____

   My thinking _____

   My plans _____

4. On a scale of 1 to 10 (with 1 representing little knowledge and 10 representing complete understanding), how would you rank your knowledge of the ministry of the Holy Spirit? Referring to the section, Our Guide: The Holy Spirit, what is one new thing you have learned?

5. With which of the following statements do you most identify. Why?

   ☐ I have been converted to Christ, but not changed much.

   ☐ I am beginning to see real changes occur in my life.

   ☐ I am in the middle of a period of radical change.

   ☐ God has wonderfully, radically changed my life.

6. Are you ready to make that entire and full consecration? If so, what is your next step? If not, what is holding you back?

BECOMING A GREAT COMMISSION CHRISTIAN

CHAPTER 17

Dear *Journal,*

For the last sixty days or so a new beggar has been working the street corner in front of my office. For the first month I was absolutely livid. "What's this town coming to? Can't they keep these bums off the streets? This will kill customer relations," I fumed.

Over the following two weeks I simmered down. I began to notice that this beggar—he didn't have legs—was quite friendly and spoke a few words to each of the few people who did stop to give him something. I began to feel strangely drawn to give him some money myself. After fighting the urge for a week I finally broke down one day and put some coins in his can. You just won't believe what happened next. He said to me, "Jesus loves you. Blessed are you when you remember the poor. I'm a Christian. Are you a Christian? Have you ever given your life to Jesus?"

My mind was reeling. I thought to myself, "What? You? A Christian? But you're just a bum! An outcast!" I was dumbfounded. Speechless.

Frankly, the possibility simply never even crossed my mind that he could be a Christian. Then he

243

pushed a small slip of paper into my hand. It was a quote that simply said:

Evangelism is just one beggar telling another beggar
where to find bread—D. T. Niles.

What have I become? Who is the person inside this skin? Lord Jesus, forgive me. Show me what it means to see people the way You see them and to love them with Your love. Reveal to me how to do this, and I will follow You. Lord, I'm begging.

Robert

THE WORLD'S GREATEST SPEECH

Can you remember the most inspiring, uplifting speech you ever heard? Can you recall the commitments you were prepared to make at that intoxicating moment?

If you were asked to pick the one speech which has had more impact upon the world than any other, what would be your choice? Would it be one by Churchill or Roosevelt? Maybe Kennedy or King? How about Luther or Augustine? Perhaps Cicero or Socrates? Some say Demosthenes gave the most perfect speech ever uttered.

Down through the ages, rousing slogans and inspiring speeches have ignited heroic responses from men and women exhilarated by the call of duty and honor. Spellbinding challenges from great leaders have fired men's imaginations, motivated Herculean efforts, and mobilized vast armies of dedicated people to accomplish virtually impossible tasks.

But by a wide margin, year in and year out, the last earthly words of Jesus have consistently mustered the singular largest response. Each year these few pregnant phrases incite men and women to devote incalculable millions of hours and incomprehensible billions of dollars to fulfill His challenge.

Easily the singlemost impactful speech of human history, the final earthly words of Jesus comprise the most compact, compressed distillation of the Christian mission ever uttered. The impact continues to reverberate down the corridors of time like peals of rolling thunder.

> All authority in heaven and on earth has been given to me. Therefore go and make disciples of all nations, baptizing them in the name of the Father and of the Son and of the Holy Spirit, and teaching them to obey everything I have commanded you. And surely I will be with you always, to the very end of the age. (Matthew 28:18–20)

It's all there. Authority. Challenge. Mission. Adventure. Power. Direction. Purpose. Comfort. Eternal Security. It is our task. It is our mission. It is our commission. It is His command for us to share the gospel with the whole world. And it is great.

"We must address all three strands of the Great Commission . . . : evangelism, discipleship, and remembering the poor. Anything less than all three is not the Great Commission, but the Good Commission."

Picture for a moment the most godly, spiritual man you know. Perhaps it's your pastor, your father, your husband, or a friend. Now, assume he gives the same speech Jesus gave, really believing what he was saying to be true. How would you respond? You would want to do one of two things: erupt in laughter or call the men in white suits and have him committed. Only with Jesus is there a third option. With Jesus we can also choose to fall down, humble ourselves, and worship the God-man who has made these radical claims.

The Great Commission sets the perimeters of our service to Him. We will have other life tasks (e.g., Jesus worked as a carpenter and healed the sick), but our chief work is to fulfill the Great Commission—in our personal life, in our home, in our neighborhood, in our workplace, in our community, in our culture, and in the world at large.

When we introduce someone to Jesus—either personally or indirectly—we have introduced them to *their only hope*. We have the answer that the whole world is looking for. Let's never stop seeking the cure for cancer, AIDS, and heart disease, but neither let us forget that the greatest disease is death. Death is the disease we all catch, and the one only Jesus can cure. Belief in Jesus is the antidote that leads to everlasting life with God.

The concept of the Great Commission is broad. Sometimes, however, we define it so broadly—"win the world"—that we lose sight of individual souls. We overlook the "world of one" next door, at the grocery store, in the next cubicle. Every person's life contains enough drama to resemble a gripping novel—a story that only Jesus can bring to a happy ending.

Other times we define the Great Commission so evangelistically that we walk past broken, hurting people who desperately need to be encouraged. Some of these people would gladly turn to Christ if only someone would first offer to help fix their "broken wing."

What exactly is involved in the Great Commission? There are three basic strands to the Great Commission:

1. *Evangelism:* Spreading the good news, exposing people to the truth claims of Jesus, assisting people in receiving Jesus Christ as Savior and Lord (Acts 1:8).

2. *Discipleship:* Making disciples, training leaders, developing accountable relationships, teaching people how to live effective Christian lives (2 Timothy 2:2).

3. *Remembering the Poor:* Meeting human needs, the social gospel, taking care of widows and orphans, feeding the hungry, clothing the naked, visiting the sick and imprisoned (Galatians 2:10; Matthew 25:31–46).

We must address all three strands of the Great Commission in our service and personal ministry: evangelism, discipleship, and remembering the poor. Anything less than all three is not the Great Commission, but the Good Commission. It may be good, but it isn't great. Let's examine these three threads of our mission.

EVANGELISM: PASSION FOR THE LOST

Have you ever heard of Edward Kimball? Neither had I. An ordinary, everyday sort of man, Kimball would never attract a crowd. His destiny was never to become famous or wealthy or powerful. But every week he faithfully taught a Sunday school class in Boston, diligently explaining Bible truths week after week to the young men in his class. One day he realized that one young man in his class, a sunny seventeen-year-old, was not a believer.

After debating what to do about it, Kimball finally started down toward Holton's shoe store where the young man worked. After walking by the store once, he finally screwed up his courage and went in. Finding the young man in the stock room, he proceeded to make what he thought was a weak plea for Christ, telling him of Christ's love and the love Christ wanted in return.

The moment was right, light broke upon the young man, and there in the back of Holton's shoe store in Boston, Dwight L. Moody gave his life to Christ.

Hardly anyone has heard of Edward Kimball. But what Christian hasn't heard of Dwight L. Moody. Few will ever turn out to be a Moody, but almost anyone could be a Kimball. The only issue is whether or not we will screw up the courage and go in.

Years later, after one of the Moody's meetings in a Worcester, Massachusetts crusade, a young seventeen-year-old introduced himself as the son of Edward Kimball.

"What! Are you the son of Edward Kimball of Boston? What is your name?"

"Henry."

"I am glad to see you. Henry, are you a Christian?"

"No sir; I do not think I am."

In the moment that followed Dwight L. Moody explained how Henry's father had once asked him to become a Christian when he, too, had been seventeen years old. When he asked Henry if he wanted to be a Christian he responded, "Yes sir, I think I do."

Sitting down together, Moody opened his Bible and at length explained the Scriptures until Henry, as Moody had done many years before, gave his life to Christ.[1]

Can you imagine the loss to the world if Dwight L. Moody had never become a Christian? On a more personal note, can you imagine the loss to Edward Kimball if his son Henry had never become a Christian? Imagine the heartbreak of Christian parents all over the world who long for their dear children to turn to Christ. Edward and Henry Kimball supply us with a vivid example of one way God will bless the Christian who senses the urgency to overcome his or her fear to share the gospel of Christ.

We must come to grips with where Jesus wants us to center our lives. What is the fulcrum of His teaching—the pivot point? On what key point does the teaching of Jesus turn? What is the central issue which concerns Him? What overarching idea epitomized His life?

Jesus came to seek and to save the lost. "Here is a trustworthy saying that deserves full acceptance: Christ Jesus came into the world to save sinners" (1 Timothy 1:15). Jesus healed the sick, cast out demons, raised the dead, and performed one-of-a-kind miracles. But were these the highest point—the ultimate end—of His life and ministry? No, these were merely the means to another end. To what end did Jesus perform these mind-boggling feats? The events in the historical life of Jesus bear witness to His *purpose* and *authority*.

Everything Jesus did contributed to His purpose. No step Jesus ever took or word He ever uttered was meant for any purpose except to point men toward the knowledge of the kingdom of God. Jesus came with the authority to offer forgiveness of sins and salvation to all who believe.

Evangelism is not a matter of mere human sympathy. Christianity is not a matter of dramatic human helps to ease the burden of daily living. That would be a good idea, but not a God idea. Instead, evangelism is a command based upon the authority of Jesus Christ to baptize and disciple sinners into everlasting life. "All authority in heaven and on earth has been given to me. Therefore . . ." Evangelism is the God idea which summarizes the Bible: redemption for sinners who repent and believe.

Evangelism is a *command*, not a *suggestion*. One day a man said to me, "I don't share my faith because I don't have the *gift* of evangelism."

It is true. Some people receive a special gift of evangelism (Ephesians 4:11). Some, then, will use their gift of evangelism to lead people to the feet of the Master. It may even come easy to them. They are the sales department. But every other department ultimately supports sales, for if nothing is sold then there is no need for service and support.

Those among us who do not have the gift of evangelism will have to rely on our willingness to obey Jesus' command to bear witness. We will work in children's ministries, reach out to the poor, teach and train new and mature believers, care for people in crisis, show mercy, and do works

---

> ## *"The ultimate purpose of God is to save lost sinners, not merely bandage humanity's mortal wounds."*

---

of service. And yet unless our service includes a sensitivity to how we may win the lost, we labor in vain, for the ultimate purpose of God is to save lost sinners, not merely bandage humanity's mortal wounds.

All of our good deeds, good works, and Christian service should be focused by and filtered through Christ's command to be witnesses to the life-changing power of faith in Jesus. Paul wrote to his young protégé Timothy words we should all apply, "Do the work of an evangelist, discharge all the duties of your ministry" (2 Timothy 4:5). Evangelism is where Jesus centered His life. By His authority, it is where He wants us to center ours. Whether we do so directly or indirectly, "He who wins souls is wise" (Proverbs 11:30).

Eternal Life, Inc.

In the church, as in every organization, different departments and committees sometimes imagine their task is the area upon which the fortunes of the organization rise or fall.

"Oh, sure," acknowledges the counseling department, "Evangelism and worship are crucial. But unless we get people's personal problems straightened out, then people won't be very useful, now will they?"

"Yes, yes. We must win souls and educate people, but unless the finance committee does its job, well, you know, the whole thing will come to a screeching halt."

"Well, if the buildings aren't kept up, then not many people will be attracted to come worship here, . . . know what I mean?"

In every organization each department from manufacturing to sales, from shipping to accounting, from administration to customer service must contribute to the ultimate end of the organization: to provide a product or service that meets a need. That ultimate end, or mission, is the organizing idea and the driving force. In the final analysis, unless people purchase a company's products and services then all else is for naught. No administrators, no bookkeepers, no shipping clerks, no widget makers are needed if no one buys the product.

The two exceptions to this rule seem to be government and the church. With limited accountability, the government and the church are able to cruise along, collecting and spending money without necessarily producing significant results. Many churches are turning their communities upside down for the gospel. But many more belong to that gigantic new denomination, cultural Christianity.

What is the chief end of the church? The product God offers is eternal life, and He is the exclusive manufacturer. The church is nothing more than the manufacturer's representative. Unless the church sees people coming to faith in Christ, it is not accomplishing God's goal. The various departments, committees, and functions—Christian education, counseling, pastoral care, physical plant, administration, finance, and so on—may produce scintillating numbers. But if "eternal life" is not being sold and bought, then the church has missed its mission. And *you* are the church.

Methods of Sharing Faith

When you discover a method of evangelism that works for you, hold fast to it. Some frown on passing out tracts on street corners—"too impersonal." Others scowl at "lifestyle" evangelism that befriends people over the long term—"too slow." But the best method of witnessing is the one you will use.

No one method or style of evangelism is more valid than another. Francis Schaeffer commented on the need for flexibility in method. He wrote, "Each generation of the church in each setting has the responsibility of communicating the gospel in understandable terms, considering the language and thought-forms of that setting."[2]

The essential issues in evangelism are these: Is it faithful to the truth? Is it honoring to God? Does it depend upon the Holy Spirit to produce fruit? Does it produce fruit? Any method that honors Christ and produces fruit is valid. Here are some examples:

- Inviting neighbors to your evangelistic church services
- Inviting associates to an evangelistic Bible study
- Taking training to learn how to share your faith
- Calling on church visitors
- Passing out tracts door to door
- Explaining "The Four Spiritual Laws" booklet to a friend
- Taking a friend to lunch to explain the gospel
- Showing the *Jesus* film to a small group in your home
- Giving Bibles to non-believers in hospitals
- Inviting associates to community outreach events
- Organizing an evangelistic prayer breakfast, luncheon, or dinner party with an outside speaker
- Giving money to evangelistic ministries
- Setting up chairs for a missions banquet
- Raising money for an evangelistic ministry or minister
- Working in a drug, alcohol, or pregnancy program that points people to Christ
- Jail ministries
- Ministry to the poor that is gospel centered

God made each of us different. We need to respect, even treasure, those differences. The Holy Spirit has anointed countless different methods to be the means of spreading the gospel. Still, though the message can be communicated through many methods, we can ill afford to ever forget that it is a single message: belief in Jesus Christ. It is why He came.

DISCIPLESHIP: SPIRITUAL MULTIPLICATION

A Gallup poll asked, "What do you believe about Jesus Christ—do you think Jesus Christ was God or the Son of God, another religious leader like Mohammed or Buddha, or do you think Jesus Christ never lived?" Eighty-four percent of Americans answered this tightly worded question by saying that Jesus is God or the Son of God.[3]

As survey questions become more *personal* and more *specific* the percentages go down abruptly. For example, while 84 percent believe Jesus is God or the Son of God—"Even the demons believe that, and shudder" (James 2:19)—66 percent say they have "made a commitment to Christ." When asked if they are evangelical or have had a "born again" experience the numbers are cut nearly in half to 38 percent. Why the discrepancy? Here are four reasons.

First, many Christians don't understand our duty to *become* disciples. One prevailing current idea is that we can pray a prayer, receive Jesus as Savior, gain a ticket to heaven, and then live our lives however we want. God is intensely interested in how we live. He inspired men to write the Bible as the most relevant blueprint for right living ever written, and He did so for a reason. "All Scripture is God-breathed and is useful for teaching, rebuking, correcting and training in righteousness, so that the man of God may be thoroughly equipped for every good work" (2 Timothy 3:16–17). He wants Christians to be properly equipped to live good lives.

Second, many Christians don't understand our duty to *make* disciples. Our lives are to be models of Christian living for new and young believers. "In everything set them an example by doing what is good" (Titus 2:7).

As evangelistic as the Apostle Paul was, he saw equal value in teaching the believers what to believe and how to live. "After spending some time in Antioch, Paul set out from there and traveled from place to place . . . strengthening all the disciples" (Acts 18:23). "He traveled through [Macedonia], speaking many words of encouragement to the people" (Acts 20:2).

Third, most Christians don't maximize their labors through *spiritual multiplication*. I must confess that until a few years ago I always thought of spiritual multiplication as a good philosophy of ministry, but never as a spiritual principle. Then one day John Tolson, founder of The Gathering of Men, was teaching our Bible study discussion leaders from 2 Timothy 2:2. I'm sure I had read this verse hundreds of times for I had it memorized, but not until that morning did it ever connect with my brain: *Spiritual multiplication is God's method for reaching the world.* "And the things you have heard me say in the presence of many witnesses entrust to reliable men *who will also be qualified to teach others*" (2 Timothy 2:2, italics added). Sometimes we will only make sheep, but we should always strive to make shepherds.

"If you really want to have a powerful ministry for God, make discipling your family your first priority."

The difference between spiritual addition and spiritual multiplication is the difference between reaching your neighborhood and reaching the whole world. If you discipled one person each year for forty years you would have forty disciples. Not bad. If on the other hand you discipled only one person who made a commitment to disciple one other person, teaching him to similarly disciple one other and so on, you would have 1,048,576 disciples in twenty years, 1,073,700,000 disciples in thirty years, and 1,099,500,000 disciples in forty years—all from your first disciple.

The sad reality, of course, is that not only do most Christians not understand spiritual multiplication, they don't understand spiritual addition either. How many Christians have forty disciples at the end of their adult lives? How many have even four? Most Christians become spiritual takers, not spiritual givers. Real love, peace, and joy comes from obeying Christ's command to go and bear much fruit. "This is to my Father's glory, that you bear much fruit, showing yourselves to be my disciples" (John 15:8).

We are to make disciples of our families, our associates, our friends, our neighbors, our church, our community, and the whole world. Not only do we pour Truth into them, but we challenge them to reproduce their lives into others. We should constantly be on the lookout for potential spiritual leaders to surface who will be especially faithful in teaching others. And if you really want to have a powerful ministry for God, make discipling your family your first priority.

Billy Graham was once asked, "If you were a pastor of a large church in a principal city, what would be your plan of action?" Anticipate his answer. How do you think he will answer? I would suspect we are about to have a large crusade. Here, however, is Dr. Graham's interesting answer:

> I think one of the first things I would do would be to get a small group of eight or ten or twelve men around me that would meet a few hours a week and pay the price. It would cost them something in time and effort. I would share with them everything I have, over a period of years. Then I would actually have twelve ministers among the laymen *who in turn could take eight or ten or twelve more and teach them.*[4]

Here is an axiom of spiritual growth: The smaller the unit, the greater the change.

Fourth, most Christians don't understand *how* to make disciples. Unless and until we ourselves become diligent students of the Bible we will not be able to fulfill our calling to make disciples. We cannot reproduce what we do not understand. Our lives must become the live model of what we believe. As someone has said, "We teach what we believe; we reproduce what we are." Every Christian should receive training on the basic beliefs of our faith and also training on how to, in turn, teach others.

Several specialty ministries have carefully developed training aids and study materials to assist the church. Campus Crusade for Christ, Ligonier Ministries, the Navigators, and Christian Businessmen's Committee, for example, all have study programs designed to disciple men and women, who will in turn be equipped to disciple other men and women, and so on.

THE POOR: REACHING OUT

The tinsel and glitter that make Christmas sparkle had infected us with merriment. As we drove from the mall toward home that warm glow of being personally satisfied with life warmed my insides. My two children punctuated their excited conversation by stabbing the air with animated gestures. We all were entranced by that intoxicating anticipation of Christmas morning. From the corner of my eye I spotted two figures—one large and one small—standing at the side of the road. They were people. There was something in their hands. My children, preoccupied with mirth over the Christmas present selected for their mother, missed seeing the two people as we drove by.

At the next corner I turned and drove back around the block. While negotiating a corner I pulled out my wallet and removed the cash—all thirteen dollars.

"What are you doing, Dad?" my daughter asked.

"You'll see. Just a minute. . . . There, look up there," I said, "Do you see those people?"

"Yea, Dad, but what are they doing?" my son said.

"Roll the window down," I told him.

"What for?"

"Just go ahead and do it. You'll see."

As we drove closer my children's eyes grew large like round saucers. The bigger figure was a man holding a sign that read: "I will work for food."

The smaller figure was a little boy about my son's age. He held a sign that read: "I will do chores for toys."

I pressed the thirteen dollars into my wide-eyed son's hands and rolled to a stop in front of this down-and-out father and son.

"Give him the money, son," I said.

A quiet hush had fallen over the infectiously excited confines of our car. The man asked if we had some work they could do for us. "No, but go ahead and take the money. We hope everything works out for you."

"Really, are you sure? We would really rather do some work for you."

"No, that's okay. Sorry we don't have more."

Silence replaced laughter as we pulled away from the curb. No one said a word for the remainder of the ride home.

The stark contrast between the poverty of the poor and the prosperity of the prosperous baffles my mind sometimes. How could there be such a wide, gaping difference in people's circumstances?

Even more puzzling: How can so many people drive on by? Certainly, everyone has their own maximum capacity. Sometimes we feel completely drained because we have over-helped others. Maybe we gave so much we are weary and need a boost of encouragement ourselves.

But sometimes we become so preoccupied with our own trifles that the significant needs of broken people go unnoticed and unmet. We still drive down the same old roads, but the thick walls of routine and familiarity screen them from our sight. We no longer "see" the people.

I realize someone may take exception to including the poor in the Great Commission. No one will deny the importance of remembering the poor, but by what biblical authority is it part of the Great Commission? I present as witnesses Jesus, Paul, Barnabas, Peter, James, John, and the rest of the Twelve. Please hear the evidence.

Jesus placed a special emphasis on the poor. The "poor" is somewhat of a misnomer, for it includes all the downtrodden, broken, weak, powerless, homeless, rejected, displaced, and despised of the world. They are the unemployed, the underemployed, and the unemployable. Jesus met both the spiritual and the physical needs of people, and He exhorts us to do the same: "For I was hungry and you gave me something to eat, I was thirsty and you gave me something to drink, I was a stranger and you invited me in, I needed clothes and you clothed me, I was sick and you looked after me, I was in prison and you came to visit me."

Then the righteous will answer him, "Lord, when . . . ."

The King will reply, "I tell you the truth, whatever you did for one of the least of these brothers of mine, you did for me" (Matthew 25:35–37, 40).

To the poor themselves Jesus said, "Blessed are you who are poor, for yours is the kingdom of God" (Luke 6:20).

Next witnesses, please. When Paul and Barnabas went to Jerusalem to meet with the church pillars, James, Peter, and John, they agreed on the strategy for spreading the gospel: Paul and Barnabas would go to the Gentiles; James, Peter, and John to the Jews. Then Paul noted, "All they asked was that we should continue to remember the poor, the very thing I was eager to do" (Galatians 2:10).

Paul was already helping the poor. The brothers in Jerusalem expressed their desire for Paul to continue doing so. Remembering the poor was important to Paul. Remembering the poor was important to James, Peter, and John. Paul reaffirmed he was eager to continue helping the poor. Thank you, Paul. No further questions.

Later, the Apostle John (reflecting perhaps on this experience?) was inspired by the Holy Spirit to write, "If anyone has material possessions and sees his brother in need but has no pity on him, how can the love of God be in him?" (1 John 3:17).

"The stark contrast between the poverty of the poor and the prosperity of the prosperous baffles my mind sometimes. . . . Even more puzzling: How can so many people drive on by?"

James, the wise and godly brother of Jesus, wrote, "Faith without works is dead" (James 2:20, KJV). And, "Religion that God our Father accepts as pure and faultless is this: to look after orphans and widows in their distress" (James 1:27).

Finally, let's call the Twelve to the witness stand. In Acts 6:1–7 the Twelve appointed seven wise, Spirit-filled men including Stephen and Philip to take care of the daily distribution of food to the poor widows (the ancient version of food stamps—though private, not government). And what happened when they fulfilled their duty to the poor? "So the word of God spread. The number of disciples in Jerusalem increased rapidly" (Acts 6:7).

We should remember the poor simply because the founders of the first-century church—Paul, Barnabas, James, Peter, John, and the rest of the Twelve—all agreed that remembering the poor should share center stage in their mission to the world.

The Great Commission is, after all, a later theological construct designed to capture and express the essence of the believer's mission in the world. Why would we be so bold to define the boundaries of our calling more narrowly than Paul, Barnabas, James, Peter, and John?

Here are the central ideas in remembering the poor. If you apply the same standards for giving money to the poor that you apply to your other giving, you will never give any money. The poor cannot perform. The poor will not be accountable. The poor are not going to miraculously change their whole life because we magnanimously give them a little money or briefly love them.

Poverty is a culture. Poverty is a lifestyle. People are not poor without reason. Giving to the poor can be discouraging. Giving to the poor is like pouring money down a rat hole. You will get little, if anything, in return. The only enduring motivation for remembering the poor is a consuming desire to please Jesus. Do it for Jesus.

What should our "stance" be toward the poor regarding the gospel? Jesus saw helping the poor as *pre-evangelism*. In other words, He never lost sight of the ultimate purpose of redeeming lost sinners. He saw value in helping the poor in and of itself, but He always meant His service to be a "pointer" toward His kingdom. Remembering the poor is valuable by itself, even more valuable if they turn to Christ.

A man desperately needed two hundred dollars to cover a bad check he had written. If he didn't settle the debt by Friday the unsympathetic debtor threatened to have a warrant sworn out for his arrest.

This man didn't need a lecture. He needed two hundred dollars. A few men chipped in and gave him the money. Waves of contented fulfillment swept over the men involved. "This is what Christianity is all about," exclaimed one man. Yes, it is. Because the Bible says, "Dear children, let us not [only] love with words or tongue but with actions and in truth" (1 John 3:18).

Who are the invisible, unseen, forgotten people you have been driving by? The men and women out of work? The widow whose paint is peeling? The young boy without a dad? The man whose cancer bills are not fully covered by insurance? The pregnant teenager? The neighbor whose spouse deserted the family?

Do you live your Christianity on a human scale? The nature of our *horizontal* relationships with people is a precise indicator of the nature of our *vertical* relationship with God. If we don't love people, we are estopped from claiming to love God. The height of our love for God will never exceed the depth of our love for another (Matthew 25:45; Luke 10:36–37; 1 John 4:19–21).

Jesus put the premium on people. People and relationships are a higher priority to Him than possessions and accomplishments. How we treat our neighbor bears witness to the depth (or shallowness) of our relationship with Christ. If we don't have pity, if we don't look after needy people, our religion is not pure and faultless and the love of God is not our trademark. Defend the cause of the poor and needy because God inquires of us, "Is that not what it means to know me?" (Jeremiah 22:16).

GOD'S DESIRE

The desire closest to the heart of our God is that sinners would come to faith and repentance. I find it interesting. The least desired, least performed service of most Christians is the very work that most pleases God. I suspect Satan has something to do with that fact.

The most difficult work to motivate Christians to do is to win the lost and make disciples of them. Jesus understood this, "The harvest is plentiful but the workers are few. Ask the Lord of the harvest, therefore, to send out workers into his harvest field" (Matthew 9:37–38). "If we really believed that God meant what He said—what should we be like!" exclaims Oswald Chambers.[5]

Robert E. Coleman, in *The Master Plan of Evangelism*, wrote,

> There is no use to pray for the world. What good would it do? God already loves them and has given His Son to save them. No, there is no use to pray vaguely for the world. The world is lost and blind in sin. The only hope for the world is for men to go to them with the Gospel of Salvation, and having won them to the Savior, not to leave them, but to work with them faithfully, patiently, painstakingly, until they become fruitful Christians savoring the world about them with the Redeemer's love.[6]

Try to do something every day that at least has the *potential* to last forever. It is not that God needs our help, but that He has chosen to use us. No one is going to hell because you don't do your part. God is not going to lose anyone on account of our unfaithfulness. God is going to do what He will do, but He offers us the joy of serving Him. The only question that remains is this: Will you be a part of what God is doing in the world?

The Great Commission must become an attitude before it can become a mission. Don't settle for the Good Commission. As someone has said, "People are waiting to see what we will do with our lives." Pray,

> God, help me to see people the way You see them, and to love them with Your love. Reveal to me how to do this, and I will follow You.
> Lord, I'm begging.

฿   ฿   ฿

DISCUSSION QUESTIONS

1. "Winning the lost—the least desired, least performed service of most Christians—is the very work that most pleases God."

   ☐ Agree   ☐ Disagree

   Why, or why not?

2. "Remembering the poor is the most overlooked part of the Great Commission."

   ☐ Agree   ☐ Disagree

   Explain your thinking.

3. Why do you think Christians generally don't devote more time and money to evangelism, making disciples, and remembering the poor? What are the other activities that siphon off our resources?

4. Would you characterize yourself as a Great Commission Christian, and why or why not?

5. In the space provided put the percentage of your ministry time you have devoted to each of the four areas mentioned. Make sure your percentages add up to 100 percent:

   ☐ Evangelism
   ☐ Making Disciples
   ☐ Helping the Poor
   ☐ Other

6. Are you satisfied with the amount of time you have devoted to Christian ministry? What changes would you like to make going forward?

DEVELOPING
A PERSONAL
MINISTRY

D*ear Journal,*

I have watched with great admiration as other people have become involved in ministry personally. Recently, though, my admiration has turned to envy. I find I have a growing desire to have a personal ministry—not something I watch someone else do, but something I do. This desire seems to come from a growing sense of gratitude, not merely a call to duty. It's as though I can't not do anything any longer. I want my life to count—to make a difference for Christ. But what can I do? I'm not a minister. I'm not a trained person. I'm only a layman. What responsibility do I bear to do good works and perform Christian service? What should I do? How can I get mobilized?

Robert

THE CASE FOR A PERSONAL MINISTRY

Most Bible characters kept their "day jobs": Adam the gardener, Abraham the rancher, David the shepherd, Gideon the wheat farmer, Jacob the herdsman, Joseph the government official, Luke the doctor, Moses the legislator, Nehemiah the statesman, Noah the zoologist, Paul the tent maker, and Peter the fisherman. They were laymen called by God to each have a personal ministry.

God has not created two classes of Christians: occupational Christians who are the *ministers* and lay Christians who are the *ministry*. Rather, all Christians are ministers and the Great Commission is the ministry—saving sinners, building believers, and nurturing the needy.

The Bible teaches the priesthood of all believers. Writing to *all* believers Peter said, "But you are a chosen people, a royal priesthood, a holy nation, a people belonging to God, that you may declare the praises of him who called you out of the darkness into his wonderful light" (1 Peter 2:9).

God's plan is for every believer to have a personal ministry. We are made for the task. "For we are God's workmanship, created in Christ Jesus to do good works, which God prepared in advance for us to do" (Ephesians 2:10). God has a particular good work, or personal ministry, for each of us.

What motivates Christians to have a dynamic personal ministry? Christians are motivated to have a personal ministry when they recognize how deeply and radically the grace, mercy, and kindness of God has touched and healed their lives.

Out of the overflow of a heart filled with an abundance of gratitude comes a desire to serve Christ. Our motivation is a need to express our gratitude to Christ. Guilt may motivate us to begin a ministry, but only gratitude will keep us going.

SIX AREAS FOR MINISTRY

There are six areas of personal ministry in which anyone with a sincere desire to serve God can help, whether trained or not: the Church, the Community, across Culture, at Work, at Home, and to the World.

I have struggled about how to best present a portrait of ministry possibilities in these areas. We could make a long list of types of ministries. We could look at different notable examples of specific ministries. I haltingly chose to give the example of one ordinary-but-serious family over a twenty-year period.

I picked one family's story because I thought you would relate to them more realistically. They are not superstars. They are *very* ordinary. You will be able to relate to them personally. And I also thought you might see more continuity by viewing a moving picture of one family rather than a collection of snapshots.

But the reason I do so haltingly is that the only family I know that well is my own. Following are the ways our ordinary but available family has been involved in each of these areas of personal ministry. My sincere prayer is that God will use this as a catalyst to spark some new ideas for your own personal ministry.

1. Ministry in the Local Church

Our first personal ministry was in the church. I was a brand new convert and Patsy was a growing Christian. We jumped in with both feet. We tried everything. I served on the finance committee. We attended the Campus Crusade for Christ *Lay Institute for Evangelism* offered at our church and learned how to share our faith. Later we went out on Sunday nights to visit the visitors. We even tried sponsoring the youth group (for about three weary weeks).

When the leadership realized we were serious, wanted to grow, and wanted to serve, they put us in charge of teaching the basics class for new believers. While we served, they also discipled us by inviting us into a home Bible Study. A few months later we started a home Bible study of our own. We couldn't get enough.

I think the best place to have a ministry, if you can, is in the church. Most people will find the right outlet for their spiritual gifts in the church, if your church believes in putting the laity into service.

2. Ministry in the Community

Our second personal ministry was in the community. A desire to see our community fully reached for Christ was brewing in my thoughts. One morning I felt led to write down the five areas in which we get involved outside the home: church, business, civic affairs, education system, and politics. Everyone is involved in church and work, so that leaves three areas for cultural impact. Several of us met together and talked about each taking a different area. Since I had no school-aged children at the time and am apolitical, I committed to become involved for Christ in civic affairs. I joined the Winter Park Chamber of Commerce. Within a few weeks they asked if I would serve on the program committee. I said, "Sure."

Within a few months the program committee chairman resigned and they asked if I would serve as chairman. I said, "Sure." I did the best possible job I could and soon they asked me to serve on the board of directors. I said, "Sure." Not long after this I was asked if I would be interested in becoming an officer. I said, "Sure."

About this time I began wondering what in the world I was doing so deeply involved in activity that had nothing whatsoever to do with Christian service. This was, after all, supposed to be a commitment to serve Christ. I began to wonder if I had made a mistake. Then one morning, as the program committee chairman, I had the most incredible idea. Why not start a prayer breakfast a few days before Thanksgiving and share Christ with all the members and their friends?

That year, 1977, the Winter Park Chamber of Commerce sponsored the first annual Thanksgiving Prayer Breakfast. It's still going strong, though now independently sponsored. Through this ministry, multiplied hundreds who would not otherwise hear the gospel have clearly heard how to receive Christ as Savior and Lord or been challenged to recommit their lives to Him.

The prayer breakfast, as you might imagine, led to other opportunities. With the help of others, there have been outreach breakfasts, luncheons, and dinners at private clubs and public hotels.

As we became trained disciples ourselves, we wanted to disciple others. Without any special skill, we have taught various Bible studies to men, women, and couples at church, at the office, at neutral locations, and in our home.

We especially wanted our home to be used by the Lord, so we had some friends in to dedicate it to the Lord and have opened it up for evangelistic desserts and Bible studies. We made office space available for Bible studies and encouraged several to meet there. Through all of this we have regularly seen people come to faith in Jesus Christ, then grow in that faith.

These experiences taught us that everything in Christianity revolves around an *event*. Whether a counseling luncheon, church service, prayer meeting, weekly Bible study, seminar, annual outreach event, or simply getting with someone for a cup of coffee—everything revolves around events. So we focus on scheduling events to which people can come and also bring their friends who may not yet know Christ.

3. Ministry Across Culture

Our third personal ministry was across the community. Through the teachings of our dear friend, Tom Skinner, I sensed a growing desire to reach out to the poor and also to reach out across racial barriers. Then in 1980 it happened. Racial tensions flared in our community.

At the time, we had a one-day-a-week black housekeeper who happened to live in the middle of the troubled area. I will never forget the day I came home for lunch during those riots. I asked her, "What do you think is going to happen with all this?"

"Oh, I don't know."

"Well, when do you think we'll ever be able to rise above this sort of thing?"

"Oh, I don't know."

"Well, what keeps you going? Where do you get your hope?"

"Oh, I don't know."

That was all. When I was alone I found myself deeply troubled. I prayed asking God to help her, to help me, and to help our city. Then an idea struck me. What if we asked twenty black men and twenty white men to come together. The idea would not be to change our city, but to change us. We could make a commitment to really try to learn how to love one other—exactly as it says in the Bible.

It was interesting. Exactly half the men came to that first meeting—ten black and ten white. Some wanted to take on the task of changing the world. Some wanted to focus on building relationships. We stuck with the notion of trying to learn how to love each other. We met one Saturday morning each month for five years. No one will ever be able say we changed our city, but I know that I will never be the same. We learned more of what it means to love with Christ's love, and what it means to share with brothers in need.

4. Ministry at Work

Our fourth personal ministry has been in our work. We had the privilege of owning a company. We never tried to be a "Christian company," but a hard working, honest company that happened to be run by Christians.

We never put Bibles on the reception table or displayed religious symbols or anything like that (not that we have anything against them). But we did try to share our faith in Christ with every employee. We invited them to Christian outreach events, gave them Christian literature, spoke openly about Christ, prayed regularly, and kept an open door if anyone wanted to talk about spiritual things.

We decided to make people a priority and, as a result, constantly had a stream of hurting people flowing through the offices. Some of them worked there; some didn't. They came with all kinds of problems: marriage problems, children problems, career problems, money problems, legal problems.

We discovered that nearly everyone has some major problem with which they are struggling to cope. Often they only need someone to listen for a while. So we encouraged the Christian employees to take time to minister to people personally. We opened the doors up for nearly anything that hinted of Christianity. As far as I know, it never hurt business one iota.

5. Ministry in the Family

Our fifth personal ministry has been in our family. While fifth chronologically, this ministry is first in our priority of ministry. Many people, especially men, are leaving a trail of broken relationships strewn along the path of their personal ambitions. We don't want to win the world but lose our family. I have learned that no amount of success at the office can compensate for failure at home.

My wife, Patsy, committed her life to the Lord as a child. In turn, she was the first to introduce me to the concept of a personal relationship with Christ. In turn, when our daughter reached the age of six I helped her personally receive Christ. In turn, when she turned eight she led our four-year-old son to Christ.

We believe making disciples of our children and each other is our top ministry priority. So we pray before meals and we pray together about major needs. During the school year we have daily devotions three or four days a week. For fifteen minutes we have a brief lesson and pray. We pray for ourselves, but we also try to pray for one person or family outside the family each day. We are teaching our children to treat every problem as at least a spiritual matter, and to pray about it. We are

---

"Grace will make a happy home, but Law only makes kids glad to turn eighteen so they can move away from home."

---

also striving to make our spiritual lives spontaneous, exciting, fun, and relevant to our children. Grace will make a happy home, but Law only makes kids glad to turn eighteen so they can move away from home.

6. Ministry to the World

Our sixth personal ministry is to help reach the whole world for Christ. In the past the only thing we could do was send money. Then we had a missionary family stay at our home and our vision grew. We realized we could also pray for missionaries. And every now and then we can write someone overseas to encourage them.

One of the greatest privileges in having a ministry is to personally travel overseas. To see other cultures is an eye opener. It forces us to think through ideas we have taken for granted. It is good to walk among the poor, to see their hunger for God, to feel the weight of their conditions, to see their humanity, to become sensitive to them *personally*. Everyone would benefit from taking a missions trip, especially among the poor. I know not everyone can go, but if you *can* go you will never be the same again.

る   る   る

I hope this paradigm gives you a picture, at least partially, of different ways God can use you. These are *personal* ministries, not something you watch someone else do from a distance, not a report from a missionary about what *they* did.

If you don't have a personal ministry, or are not satisfied with what you have been doing, take some bold steps. Make some phone calls. Visit your pastor. Drop by and visit the shelter for the homeless, the local soup line, the high school campus ministries, the drug rehab program, the pro-life counseling center. You may find your niche in the church, in an existing organization, or you may feel most comfortable serving as an individual.

Add the category of "personal ministry" to your lexicon. God will work through you if you offer Him your hands to serve, your mind to think, and your lips to speak. The rest of this chapter will outline some boundaries for your good deeds, and how one goes about finding their personal ministry.

SPIRITUAL GIFTS

The first step to find your niche in effective service is to understand your spiritual gifts. It would be foolish to try to become a salesman if you prefer to work with numbers. In the same way we pursue vocational employment based upon our aptitudes and abilities, we pursue our spiritual service based on an understanding of how God has gifted us.

Every believer receives at least one spiritual gift. "Now *to each one* the manifestation of the Spirit is given for the common good" (1 Corinthians 12:7, italics added). The Holy Spirit determines our spiritual gifts. "He gives them to each one, just as he determines" (1 Corinthians 12:11). "Each man has his own gift from God" (1 Corinthians 7:7).

The purpose of our spiritual gifts is to serve Christ by serving others, helping to fulfill the Great Commission. "Each one should use whatever gift he has received *to serve others* . . . ." Our responsibility is to be faithful. ". . . to serve others, *faithfully* administering God's grace in its various forms" (1 Peter 4:10, italics added).

Spiritual gifts include *service* gifts, *speaking* gifts, and *signifying* gifts. While theologians and teachers often differ on how to precisely classify and name these gifts, the following generally captures the gist of the different gifts.

1. Service Gifts

Service gifts are the ligaments and muscle tissue that hold the church of Jesus Christ together. Service gifts are often low profile, behind-the-scene gifts. They include showing mercy, service (or helps), hospitality, giving, administration, leadership, faith, and discernment.

People who serve are eager for God to receive the credit for whatever good comes. "If anyone *serves*, he should do it with the strength God provides, so that in all things God may be praised through Jesus Christ" (1 Peter 4:11, italics added). Here are brief definitions of the service gifts with a few examples of how each gift may be used. These, along with the definitions of speaking and signifying gifts that follow, are adapted from the work of Carl Smith, Kenneth O. Gangel, and Leslie B. Flynn:

- *Mercy:* Special ability to show sympathy to the suffering saints. Meals to the sick, hospital visits, phone calls, and visits to the hurting.
- *Service:* Special ability to joyfully serve behind the scenes. Set up chairs, ushering, assist leaders.
- *Hospitality:* Special desire to offer home, food, and lodging. Host missionaries, Bible studies, singles to dinner.
- *Giving:* Special desire and financial ability to give above and beyond a tithe. Generosity toward youth mission trips, deacon fund offerings, para-church ministries, a suit for the pastor.
- *Administration:* Special ability to orchestrate program details. Committee work, volunteer for church office, conference/seminar supervision.
- *Leadership:* Special ability to preside or govern wisely. Boards of Christian ministries. Visible roles, elders, deacons, committee chairmen, run nursery program, fund-raising.
- *Faith:* Vision for new projects that need doing and perseverance to see them through. Building programs, new ministries.
- *Discernment:* Ability to detect error. Meet with teachers who may be teaching incorrectly, letters to the editor.

2. Speaking Gifts

Speaking gifts include knowledge, wisdom, preaching, teaching, evangelism, apostleship, shepherding, and encouragement. "If anyone *speaks*, he should do it as one speaking the very words of God" (1 Peter 4:11). Here are definitions and examples of the spiritual gifts of speaking:

- *Knowledge:* Spiritual ability to search and acquire Scriptural truth. Academic pursuits, writing, teaching
- *Wisdom:* Special insight into applications of knowledge. Counseling, teaching, discussion group leader, accountability groups, friendship.
- *Preaching:* Special ability to rightly proclaim and expound God's truth. Preachers, lay preachers.
- *Teaching:* Special ability to explain Scripture in edifying way. Sunday school teachers, Bible studies, home groups, children, and youth programs.
- *Evangelism:* Special ability to clearly present the gospel to non-believers. Sunday night church visitation program, share faith with contacts on job, sponsor outreach events.
- *Apostleship:* Special ability to begin new works. Missionaries, church planters, Christian service organizations.
- *Shepherding:* Unique ability to care for a flock of believers over the long haul. Pastors, elders, nursery program.
- *Encouragement:* Special skill to inspire, encourage, and comfort. Being a friend, counseling, writing letters.

People who have been given speaking gifts are able to help equip others to have a personal ministry of service. "It was he who gave some to be apostles, some to be prophets, some to be evangelists, and some to be pastors and teachers, *to prepare God's people for works of service,* so that the body of Christ may be built up" (Ephesians 4:11–12, emphasis added).

3. Signifying Gifts

The signifying gifts are miracles, healing, speaking in tongues, and the interpretation of tongues.

- *Tongues:* Spiritual ability to speak in a language foreign to speaker.
- *Interpretation of Tongues:* Spiritual ability to interpret the message of one speaking in tongues.
- *Miracles:* Spiritual ability to actuate the supernatural intervention of God against the laws of nature.
- *Healing:* Spiritual agency of God in curing illness and disease and restoring to health supernaturally.

If you have never studied and understood your own spiritual gifts, let me make two recommendations. First, study the four passages of Scripture which deal with spiritual gifts: Romans 12:3–8; 1 Corinthians 12:1–31; Ephesians 4:11–13; and 1 Peter 4:9–11. You may want to study the context by examining the verses before and after these specific references.

Second, I have read two books which helped me tremendously: *Unwrap Your Spiritual Gifts*, by Kenneth O. Gangel (Wheaton: Victor Books, 1974), and *19 Gifts of the Spirit*, by Leslie B. Flynn (Wheaton: Victor Books, 1983). You may want to read one or both of them.

A PART OF THE BODY OF CHRIST

After discovering our spiritual gifts, the next step is to find how we fit into the body of Christ—the church.

Using our spiritual gifts effectively is linked to participating in the body. "Just as each of us has one body with many members, and these members do not all have the same function, so in Christ we who are many form one body, and each member belongs to all the others" (Romans 12:4–5; see also 1 Corinthians 12:12–27).

Every believer is part of the body of Christ, which is the church. "Now you are the body of Christ, and each one of you is a part of it" (1 Corinthians 12:27). God has arranged our position in the body as He sees best. "But in fact God has arranged the parts of the body, every one of them, just as he wanted them to be" (1 Corinthians 12:18). A diversity in the body of Christ is normal and healthy. "If they were all one part, where would the body be?" (1 Corinthians 12:19).

To ensure that people with different spiritual gifts will accomplish His desired end results, God established the concept of the body of Christ—the church. This includes both the local church and the work He is doing through the church worldwide. How does this body work?

> The body is a unit, though it is made up of many parts; and though all its parts are many, they form one body. . . . The eye cannot say to the hand, "I don't need you!" And the head cannot say to the feet, "I don't need you!" On the contrary, those parts of the body that seem to be weaker are indispensable. . . . There should be no division in the body, but . . . its parts should have equal concern for each other. If

one part suffers, every part suffers with it; if one part is honored, every part rejoices with it. Now you are the body of Christ, and each one of you is a part of it. (1 Corinthians 12:12, 21–22, 25–27)

For the body of Christ to run smoothly there must be a *division of labor* based upon different gifts. When a dispute in the early church arose over discrimination against the poor widows, the Twelve suggested they give up the responsibility for the daily distribution of food to a committee of seven. "This proposal pleased the whole group" (Acts 6:5).

This division of labor solved the dispute, gave additional people the opportunity to develop a personal ministry, and caused the overall ministry to expand. "So the word of God spread . . . and a large number of priests became obedient to the faith" (Acts 6:7). The body of Christ works best when every part is put to use. The muscles of an unused limb will atrophy.

God wants us involved in all of His plan and purpose, narrowed according to our own gifts, broadened by our participation in the body of Christ. How much should one person do?

Setting Priorities

As committed Christians we are to be devoted to all of God's agenda. On the other hand, there is obviously no way one person can master all aspects of the Great Commission. How can one person be effectively involved in all three of these areas: saving sinners, building believers, and nurturing the needy? What is the balanced, prioritized approach?

Based on the *spiritual gifts* God gives you, the *body of believers* in which He places you, and *the gifts of your co-laborers*, my opinion is that each person should have *one major personal ministry*. Do this ministry with every ounce of diligence, faithfulness, and excellence you can muster. Start with a maximum one hour commitment. As your conviction grows, so can your time commitment. A good target for personal ministry for someone who works and has a family is four or five hours per week. Think of it as a tithe of your time. Include the family whenever you can. But never let your ministry have a higher priority than your family. For many of us, especially mothers, our family *is* our primary ministry.

Then, keep a finger in the other areas of the Great Commission by considering *minor support ministries*. These may include donating a limited amount of time (regularly or project oriented), prayer support, speaking favorably for a ministry in the community, giving advice, or financial support.

"Never let your ministry have a higher priority than your family."

In this way we do not personally do all the work of ministry, but synergistically leverage our strengths with the strengths of our co-laborers.

Christian Versus Secular Service

Should Christians work on secular projects? Non-Christians prefer to work on projects not identified as distinctly Christian; Christians, on the other hand, acknowledge that everything belongs to God. "For everything in heaven and earth is yours" (1 Chronicles 29:11). Therefore, all noble projects are spiritual. All good deeds are spiritual. Said differently, no project God calls the Christian to do is secular.

There are two kinds of fruit the Christian will produce—one that lasts and one that doesn't. We are to be *ambassadors* for the kingdom of God (producing lasting fruit) and *stewards* of creation (which will pass away). The highest goal of the most noble humanist is to make the world a better place. This, too, is a fruit of Christian service, but it must be kept in perspective.

Our stewardship of culture and society is a means to an end; it must never be confused with fruit that lasts. "The elements will be destroyed by fire, and the earth and everything in it will be laid bare" (2 Peter 3:10). Only God and people who turn to Christ live forever—that is lasting fruit. So always keep the end in view.

Christians are a "special interest group," and the Great Commission is the special interest; it should receive a special emphasis. Jesus hand-picked us to do good works that will last. "You did not choose me, but I chose you to go and bear fruit—fruit that will last" (John 15:16). We will receive no help from non-Christians to produce fruit that will *last*, so we alone must do it.

Success in Ministry

The success of much Christian ministry gets evaluated on the same basis as secularized work—growth, numbers, budget, performance, externals. So naturally the question comes up: Just exactly what is success in ministry, anyway?

Since we are in the service of the kingdom of God, the intelligent answer will certainly reflect what is important to God. Here is the revealing question upon which to meditate: What will have mattered one hundred years from now? The correct answer is this: The only thing that will matter one hundred years from now is changed lives.

Success in ministry is changed lives. That is the supreme test. We should each try to do something every day which at least has the potential to last forever. Whether sharing our faith with a co-worker or setting up chairs for the missions meeting, these contribute value to the work of bringing the kingdom of God to the world.

The World of Fifty Feet

We each stand in the center of a world of fifty feet. That's about how far our voice will carry without shouting. Fifty feet in any direction. Who are the people who live within your world of fifty feet?

Our world of fifty feet is a moving target: from the bed to the breakfast table, from the office to the store, from the church to the school, from the neighborhood to the civic club.

Who are the people in your world of fifty feet who are unlovable? Perhaps they are unattractive. Maybe they are poor communicators. They may have an abrasive personality. Anyone can love someone who first loves them. But we are to love because we are already loved. Jesus said, "As I have loved you, so you must love one another."

Would it make sense to take a piece of paper and write down the different spheres in which you move (e.g., home, work, school, grocery store, team tennis)? In your mind's eye look for the faces of the unlovable in each of those arenas. Write down their names, or a code word if you don't know their names. Write down one step you can take with each person to love them. Help them to know Christ as Savior, become disciples, and don't forget to make sure they have enough to eat.

Every Christian is called to have a personal ministry. How we minister depends upon an assessment of our spiritual gifts and the place in the body of Christ where He places us. Have you had a dynamic, personal ministry? Is your life changing other people's lives? If not, prayerfully ask the Lord to show you the good works which He prepared in advance for you to do. *Do something every day which at least has the potential to last forever.*

🙚 🙚 🙚

DISCUSSION QUESTIONS

1. How have you viewed ministry in the past? As something you personally do, or as the work we pay ministers to do?

2. Do you have a personal ministry? If yes, describe it.

3. What is the key point from each of the following verses:

   Ephesians 2:10 _____

   1 Peter 2:9 _____

   John 15:16 _____

   1 Corinthians 12:7 _____

   1 Peter 4:10 _____

   Romans 12:4–5 _____

4. Have you ever determined your spiritual gifts? How important to your service do you think it is to know your gifts? From the listings in this chapter, describe what you think/know are your spiritual gifts.

5. Does the concept of being a member of the body of Christ make sense to you? Explain your answer.

6. Based upon your spiritual gifts and your place in the body of Christ, which of the following areas might give you the opportunity to develop a personal ministry? Write down possible specific ideas in the space provided.

   At Home _____

   The Church_____

   At Work _____

   The Community _____

   Across Culture_____

   To the World_____

THE 80/20
CHRISTIAN

Remember the 80/20 rule? Italian economist, Vilfredo Pareto, first noted the principle that 20 percent of our efforts produces 80 percent of our results, and vice versa. And the rule (which is actually not a rule at all but a useful working generalization) extends into every nook and cranny of life. You know. Twenty percent of the people do 80 percent of the work, 20 percent of the people give 80 percent of the money, 20 percent of the people accumulate 80 percent of the wealth, and so on.

❧   ❧   ❧

There was an 80/20 man who lived an 80/20 life. He was the kind of man you could always count on to give a full 80 percent to everything he undertook. Well, actually not always, but at least 80 percent of the time.

One day the 80/20 man decided he would like to become a Christian or, should we say, 80 percent of him did. For he could only bring himself to believe about 80 percent of what the Bible says about the historical life of Jesus. You know, the virgin birth ("I mean, Come on"), the atonement for the sins of people not even born yet, the human incarnation of the unseen God ("Give me a break"). And then there is that part about rising from the dead ("Puh . . . lleezze!").

But he was highly motivated (to the 80th percentile) to see his faith change his life. He secretly hoped for an 80 percent improvement. *That would meet 100 percent of my expectations*, he thought.

279

He began attending church (four out of every five Sundays—a splendid record, indeed) which he thoroughly enjoyed or, should we say, at least 80 percent of the time. When he went he stayed for the whole service (a remarkable achievement in itself), but he could only bring himself to listen to about 80 percent of the sermons. He sang 80 percent of the hymns with 80 percent enthusiasm, and prayed 80 percent of the prayers with four-fifths of his heart.

One day he said to his friend, "You know, I really like this Christianity stuff, at least 80 percent of it. About 20 percent of it, though, is pretty hard to swallow." He felt that way four-fifths of the time. He added, "I believe about 80 percent of the Bible is true." The Bible carried a lot of weight with him, about three pounds. He was an 80/20 Christian.

But you know how the 80/20 rule works. And so his brand of Christianity relieved only 20 percent of his fears, removed a mere 20 percent of his angry outbursts, and he found just 20 percent of the sense of purpose and meaning for which he longed. *This is a lot of work for a little result,* he thought.

Eighty percent of the time he found himself in a surly mood, criticizing his wife, yelling at his kids, disagreeing with his pastor, hating his boss, angry at the hand fate had dealt him, exhausted beyond words, paralyzed with fears, anxious about the future, teetering on the brink of financial disaster, and otherwise generally frustrated with his life.

One day he was reading his Bible (which he did 20 percent of the time). He usually skipped over about 80 percent of the verses looking for something visceral, something that would invigorate his emotions. He was paying about 80 percent attention to the verses he was reading when, lo and behold, these razor-edged words thundered off the page, sending shivering echoes down the halls of his mind (80 percent of which were empty):

> I warn everyone who hears the words of the prophecy of this book: If anyone adds anything to them, God will add to him the plagues described in this book. And if anyone takes away from this book of prophecy, God will take away from him his share in the tree of life and in the holy city, which are described in this book (Revelation 22:18–19).

The 80/20 man was quite astonished . . . astonished that these words were the last words of the Bible . . . surprised that he had made it that far—past the first 80 percent. He figured the chances of that happening were even less than one in five.

If this is how God decided to summarize the Bible, then these must be very important words, indeed: Don't add to His words. Neither subtract anything away. Uh, oh.

Yes, yes. I want to share in the tree of life. I want to walk along the avenues of the holy city. I want to stand ankle deep in the river of life and feel the cool, refreshing waters swirl around my feet.

Suddenly it occurred to the 80/20 man that he was either for God or against Him. Instantly his eyes were opened and he clearly saw that 80 percent "in" is still "out." His body convulsed and he shrieked as a jagged, white-hot saber of pain lanced the throbbing, festered 20 percent of his unyielded soul.

He fell on his knees with 100 percent of his weight, he cried out to God with 100 percent of his heart, he wept 100 percent of the tears within him, he repented 100 percent of his spiritual blindness and sin, he surrendered 100 percent of his life, he pledged 100 percent loyalty, he dedicated 100 percent of his time and money, he committed to seek after 100 percent obedience, and he submitted 100 percent of his being to 100 percent of the authority of 100 percent of the Bible. It was the first 100 percent moment of his 80 percent life. It was supremely beyond all he had dared ask or imagine.

When 80 percent of the euphoria had worn off he noticed he had only lost 20 percent of the glow. From deep inside he remembered a verse of hymn, "Something's happened, and now I know. He touched me. My Savior made whole."

In the days that followed he found an enigma. Eighty percent of the time he rode the crests of the waves. But 20 percent of the time his circumstances seemed insurmountable, unconquerable, unsolvable. Yet, even in the midst of grueling anguish, pain, and tears he found welling up within him springs of living water, peace, and joy. Yes, he experienced the same veneer of mortal emotions he did before, but beneath that shallow facade immortal joy audibly but softly hummed like a giant, powerful turbine with unending reserves of power.

During those storms—those 20 percenters—as the tiny ship of his circumstances was buffeted to and fro by life's high seas, Robert noticed that the anchor of God's immovable, sovereign, authoritative, infallible, holy Word held him fast in the hollow between the waves as though in the very hand of the living God. And it happened 100 percent of the time.

Introduction: An Authentic Christian Life

1. Edward E. Plowman, ed., *National & International Religion Report*, May 20, 1991.

Chapter Two: The Two Spirits of Our Age

1. Francis A. Schaeffer, *Escape From Reason* (Downers Grove: InterVarsity Press, 1968), 40.

2. Gordon H. Clark, *Thales to Dewey* (Jefferson: The Trinity Foundation, 1957), 534.

3. R. C. Sproul, class notes from *History of Philosophy and Christian Thought*, 1989.

4. The Barna Research Group, *The Church Today: Insightful Statistics and Commentary* (Glendale: Barna Research Group, 1990), 34.

5. Os Guinness, *Winning Back the Soul of American Business* (Washington: Hourglass Publishers, 1990), 30.

Chapter 3: Three Dangerous Ideas

1. Jean-Paul Sartre, "Existentialism is a Humanism," in Walter Kaufmann, ed., *Existentialism from Dostoevsky to Sartre* (New York: A Meridian Book, 1975), 349.

2. Ibid., 359.

3. Allan Bloom, *The Closing of the American Mind* (New York: Simon and Schuster, 1987), 25.

4. S. I. McMillen, M.D., *None of These Diseases* (Old Tappan: Spire Books, 1963), 13–15.

5. Roland H. Bainton, *Here I Stand: A Life of Martin Luther*, (Nashville: Abingdon Press, 1950), 144.

6. St. Augustine, *City of God*, Vernon J. Bourke, ed. (New York: Doubleday, 1958), 87–88.

Chapter Five: Born Again "Again"

1. George Gallup, Jr., *100 Questions and Answers: Religion in America* (Hermitage Press, 1989), 180–181.

2. Kenneth L. Woodward, "A Time to Seek," *Newsweek*, December 17, 1990, 56.

3. Richard Baxter, *The Puritan Pastor*, William Brown, ed. (Carlisle: The Banner of Truth Trust, [1656], 1974), 97–99.

4. Jeff Kleinhuizen, "Drug May Give Fast Relief from Migraine," *USA Today*, April 24, 1991, 1.

5. Soren Kierkegaard, *Existentialism from Dostoevsky to Sartre*, in Walter Kaufmann, ed. (New York: A Meridian Book, 1975), 87–88.

Chapter Six: Seven Steps to a Wise Life

1. William J. Bouwsma, *John Calvin: A Sixteenth Century Portrait* (New York: Oxford University Press, 1988), 19.

2. The Barna Research Group, *The Church Today: Insightful Statistics and Commentary*, 29.

3. Richard Dobbins, "Why Do Ministers Fail?" *Ministries Today*, (May/June, 1989), 24.

Chapter Seven: An Apology for Doctrine

1. Max Anders, *30 Days to Understanding the Bible* (Brentwood: Wolgemuth & Hyatt, Publishers, Inc., 1988), 164.

Chapter Eight: Thinking in Biblical Categories

1. George Sweeting, *Great Quotes & Illustrations*, (Waco: Word Books, 1985), 32.

2. Ibid., 33.

3. Charles R. Swindoll, *The Grace Awakening* (Dallas: Word Publishing, 1990), 159–160.

4. Joseph F. Girzone, *Joshua* (New York: Collier Books, 1987), 67.

Chapter Nine: The God Who Is

1. Adapted from Heinrich Von Loon, *The Land of Svithjod*, no longer in print, no data available.

Chapter Ten: The Radical Effect of the Fall

1. Francis A. Schaeffer, *Escape From Reason* (Downers Grove: InterVarsity Press, 1968), 90.

2. Albert M. Wells, Jr., *Inspiring Quotations* (Nashville: Thomas Nelson Publishers, 1988), 235.

3. Leighton Ford, *The Greatest Lesson I've Ever Learned*, Bill Bright, ed. (San Bernandino: Here's Life Publishers, Inc., 1991), 73.

4. Francis A. Schaeffer, *Letters of Francis A. Schaeffer* (Westchester: Crossway Books, 1985), 108.

Chapter Eleven: The Content of the Gospel

1. Billy Graham, *Ministries Today* (September/October 1989), edited from *The Work of an Evangelist*, (World Wide Publications, 1984), 50.

2. J. B. Phillips, *Your God Is Too Small* (New York: Collier Books, MacMillan Publishing Company, 1961), 112.

3. C. S. Lewis, *Mere Christianity* (New York: MacMillan Publishing Co., Inc., 1952), 56.

4. Lloyd John Ogilvie, *Autobiography of God* (Ventura: Regal Books, 1979), 33.

5. Martin Luther, *The Bondage of the Will* (Old Tappan: Fleming H. Revell Company, 1957), 170–171.

Chapter Thirteen: The Most Important Thing

1. Albert M. Wells, Jr., compiler, *Inspiring Quotations* (Nashville: Thomas Nelson Publishers, 1988), 119.

2. James C. Dobson, *Straight Talk to Men and Their Wives* (Waco: Word Books, 1980), 44–45.

Chapter Fourteen: God's Blueprint for Living

1. W. R. Moody, *Dwight L. Moody* (Westwood: Barbour and Company, Inc., 1985), 39.

Chapter Fifteen: Seven Ways to Find God's Will

1. Leslie B. Flynn, *19 Gifts of the Spirit* (Wheaton: Victor Books, 1974), 141–142.

2. J. I. Packer, *Knowing God* (Downers Grove: InterVarsity Press, 1973), 209.

3. George Sweeting, *Great Quotations & Illustrations* (Waco, Word Books, 1985), 129.

4. H. H. Halley, *Halley's Bible Handbook* (Grand Rapids: Zondervan Publishing House, 1965), 807.

Chapter Sixteen: How to Change

1. William J. Bouwsma, *John Calvin* (New York: Oxford University Press, 1988), 11.

2. Oswald Chambers, *My Utmost for His Highest* (Westwood: Barbour and Company, Inc., 1963), 270.

3. W. R. Moody, *Dwight L. Moody* (Westwood: Barbour and Company, Inc., 1985), 122.

4. Oswald Chambers, *My Utmost for His Highest* (Westwood: Barbour and Company, Inc., 1963), 83.

5. Richard J. Foster, *Celebration of Discipline* (San Francisco: Harper and Row, 1978), 153.

6. John Calvin, *Calvin: Institutes of the Christian Religion*, John T. McNeill, ed. (Philadelphia: The Westminster Press, 1960), 47.

Chapter Seventeen: Becoming a Great Commission Christian

1. W. R. Moody, *The Life of Dwight L. Moody* (Westwood: Barbour and Company, Inc., 1985), 39–41.

2. Francis A. Schaeffer, *Escape from Reason* (Downers Grove: Inter-Varsity Press, 1968), 93–94.

3. George Gallup, Jr., *100 Questions and Answers: Religion in America* (Hermitage Press, 1989), 6.

4. Robert E. Coleman, *The Master Plan of Evangelism* (Old Tappan: Fleming H. Revell Company, 1963), 120.

5. Oswald Chambers, *My Utmost for His Highest* (Westwood: Barbour and Company, Inc., 1963), 139.

6. Robert E. Coleman, *The Master Plan of Evangelism* (Old Tappan: Fleming H. Revell Company, 1963), 109.

Breese, David. *Seven Men Who Rule the World From the Grave*. Chicago: Moody Press, 1990.

Clark, Gordon H. *Thales to Dewey*. Jefferson: The Trinity Foundation, 1957.

Guinness, Os. *Winning Back the Soul of American Business*. Washington: Hourglass Publishers, 1990.

Kaufmann, Walter, editor. *Existentialism from Dostoevsky to Sartre*. New York: A Meridian Book, 1975.

LaHaye, Tim. *Faith of Our Founding Fathers*. Brentwood: Wolgemuth & Hyatt, Publishers, Inc., 1987.

Marshall, Peter and David Manuel. *From Sea to Shining Sea*. Old Tappan: Fleming H. Revell Co., 1986.

Schaeffer, Francis A. *Escape from Reason*. Downers Grove: InterVarsity Press, 1968.

Sproul, R. C. *Lifeviews*. Old Tappan: Fleming H. Revell Company, 1986.

(These sources are specifically related to the material covered in chapters 2 and 3.)

SELECTED BIBLIOGRAPHY

SUBJECT INDEX

*P*ATRICK M. MORLEY is author of the two best-selling books *The Man in the Mirror* and *I Surrender*. A businessman from Florida, he has been the President or Managing Partner of 59 companies and partnerships. Mr. Morley graduated with Honors from the University of Central Florida and is a graduate of the Harvard Graduate School of Business Owner/President Management Program.

He serves on the Board of Directors of Campus Crusade for Christ and is Chairman of the Orlando Thanksgiving Prayer Breakfast which he founded in 1978. Pat regularly speaks at evagelistic outreach events. He lives in Orlando, Florida, where he teaches a weekly Bible Study to 125 businessmen and is an active member with his family at Orangewood Presbyterian Church.